Praise for *Mindfu*

Anālayo's first-person experience with meditation practice saturates this offering, which is dedicated to explaining in practical detail how various ancient texts, many translated into English by the author for the first time and selected because of their focus on the subjects of ill health and death, present the Buddha's and his disciples' explicit teachings on how to wisely and compassionately approach the challenges inherent in these inevitable dimensions of human experience. This book is a practice manual both for individuals facing sickness and death and for those motivated to assist others in those circumstances. The subject takes on a broader global relevance at this time on the planet, given the fact that mindfulness as a meditation practice and as a way of being has become progressively integrated into the mainstream of modern medicine, psychology, and health care over the past four decades, and there is a growing scientific literature on its effects. – **from the Foreword, Jon Kabat-Zinn,** co-editor with Mark Williams of *Mindfulness: Diverse Perspectives on Its Meaning, Origins, and Applications*

Mindfully Facing Disease and Death is an indispensable book for serious students of Buddhism. In the first noble truth, the Buddha doesn't mince words when he declares that the path to liberation begins by coming to terms with two of life's stark realities: sickness and death. In his new book, Bhikkhu Anālayo translates the Buddha's original teachings on mindfully preparing for the inevitable appearance of these two life events. Bhikkhu Anālayo's commentary on these teachings reflects his rigorous scholarship and years of meditative practice. That scholarship and meditative practice combine to produce a book that is, at once, easy to understand and deeply insightful.

The book is impressively comprehensive. Would you benefit from concrete practices for coping with pain? See Chapters 6 and 7. Do you experience fear when you get sick? See Chapter 9. Do you wonder if the divine abodes could help ease the process of dying? See Chapter 15. Bhikkhu Anālayo addresses these inquiries and many more with clarity and compassion. This book has the potential to transform the lives of everyone who reads it. – **Toni Bernhard**, author of *How to Live Well with Chronic Pain and Illness: A Mindful Guide*

As I began to read this book I found myself moved to tears. Aming Tu of Dharma Drum Mountain, when confronted by cancer, turned to the Buddhist texts he had been studying for decades and discovered, of course, great treasure and much practical advice on how to address sickness and death. As he sorted through these texts and applied them to his own predicament, he developed an understanding that is of inestimable value, one that he knew would be of great benefit to the world: each and every one of us will, at one time or another, be faced with sickness old age and death, and each and every one of us will benefit from turning to the pragmatic and profound teachings of the Buddha – sometimes known as 'the Great Physician'.

He asked Anālayo – his friend, colleague, renowned Buddhist scholar and writer – to help bring these texts to the world in an easily accessible form. This book is the fruit of this remarkable and deeply moving collaboration. *Anukampā* – the active expression of compassion – is a central theme of this book, and it seems to me that this whole book is a living expression of *anukampā*: as it flows from Aming Tu, through Anālayo, to us, the reader.

I believe the Buddha would rejoice in this book and exhort all of us to read it and apply the 'medicine' within. This will help to bring about the deepest healing of all – the healing of the mind and the heart – even if we are slipping over the final frontier of death itself. What greater gift could we ever be given? Truly, this is a remarkable and wonderful book. – **Vidyamala Burch**, author of *Living Well with Pain and Illness*, Co-Founder and Managing Director, Breathworks

An invaluable and extraordinary resource on the profound teachings by the Buddha on dying, death, and grieving. Bhikkhu Anālayo has given a great gift to all of us by bringing together in this book the compassionate wisdom of the Buddha on our mortality. – **Roshi Joan Halifax,** Abbot, Upaya Zen Center

Bhikkhu Anālayo has offered a wonderful resource for those wishing to approach illness and death from a contemplative perspective. The meditative mind tends to go out the window when we're sick or hurting. With his skillful translation of source texts, and insightful commentary, Anālayo shows us how to stay fully present when every instinct is to run. Elegant, rigorous, and compassionate, this is a fine addition to the conscious dying movement that will help you transform obstacle into opportunity. – **Andrew Holecek**, author of *Preparing to Die*

Ven. Anālayo has assembled a series of early Buddhist suttas covering the topic of disease and death and how mindfulness can be applied in these circumstances. The reader is reminded of a range of fundamental Buddhist teachings in a context where their relevance to the problem of suffering becomes clear. The Buddha's humanity and compassion jump off the pages as one reads his simple advice to his monks and ordinary people on how to help the sick and dying in practical ways. Anālayo then applies the deep and subtle teachings on mindfulness found in the *Satipaṭṭhāna* and elsewhere to show how mindfulness in the situation of sickness and death can be liberating.

I am personally very grateful to Ven. Anālayo for all his work in bringing together the early sources of the Buddha's teachings and painstakingly examining all possible interpretations from a range of versions (not only Pāli, but Chinese and Tibetan) in a way that allows for alternative interpretations and approaches. This enables a reader like myself (from the Tibetan Buddhist tradition) to examine the texts with a sense of ever deepening knowledge and understanding both of the early sources as well as of my own tradition. Ven. Anālayo is able to do this for me because his fine analysis combines the detached objectivity of the academic scholar with the engaged concern of the Buddhist practitioner for whom the texts are a source of genuine spiritual advice, as relevant today as when they were written. – **Lama Shenpen Hookham,** author of *There Is More to Dying than Death,* founder of the Awakened Heart Sangha

Bhikkhu Anālayo's wonderful work will prove of great value not only to professionals working with chronic pain management and hospice service, but also provides very useful and practical insights for spiritual people of all traditions. – **Glenn Mullin,** author of *Death and Dying: The Tibetan Tradition*

In this wonderfully accessible and compassionate book Bhikkhu Anālayo illuminates classic Buddhist teachings and offers practical counsel for facing death with clarity and kindness. Ancient wisdom to prepare us for the adventure of a lifetime. – **Frank Ostaseski,** co-founder of the Zen Hospice Project, founder of the Metta Institute

When a person is as skilled as Bhikkhu Anālayo as both a practitioner and scholar of Buddhism, an unexpected richness pours forth that compels the reader further into the Buddha's teachings on the frailties of body and mind. In this remarkable book on mindfully facing disease and death we are guided by Anālayo's insightful courage and conviction that death and illness can be a gateway to the cessation of all human struggles. – **Rodney Smith,** Buddhist teacher and author of *Lessons from the Dying*

Also by Anālayo

Satipaṭṭhāna: The Direct Path to Realization
The Genesis of the Bodhisattva Ideal
A Comparative Study of the Majjhima-nikāya
Excursions into the Thought-world of the Pāli Discourses
Madhyama-āgama Studies
Perspectives on Satipaṭṭhāna
The Dawn of Abhidharma
Compassion and Emptiness in Early Buddhist Meditation
Saṃyukta-āgama Studies
Ekottarika-āgama Studies
The Foundation History of the Nuns' Order

Mindfully Facing Disease and Death

Compassionate Advice from Early Buddhist Texts

Anālayo

Windhorse Publications

Windhorse Publications
169 Mill Road
Cambridge
CB1 3AN
UK

info@windhorsepublications.com
www.windhorsepublications.com

As an act of Dhammadāna, Anālayo has waived
royalty payments for this book.
The index was not compiled by the author.

Cover design by Dhammarati

Typesetting and layout by Ruth Rudd
Printed by Bell & Bain Ltd, Glasgow

British Library Cataloguing in Publication Data:
A catalogue record for this book is available from the British Library.

ISBN: 978 1 909314 72 6

CONTENTS

ABOUT THE AUTHOR

Born in 1962 in Germany, Bhikkhu Anālayo was ordained in 1995 in Sri Lanka, and completed a PhD on the *Satipaṭṭhāna-sutta* at the University of Peradeniya, Sri Lanka, in 2000 – published in 2003 by Windhorse Publications under the title *Satipaṭṭhāna: The Direct Path to Realization*.

Anālayo is a professor at the University of Hamburg; his main research area is early Buddhism and in particular the topics of the Chinese *Āgama*s, meditation, and women in Buddhism. Besides his academic pursuits, he spends about half of his time in meditation under retreat conditions and regularly teaches meditation.

ACKNOWLEDGEMENT

I am indebted to Shaila Catherine, Bhikkhunī Dhammadinnā, Linda Grace, Jon Kabat-Zinn, Hedwig Kren, Mike Running, Syinchen Shi, Christiane Steffens-Dhaussy, and Matt Weingast for comments on draft versions of this study. Any shortcomings in the following pages are due to my own ignorance.

PUBLISHER'S ACKNOWLEDGEMENTS

Windhorse Publications wishes to gratefully acknowledge a grant from the Triratna European Chairs' Assembly Fund towards the production of this book.

Triratna European Chairs Assembly

Windhorse Publications also wishes to gratefully acknowledge and thank the individual donors who gave to the book's production via our "Sponsor-a-book" campaign.

DOCTRINAL TOPICS INTRODUCED IN EACH CHAPTER

FOREWORD

The Dharma world owes a debt of gratitude to Bhikkhu Anālayo for his meticulous, prolific, and surpassingly clear scholarly work over the past decades translating and elucidating important Buddhist texts and bringing the richness of the early Buddhist canon to life, particularly where it concerns the teachings on *satipaṭṭhāna* (mindfulness) and *karuṇā* (compassion). In addition to being a renowned scholar and translator, Bhikkhu Anālayo has been an ardent practitioner of mindfulness for decades. The fact that he lives and practices as a renunciant monk in accordance with rigorous monastic precepts infuses an additional dimension of authenticity, dedication, and relevance into his remarkable body of work. His first-person experience with meditation practice saturates this offering, which is dedicated to explaining in practical detail how various ancient texts, many translated into English by the author for the first time and selected because of their focus on the subjects of ill health and death, present the Buddha's and his disciples' explicit teachings on how to wisely and compassionately approach the challenges inherent in these inevitable dimensions of human experience. This book is a practice manual both for individuals facing sickness and death and for those motivated to assist others in those circumstances. The subject takes on a broader global relevance at this time on the planet, given the fact that mindfulness as a meditation practice and as a way of being has become progressively integrated into the mainstream of modern medicine, psychology, and health care over the past four decades,[1] and there is a growing scientific literature on its effects.[2]

I take Anālayo's invitation to write the foreword to this book as emblematical of his openness and commitment to catalyzing a wider receptivity to the dharma and its wisdom on the part of the world, with all its endemic suffering and the global urgency of our human and planetary predicament. It is also clear from his writings here and elsewhere that Anālayo is taking on the task of articulating these early Buddhist teachings in new and imaginative ways[3] that, while completely congruent with the texts themselves, reveal new ways of working with them that might make their wisdom accessible to a wider range of people. He also clearly recognizes that the rigor and depths of Buddhist wisdom reside in the living practice of those who are inspired by it, and who are touched by the intrinsic universality of these teachings about the nature of the mind and body, and the nature of suffering, and who also recognize the importance of the ethical foundations of these teachings and their promise in the face of seemingly endless greed, hatred, and delusion in the age in which we find ourselves. This book is an invitation to systematically deepen our own lived understanding of mindfulness in relationship to human wellbeing and health, to wisdom and compassion embodied, or, as Anālayo puts it in this book, "to learn to face one's own being subject to disease and death, in order to be able to assist others in the same task". Easy to say. Not so easy to live. That is why this book is so welcome, and so necessary at this point in time.

When I decided, in the late 1970s, to see if it might be possible to introduce the practice of mindfulness into the mainstream of medicine and health care in a major academic medical center and hospital, it was in part because of my own direct experience of physical pain years earlier on a two-week-

1 Anālayo mentions this phenomenon in a scholarly paper on healing in early Buddhism which cites some of the early work on Mindfulness-Based Stress Reduction (MBSR) for people with chronic pain conditions; see Anālayo 2015c.

2 Kabat-Zinn 1982, Kabat-Zinn et al. 1985 and 1986, and Zeidan et al. 2015 and 2016.

3 Anālayo 2014c.

long *vipassanā* meditation retreat conducted in the Burmese tradition of Sayagyi U Ba Khin --- and the direct discovery, out of necessity, that there were practical ways of working with what felt unbearable without moving my body or trying to escape the discomfort. Although in my case, shifting my posture (we were taking vows of not moving voluntarily for up to several hours at a time) would have ended the experience of intense bodily pain and its attendant suffering, it struck me that for people for whom their suffering due to chronic pain conditions was constant and not so easily dispelled, what I was learning about pain and the body and the mind through the systematic cultivation of *samatha* and *vipassanā* under the umbrella of "mindfulness" could have potentially profound and liberative benefits in medical settings. I came to see that hospitals and medical centers function in society as what we might call *dukkha magnets*, drawing virtually all of us to them once our symptoms, level of pain, disease, or injury reach a certain point. What better place then to offer a relatively intensive systematic exposure over a period of time to what the Buddha discovered through his own arduous and rigorous investigations but in a form and language that was not classically Buddhist but nevertheless designed and calibrated to teach the meditative cultivation of open-hearted awareness while igniting strong motivation to practice in the face of all aspects of the human condition and human suffering?

The synergies are evident, and compelling. Recall, as Anālayo points out in the opening chapter, that the Buddha is sometimes referred to as the physician of the world, and that the four noble truths were articulated in a classical medical form that pertains to this day: (1) diagnosis; (2) etiology; (3) prognosis; (4) treatment plan. While in a mainstream medical setting such as a hospital, "mindfulness" could not and should not be offered as Buddhism or as philosophy, it was definitely within the realm of possibility, I thought, to take a cue from the non-dual Chan traditions and let the universal essence of the Dharma and its elucidation unfold out of the practice of the meditation itself.[4] This insight came on a two-week retreat at the Insight Meditation Society in Barre, Massachusetts, a place that is dear to Anālayo's heart and where

4 Kabat-Zinn 2013.

he teaches regularly. The vision was to articulate the practice of mindfulness in ways that any ordinary person could understand, as a way to cultivate and strengthen innate qualities and capacities, rather than the imposition of a framework based on texts of any kind, whether it be the four noble truths, the eightfold path, the four establishments of mindfulness, the seven factors of awakening, or any other teachings we might as committed meditation practitioners be drawing on to support and deepen our own practice. As "mindfulness instructors" within modern medicine and health care, we would have to teach out of our own experience rather than citing authoritative Buddhist sources or texts, or, for that matter, drawing on inspiring or endearing Buddhist stories. Nevertheless, we ourselves would have to be grounded in our own dharma practice based on classical teachings from various Buddhist traditions, while continuing to learn from and practice with recognized Buddhist Dharma teachers. That meant we would be *translators* of Dharma and Dharma practice in a universal idiom that would nevertheless be as congruent with those classical teachings as we could manage to live up to in our own lives. In MBSR and the other mindfulness-based interventions that have proliferated over the past decades, this is referred to as "teaching out of our own practice and experience". But this does not mean teaching whatever one likes, or making up your own private version of the Dharma. It means immersing yourself in the classical teachings to undergird and reinforce your own commitment to living an awakened life via the practice of mindfulness/heartfulness.[5]

In the early days of MBSR, the book I found most helpful and supportive in deepening my own first-person understanding of mindfulness and its cultivation, and how such practices fit into the larger framework of Buddhadharma, was Nyanaponika Thera's *The Heart of Buddhist Meditation*,[6] a systematic explication of the *Satipaṭṭhāna-sutta* and the only one readily available at that time. I also found Nyanaponika's book invaluable in another way. It helped clarify and deepen my own intuitions and experience, based on years of practice and study both in the Chan/Zen/Sŏn tradition and in the

5 Kabat-Zinn 1990/2013, 2005, and 2010.
6 Nyanaponika 1962.

Theravāda *vipassanā* tradition, regarding the potential value of a disciplined daily cultivation of mindfulness in everyday life in the face of stress, pain, and illness. The challenge was to discern how such meditative practices might be presented and described in ways that would appeal to Westerners with no particular interest in Buddhism or classical Buddhist teachings, but who were suffering greatly and might benefit from taking up the practice of mindfulness in their own lives, especially if it could be engaged in wholeheartedly and consistently over time. The idea was to make mindfulness as a disciplined meditation practice and a way of living completely commonsensical and worth engaging in as an experiment, especially for people with chronic medical problems who were falling through the cracks of the health-care system and not getting the benefits from traditional treatments that they had hoped for. Of course, the challenge is always that of not losing or denaturing the essence and depth as one explores new ways of presenting and languaging the dharma in its most universal manifestations. I see this as an ongoing evolutionary challenge, for Buddhism, for the world, and for those who love and live and teach the dharma, as mindfulness – for better or for worse – enters the mainstream of society globally, as is presently happening at an exponential rate.

Now, with this book, more than fifty years after Nyanaponika's offering, Bhikkhu Anālayo, who was born in Germany, as was Nyanaponika – in their times both deeply rooted to monastic life in Sri Lanka – offers us a much higher-resolution microscope with which to investigate how a mindfulness-based wisdom approach might be cultivated in the face of sickness, pain conditions, disease, and death. It taps early Buddhist textual sources mostly from the Chinese, carefully selected and sequenced here for their explicit focus on these specific concerns, and translated for the first time by the author. Each introduction and discussion, bookending a central text, invites deep reflection. The instructions for dealing with sickness, pain, and/or death, one's own and others', in all twenty-four selections, contain clear, uncompromising, and practical advice for any practitioner. They are concise, precise, and at the same time challenging even to long-time practitioners, even as they are also straightforward and intimately accessible. If enacted in practice, they provide profound step-by-step instruction in the cultivation of insight, wisdom, and healing. Above all, these teachings invite us to integrate their guidance directly into the laboratory of our own meditation practice and life, in the spirit of deep investigation and inquiry. As committed meditation practitioners know first hand, there is no more worthy or meaningful introspective undertaking in the world, nor a more difficult challenge for human beings to adopt and sustain throughout life.

For just these reasons, and the fact that this book is in a Buddhist idiom and vocabulary based on classical Buddhist texts, it will probably not be of great interest or practical utility to the general public, nor to the people we see every day in MBSR programs, no matter how severe their suffering. The barriers for most will simply be too high. However, these texts and Anālayo's commentaries can and hopefully will serve as a powerful resource for those of us, worldwide, who are MBSR instructors and instructors-in-training, or instructors of other mindfulness-based interventions, in supporting our own meditation practices, understanding, and teaching, just as Nyanaponika's book was for me at the beginning of MBSR. Anālayo's book will certainly challenge us to look more deeply into our own relationship to these classical dharma teachings and to our own experiences of suffering within the framework of our meditation practice and of life itself unfolding – and hopefully recognize over and over again that these are essentially one and the same. While the material itself may not be directly applicable in teaching mindfulness in mainstream settings, the insights and transformations it might catalyze in those of us who study these texts and commentaries may lead to new ways of highlighting and bringing out in class discussions some of these deep teachings in ways that can be very much heard and adopted by medical patients and others suffering ill health.[7]

7 For instance, as concerns the four establishments of mindfulness, they are never taught as such in MBSR. However, in our experience, the essence emerges on its own in class discussions as we share and discuss our experiences with the body, with pleasant and unpleasant experience, and

This work will, of course, also and primarily be welcomed and hopefully celebrated widely by Buddhist scholars and by Buddhist meditation teachers and practitioners across all traditions who might be looking for new opportunities to explore and deepen their understanding of Dharma in their own lives and work, and, more specifically, its implications in regard to heath and healing, writ large in the form of unbounded wakefulness and a constitutive intimacy with the *brahmavihāras*. Anālayo eschews orthodoxy throughout, and his humility shines through in his explicit acknowledgement that the perspective he offers here is only *one* perspective on these texts, not *the* perspective.

Tying together and unifying the twenty-four texts and major themes Anālayo has selected for exploration and exegesis in a logical and compelling sequence is a final chapter with a skillful and encompassing summary, accompanied by his powerful meditation instructions, commentary, and recommendations. Anchored in the *Girimānanda-sutta*, these instructions encapsulate and distill the essence of all the topics covered in the selected texts, basically offering a rigorous and overarching condensed curriculum of what has come before. This concluding section maps the liberative dimensions of mindfulness as a practice, and how to optimize its potential for healing, here used in the sense of *coming to terms with things as they are*,[8] at the level of both body and mind.[9] These practice recommendations invite careful study and exploratory enacting in one's own life. Mindfulness of breathing, in Anālayo's words, "functions as a culmination point of practice". Explicitly scanning the body and isolating awareness of different groupings (skin, flesh, bones), as he recommends, is one more instance of the strong overlap with mindfulness-based approaches in medicine, although,

---

with awareness of thoughts and emotions. This is a natural progression. It often feels in teaching this way as if the deep dharma wisdom emerges on its own, most often in conversation and dialogue among the class participants, when the ground is prepared in practice, and when the instructor is practiced enough to draw out these themes from the actual reported experiences of the participants in their formal cultivation of mindfulness and in its moment-to-moment extension into everyday life.

8 Kabat-Zinn 2013, p.27.

9 See Aming Tu's postscript below p.251, in which he uses the phrase to "come to terms" in regard to facing his own life and death.

when it comes to body scans, we emphasize the virtues of lying-down meditations (in the *corpse* pose)[10] for falling awake and for befriending the life and constant flux of the body,[11] as well as a more conventional sequence of body regions. Anālayo also strongly encourages awareness of the body as a whole, and aptly describes it as *proprioceptive awareness*. He goes on to make skillful use of it to explore the five aggregates and highlight impermanence, with the invitation to ultimately, in his words, "rest in awareness of all aggregates in combination as a mere flux". This is similar to the practice we call *choiceless awareness* in MBSR, and others term *shikantaza*,[12] *silent illumination*,[13] or *present fresh wakefulness*.[14]

I am struck by some deep synergies in these texts with Mahāyāna teachings. The *Heart-sūtra* comes to mind, with its radical non-dual treatment of the five aggregates, the senses, even the four noble truths,[15] as does the radical non-dualism of the *Xìnxīn Míng* (*Verses on the Faith Mind*) by Sēngcàn, the third Chan patriarch.[16] Also, in a different vein, the *Vimalakīrti-sūtra*,[17] in which the Buddha asks person after person in his retinue to go and inquire after the health of the layman Vimalakīrti, who is reported to be sick.[18] However, so great is Vimalakīrti's prowess in non-dual Dharma that all are intimidated and decline to deliver the Buddha's message until Mañjuśrī, the wisest of the bodhisattvas, assents to go. At that point, all 500 of the Buddha's closest disciples and 8,000 bodhisattvas who are present tag along to listen in on the conversation and benefit from Vimalakīrti's unparalleled Dharma wisdom. What follows is a series of teachings very similar to those offered in the early

---

10 The name itself invites investigation of dying, as in "dying to the past and the future", for instance, and dying to who one thinks one is, as well as inquiring into "Who dies?"

11 This is especially valuable for people with chronic pain or other conditions that make sitting for extended periods of time difficult.

12 Kapleau 1967.

13 Sheng Yen 2012.

14 Chokyi Nyima 2002.

15 Tanahashi 2014.

16 Mu Soeng 2004.

17 Thurman 1976.

18 See below p. 185 on the lay disciple Citta, who can be seen as a forerunner of Vimalakīrti.

Buddhist texts Anālayo presents for us here: on impermanence, emptiness, equanimity, and selflessness, and our potential for full awakening through the cultivation of mindfulness.

A Chinese Chan master aged ninety-seven once said to me:[19] "There are an infinite number of ways in which people suffer. Therefore, there have to be an infinite number of ways in which the Dharma is made available to them." This book provides a new and welcome way to familiarize ourselves with and understand the Buddha's explicit teachings on how to approach the inevitability of stress, pain, disease, dying, and death, in others and in ourselves. May we all be its beneficiaries. And may it be instrumental in pointing the way to bring greater solace, peace, and wisdom for all.

Jon Kabat-Zinn, Ph.D.
Northampton, Massachusetts
30 March, 2016

Professor of Medicine emeritus
Founder, Center for Mindfulness in
Medicine, Health Care, and Society
University of Massachusetts Medical School

19 Ven. Ben Huang, Shenzen, China, 2004.

Suppose a person comes and, standing to one side, sees that a traveller on an extended journey along a long road has become sick halfway, is exhausted and suffering extremely. He is alone and without a companion. The village behind is far away and he has not yet reached the village ahead. [The person thinks]: "If he were to get an attendant, emerge from being in the wilderness far away and reach a village or town, and were to be given excellent medicine and be fed with nourishing and delicious food, be well cared for, then in this way this person's sickness would certainly subside." So that person has extremely compassionate, sympathetic, and kind thoughts in the mind towards this sick person.

INTRODUCTION

Disease and death are undeniably integral parts of human life. Yet, when they manifest one is easily caught unprepared. To prepare oneself for what one will certainly encounter at some time, there is a definite need to learn how to face the time of illness and passing away skilfully. In support of such learning, a source of practical wisdom can be found in the early discourses that record the teachings given by the Buddha and his disciples.

The chief aim of this book is to provide a collection of passages from the early discourses that provide guidance for facing disease and death. The present anthology thereby continues the theme of compassion, whose meditative cultivation as part of the four divine abodes I studied in a monograph on *Compassion and Emptiness in Early Buddhist Meditation*.[1] Whereas in that study my focus was on the meditative cultivation of compassion, *karuṇā*, the present study is concerned with its complement in *anukampā*, compassion as the underlying motivation in altruistic action.[2]

A discourse passage illustrating how compassion can arise, with which I started my other study,[3] describes seeing a person who is sick. I have placed this same passage at the outset of the present book, since it similarly serves as the starting point of my study of disease and death. Precisely such compassionate,

1 Anālayo 2015b.
2 On the two terms see in more detail Anālayo 2015b: 13.
3 MĀ 25 at T I 454b20 to 454b25, quoted in Anālayo 2015b: 5f.

sympathetic, and kind thoughts on seeing someone else afflicted are what motivates one's wish to assist those who are sick or on the verge of death. In order to be able to do so, however, it is indispensable that one also learns to face one's own sicknesses and mortality. This will be a recurrent theme of my exploration throughout this book.

The passages translated below at times explicitly mention compassion, *anukampā*, as part of an invitation to the Buddha or one of his disciples to come and visit someone who is sick or on the verge of death. When the Buddha or his disciples pay such visits without prompting, the same motivation is implicit. Those motivated by such compassionate concern are monastic disciples who are arahants or who are still in training, as well as lay disciples. In early Buddhist thought the compassionate concern to assist those who are sick or on the verge of death is common to these different types of disciples.

The four noble truths, which according to tradition correspond to the first teaching given by the recently awakened Buddha, provide the framework for the early Buddhist perspective on disease and death. The presentation of these four noble truths in this first teaching takes the form of "twelve turnings", a count that results from analysing the realization of each of the four truths into three distinct aspects. For the ground plan of this study I have adopted the same number twelve,[4] allocating twelve chapters to the topic of disease and another twelve chapters to the topic of death. Each of these two sets of twelve starts with a discussion of the four noble truths and culminates in a discourse on meditation practice. The two sets together are followed by a conclusion that offers practical meditation instructions. These bring together the chief themes explored in the preceding chapters in actual meditative practice, thereby catering to the need mentioned above to learn to face one's own being subject to disease and death, in order to be able to assist others in the same task.

Chapter 1 takes up a comparison between the Buddha teaching the four noble truths and a physician, thereby underlining the pragmatic orientation of this central doctrine in

4 On the symbolic significance of the number twelve in ancient India in general see Spellman 1962.

Buddhist thought that serves as the basic framework for facing disease and death. Chapters 2 and 3 draw attention to the need to protect the mind from being afflicted by bodily pain. Chapter 4 presents a listing of qualities of a patient and a nurse that enable speedy recovery. The qualities that bring about mental health through awakening are the topic of Chapter 5, followed by a focus on the role of mindfulness in facing pain in Chapters 6, 7, and 8.

Chapter 9 explores the theme of one's virtue leading to fearlessness when ill and Chapter 10 turns to concentration and insight at the time of sickness. Chapter 11 features instructions given by a patient to those who had enquired about his health. A whole meditation programme emerges from instructions to a sick monk in Chapter 12, whose practical implementation I explore in detail in the conclusion to this book.

Grief for dear ones is the theme of Chapters 13 and 14, with which my exploration turns from the theme of disease, explored in the first twelve chapters, to the topic of death studied in the remaining twelve chapters. The divine abodes as a way of passing away peacefully feature in Chapter 15; Chapter 16 presents deathbed instructions on insight. Chapter 17 takes up the impact of family relationships at the time of death; instructions on palliative care can be found in Chapter 18.

Chapter 19 provides instructions on mindful dying, and Chapters 20 and 21 record instances when the moment of death led to high realizations. An account of the exemplary passing away of an accomplished lay disciple can be found in Chapter 22. Chapter 23 turns to the Buddha's meditative passing away, and Chapter 24 shows how to cultivate recollection of death with diligence and offers practical instructions.

Following these two sets of twelve chapters, the conclusion presents detailed meditation instructions based on the discourse translated in Chapter 12. This is followed by an appendix with translations of the sixteen steps of mindfulness of breathing in two *Vinaya*s, which by way of inculcating continuous awareness of impermanence is a meditation practice of considerable importance to the topics covered in this book. In this way, besides completing my study of the meditative cultivation of compassion (*karuṇā*) with an exploration of active expressions of compassion (*anukampā*), the present book also complements my early surveys of mindfulness of breathing from the viewpoint of *satipaṭṭhāna* meditation.[5]

As a general pattern, in each of the twenty-four chapters a whole discourse, or at least substantial parts of it, is translated, preceded by an introduction and followed by a discussion. The introduction and discussion parts are only meant to provide a starting point for readers to develop their own reflections and do not claim to offer full coverage of the various implications and nuances of the translated discourse. The majority of the passages chosen are based on Chinese originals and, with a few exceptions, are here translated into English for the first time. The choice of relying on passages from the Chinese *Āgama*s reflects the fact that several English translations already exist of the corresponding Pāli versions. By translating their Chinese counterparts, my intention is to allow the reader to compare the parallel versions in English translation and get a first-hand impression, beyond the selected observations that I provide regarding variations between them.

The bulk of discourses relevant to the topic of disease and death are from the *Saṃyukta-āgama* and thereby from a textual lineage transmitted by a Buddhist school known as Mūlasarvāstivāda.[6] The Mūlasarvāstivāda *Vinaya* is still followed nowadays by monastics in the Tibetan tradition. Although Tibetan and Theravāda Buddhism take at times quite distinct positions, when it comes to the issue of facing disease and death the teachings recorded in the early discourses of these two traditions show close agreement alongside interesting variations in details.

In the discourses translated in this book, often the original gives the full exposition only for the first and perhaps last item

5 Anālayo 2003: 125–36 and 2013b: 227–40.

6 This *Saṃyukta-āgama*, found in the Taishō edition as entry 99, shows ample evidence of the influence of a general penchant among Chinese translators for introducing some variation in their renderings of what in the Indic original must have been the same formulations or expressions. Even quotes of a sentence found just a few lines earlier are often given in slightly different wording, and standard expressions are at times rendered in a different way.

in a list, and the rest is abbreviated. At times whole descriptions are abbreviated, and an indication is given regarding what other discourses the full treatment should be supplemented from. In my translations I replace such abbreviations with the full passage, marking the fact that this part has been supplemented by putting it into italics.[7] In this way I intend to enable those who wish to approach the translated text in a more contemplative spirit to do a full reading and thereby let the instruction sink in with each of the items in such a list in turn. At the same time I hope the use of italics will facilitate reading for those more inclined to read for information, making it easy to jump to the end of the supplemented part in italics and continue reading where the translation from the original sets in again. In the case of supplementations that are my own choice, adopted in order to enable a better understanding of a somewhat cryptic Chinese passage, I use square brackets [ ] instead of italics, and for emendations I employ angle brackets ⟨ ⟩.

So as to avoid gendered terminology and to ensure that my presentation does not give the impression that it is meant for male practitioners only, I translate equivalents of the term *bhikkhu* with "monastic".[8] I have not been able to avoid the fact that the passages presented are predominantly populated by male characters. In texts of this time and culture, women generally feature more rarely as participants in discussions and as recipients of teachings. In the case of the early Buddhist texts, of the few instances related to disease and death that do involve females, several have no parallel in other textual traditions and for this reason have fallen outside of the scope of my selection.[9]

---

7 In order for this to work, in translated passages throughout Indic terms are not in italics.

8 See also p. 66 note 1 and p. 131 note 11.

9 In the case of the story of Nakulamātā attending to her dying husband in AN 6.16 at AN III 295,12 (translated Bodhi 2012: 871), no parallel is known. The tales of the long pregnancy of Suppavāsa and of Visākhā mourning the death of a grandchild, Ud 2.8 at Ud 15,6 and Ud 8.8 at Ud 91,12 (translated Ireland 1990: 28 and 121), are without a counterpart in T 212, the only *Udāna* collection preserved in Chinese that does accompany *udāna*s with prose narrations, similar to the case of the Pāli *Udāna* collection; see in more detail Anālayo 2009a.

In order to present the early Buddhist perspective on disease and death in a way that goes beyond the confines of one particular Buddhist tradition, I have endeavoured to include only texts that are extant from more than a single lineage of transmission. Three special cases are the discourse chosen for Chapter 1, which is unknown in Pāli but found in a range of sources that clearly fall into two distinct transmission lineages, and two discourses translated from a Tibetan original in Chapters 5 and 11. These two discourses are not part of the Mūlasarvāstivāda textual tradition, but rather have their origin in Theravāda texts that were brought to Tibet and translated there.[10] Both differ in several respects from their Pāli counterpart, making them representatives of different transmission lineages within the same Theravāda tradition.

In my translations I employ Pāli terms for the sake of ease of comparison, without thereby intending to take a position on the language of the original that formed the basis for the translation into Chinese. Exceptions are terms like Dharma and Nirvāṇa, both of which are now commonly used in Western publications.

In the hope of making my presentation easily accessible to readers who may not necessarily be familiar with some of the intricate details of early Buddhist doctrine, I give brief introductions to chief doctrinal terms or aspects of early Buddhist thought in each chapter, inasmuch as these are relevant to the discourse taken up. For ease of cross-reference, a list of these terms and aspects according to chapter can be found above, p. xv.

I owe the inspiration to compile this book to my friend and colleague Aming Tu of Dharma Drum Mountain. As a professor of Buddhist informatics and a dedicated practitioner of Chan meditation, Aming Tu found the discourses on disease and death in the Chinese *Āgama*s to be an immense resource when having to live with the gradual deterioration caused to his body by cancer. In awareness of the benefit he derived from these texts, he had the compassionate wish for these teachings to be made more widely available to the general reader through being translated and explained. When he

10 On the transmission of these texts see Skilling 1993.

shared his idea with me, I was only too happy to follow it up, and the present book is the result of putting into practice the basic plan we developed together. In a postscript to this book he shares his personal experience, describing how he found the discourses from the Chinese *Āgama*s helped him to face disease and death.[11]

---

11 See below p. 250.

I

THE BUDDHA AS A SUPREME PHYSICIAN

I.1 INTRODUCTION

The discourse translated in the present chapter, which forms the starting point for this whole book, presents a comparison between the Buddha and a physician. This comparison is significant in so far as it involves a central teaching in Buddhist thought: the four noble truths. These are concerned with *dukkha*, a term whose meaning ranges from what is outright painful to what is of an unsatisfactory nature. Elsewhere I have argued that the standard translation "suffering" can be misleading.[1] Instead of imposing what in my view is a preferable translation on the reader, in what follows I simply use the Pāli term *dukkha*. The four noble truths are as follows:

- the noble truth of *dukkha*,
- the noble truth of the arising of *dukkha*,
- the noble truth of the cessation of *dukkha*,
- the noble truth of the path leading to the cessation of *dukkha*.

According to tradition, this is the teaching which the recently awakened Buddha disclosed to his first disciples.[2] This teaching

1 Anālayo 2003: 243–5.
2 For a detailed study of the various accounts of this first teaching see Anālayo 2012a and 2013a.

appears to be modelled on an ancient Indian scheme of medical diagnosis. Although we do not have incontrovertible proof that ancient Indian medicine had such a scheme,[3] the absence of such proof needs to be considered in light of the fact that extant ancient Indian medical treatises in general stem from a later period than the early Buddhist discourses. The presentation in the discourse translated in this chapter and other relevant early discourses makes it fairly probable that some such diagnostic scheme was in existence at the popular level.[4] The correlation between this medical diagnosis and what is perhaps the most central Buddhist doctrine can be visualized as follows:

- disease: *dukkha*,
- pathogen: arising of *dukkha*,
- health: cessation of *dukkha*,
- cure: eightfold path.

The correlation of the four noble truths with a fourfold medical diagnosis and the comparison between the Buddha and a physician are found in several discourses. In addition to the discourse from the *Saṃyukta-āgama* which I translate below, another two discourse versions are extant in Chinese translation.[5] Partial discourse quotations are preserved in works in Sanskrit,[6] and a complete discourse quotation exists in Tibetan.[7] In addition, yet another version has been preserved in fragments in Uighur, an ancient Turkish language, presumably having been translated from Chinese translations in turn.[8] From the viewpoint of textual transmission, these different versions fall into two main groups, making it clear that the basic presentation of the Buddha as a physician is not just a case of a single version being preserved in different languages.

3 See Har Dayal 1932/1970: 159, Filliozat 1934: 301, and Wezler 1984: 312–24.
4 See in more detail Anālayo 2011b.
5 SĀ[2] 254 at T II 462c9 and T 219 at T IV 802a16; for a translation of both see Bingenheimer forthcoming.
6 These are found in the *Abhidharmakośavyākhyā*, Wogihara 1936: 514,27, and in a commentary on the *Arthaviniścaya-sūtra*, Samtani 1971: 159,6.
7 D 4094 *nyu* 1b1 or Q 5595 *thu* 32b6.
8 Kudara and Zieme 1995: 47–52.

Instead, there are clearly at least two distinct transmission lineages attesting to the present discourse.

Even though no direct Pāli parallel to the present discourse is known, other Pāli discourses regularly refer to the Buddha as a physician. A discourse in the *Aṅguttara-nikāya*, moreover, illustrates the dispelling of one's sorrow and grief through hearing the Buddha's teaching with the example of being quickly relieved from a disease by a skilled doctor.[9] In short, comparing the Buddha to a physician and his teaching to a medical cure is a common theme in the early discourses.

The chief teaching of the four noble truths provides the foundation and framework within which a solution to the pressing problem of disease and death can be found. It not only does so in the sense of providing a framework for assisting others and oneself in facing sickness and loss of life, but also offers a perspective that goes beyond all types of affliction caused by illness and mortality. This is the perspective of the final goal of practice being a condition of total mental health through awakening.

In the discourse below the Buddha refers to himself as the Tathāgata, thereby employing a term in common use in the ancient Indian setting for someone who had reached full realization.[10] The term itself could be understood in two ways, as describing an accomplished one either as being "thus gone" or as "thus come". Both senses converge on conveying the sense of a thorough transcendence of worldly limitations by the one designated as Tathāgata.

I.2 TRANSLATION[11]

Thus have I heard. At one time the Buddha was staying at Benares in the Deer Park at Isipatana. At that time the Blessed One told the monastics:

---

9 AN 5.194 at AN III 238,5 (translated Bodhi 2012: 811).
10 On the term see in more detail Anālayo 2008b.
11 The translated discourse is SĀ 389 at T II 105a24 to 105b20, which I have already translated in Anālayo 2011b: 23f.

"By accomplishing four principles one is reckoned a great royal physician, worthy of being the possession of a king and of being a member of the king's [retinue]. What are the four?

"One: being skilled in understanding a disease; two: being skilled in understanding the source of a disease; three: being skilled in understanding the cure for a disease; four: being skilled in understanding when a disease has been cured and will not appear again.

"How is someone reckoned to be a good doctor who is skilled in understanding a disease? That is, a good doctor is skilled in understanding various types of disease as they are; this is reckoned to be a good doctor who is skilled in understanding a disease.

"How is someone a good doctor who is skilled in understanding the source of a disease? That is, a good doctor is skilled in understanding that this disease has arisen because of wind, this has arisen due to phlegm,[12] this has arisen due to mucus, this has arisen due to various colds, this has arisen because of an actual event,[13] this has arisen due to seasonal [influence]; this is reckoned to be a good doctor who is skilled in understanding the source of a disease.

"How is someone a good doctor who is skilled in understanding the cure of a disease? That is, a good doctor is skilled in understanding that for various types of disease one should administer medication, or should [bring about] vomiting, or should [administer] a laxative, or should [undertake] nasal instillations, or should [administer] fumigation, or should bring about perspiration; on [administering] in this manner various cures, one is reckoned a good doctor who is skilled in understanding the cure of a disease.

"How is someone a good doctor who is skilled in understanding when a disease has been cured and will never appear again in the future? That is, a good doctor is skilled in curing various types of disease so that they are completely eliminated and will never arise again in the future; this is reckoned to be a good doctor

12 The translation "phlegm" is based on adopting a variant; see also Yìnshùn 1983b: 115 note 2.

13 I suppose this means an accident.

who is skilled in understanding how to cure a disease so that it will not appear again.[14]

"A Tathāgata, who is an arahant and fully awakened, is also just like that, being a great royal physician who has accomplished four qualities to cure the disease of living beings. What are the four?

"That is, the Tathāgata understands that this is the noble truth of dukkha, knowing it as it really is; that this is the noble truth of the arising of dukkha, knowing it as it really is; that this is the noble truth of the cessation of dukkha, knowing it as it really is; and that this is the noble truth of the way to the cessation of dukkha, knowing it as it really is.

"Monastics, the secular good doctor does not understand as it really is the fundamental cure for birth, *does not understand as it really is the fundamental cure* for old age, *does not understand as it really is the fundamental cure* for disease, *does not understand as it really is the fundamental cure* for death, *does not understand as it really is the fundamental cure* for sadness, *does not understand as it really is the fundamental cure* for sorrow, *does not understand as it really is the fundamental cure* for vexation, and does not understand as it really is the fundamental cure for dukkha.[15]

"The Tathāgata, who is an arahant and fully awakened, being a great royal physician, does understand as it really is the fundamental cure for birth, *does understand as it really is the fundamental cure* for old age, *does understand as it really is the fundamental cure* for disease, *does understand as it really is the fundamental cure* for death, *does understand as it really is the fundamental cure* for sadness, *does understand as it really is the fundamental cure* for sorrow, *does understand as it really is the*

14 The above detailed exposition of the four principles is absent from the discourse parallel SĀ² 254, which after enumerating these four principles in short at T II 462c13 directly proceeds to the comparison with the Tathāgata. The discourse quotations in the *Abhidharmakośavyākhyā* and the *Arthaviniścaya-sūtra*, Wogihara 1936: 514,31 and Samtani 1971: 160,3, also do not go into the details regarding what the four qualities of a skilled doctor imply. T 219 at T IV 802a26 and D 4094 *nyu* 1b5 or Q 5595 *thu* 33a2, however, do have such a detailed exposition.

15 SĀ² 254 at T II 462c17 compares the predicament of the first truth to a poisoned arrow, a simile also found in the Uighur version, Kudara and Zieme 1995: 48; see also Samtani 1971: 160,1.

fundamental cure for vexation, and does understand as it really is the fundamental cure for dukkha. For this reason the Tathāgata, who is an arahant and fully awakened, is reckoned a great royal physician."[16]

When the Buddha had spoken this discourse, hearing what the Buddha had said the monastics were delighted and received it respectfully.

I.3 DISCUSSION

The correlation between the four noble truths and a diagnostic scheme taken from the realm of medicine adds a pragmatic flavour to what tradition reckons the central teaching delivered by the recently awakened Buddha. This teaching begins by clearly acknowledging that there is "dis-ease" in life. That this is indeed the case becomes quite plain when one falls ill or ages, and even more so when one has to face death, be it one's own or another's.

But even at other times there is a continuous "dis-ease", since, however pleasurable an experience may be at present, it will not last. Sooner or later it will cease; therefore it is incapable of providing lasting satisfaction. One will not always get what one wishes, but instead will often experience the frustration of unwanted experiences. At times one will have to leave the company of those one likes and be with those with whom one would rather not be associating. The early Buddhist teaching of the first noble truth sums up all these problems under a single term: *dukkha*.

Whereas the first of the four noble truths involves the honest recognition of the fact of *dukkha*, the second noble truth points out that one contributes to *dukkha* oneself. Even though everyone wants to be happy and at ease, the way many go about trying to achieve this can be rather unskilful. One clings and craves, and as a result is bound to suffer, precisely because of craving and clinging.

16 SĀ² 254 at T II 462c26 and the Uighur version, Kudara and Zieme 1995: 48–52, continue by reporting that a monastic by the name of Vaṅgīsa proclaimed a set of stanzas in praise of the Buddha, paralleling SĀ 1220 at T II 332c16.

Following the disconcerting realization that one's own craving makes a substantial contribution to the actual experience of *dukkha*, the third noble truth discloses an alternative to this predicament. It does so by announcing that there is a condition that is entirely free from craving, where the mind has become totally "healthy" in all respects by completely leaving behind the influence of what is unwholesome. With all the parallels to medicine, this third noble truth makes it clear that the early Buddhist conception of mental health goes far beyond what modern psychology would consider a healthy condition of the mind.

The fourth noble truth delineates the practical path to be undertaken to reach this condition of mental health. This path is presented as eightfold, in the sense that it covers eight complementary aspects of development:

- right view,
- right intention,
- right speech,
- right action,
- right livelihood,
- right effort,
- right mindfulness,
- right concentration.

Based on a preliminary appreciation of the four noble truths, one establishes right *view*, in the sense of a perspective on one's own predicament as well as that of others that has the potential to lead out of this predicament. This is what makes such view "right" or "correct". Implementing such rightness or correctness of view runs counter to being obsessed with the wrongdoings of others or the unfairness of adverse circumstances. Instead the focus provided by right view is on what one can do oneself within circumstances as they are at present, in particular in terms of lessening one's own clinging and attachment.

Applied to the actual situation of being confronted with a distressing or painful experience, one begins with the frank recognition that this is indeed a manifestation of *dukkha*. Next comes the question of the extent to which one contributes oneself, in whatever way this may be, to the distressful and painful nature of this experience. This type of enquiry takes courage and honesty. The reward is immediate, though, since taking responsibility for what one has done or is doing oneself in turn empowers one to "undo", to change and find an alternative approach to this same situation. The adjustments needed for this alternative to have a substantial impact on the situation at hand do at times require a gradual approach, a path of practice. Yet, as long as the basic perspective is brought into being and maintained, based on realizing how one has become an unwitting accomplice in the genesis of one's own *dukkha*, every step taken leads forward in the right direction. How all this relates to pain will be explored in the next chapters.

In this way the curative perspective afforded by right view informs one's *intentions*, the way one *speaks* and *acts*, and even the way one earns one's *livelihood*. The same perspective also underpins a systematic cultivation of the mind, which requires the *effort* to emerge out of defiled mental conditions, the *mindfulness* to know one's own mental situation, and the calmness of the mind that comes with the development of *concentration*.

Out of these, it is in particular right mindfulness in the form of practice of the four establishments of mindfulness, the four *satipaṭṭhāna*s, that is of considerable relevance to facing disease and death. The significance of mindfulness in this respect is a topic to which I will come back repeatedly in the next chapters, which show that the potential of the practice of mindfulness to bring about actual healing and help in facing pain was clearly recognized in early Buddhist thought. At the same time, however, the function of right mindfulness as an integral aspect of the noble eightfold path goes further. Its aim is to bring about the achievement of total mental health by eradicating all defilements in the mind through full awakening.

II

SICK BODY AND HEALTHY MIND

II.1 INTRODUCTION

Based on the diagnostic perspective provided by the four noble truths, different possible approaches emerge for handling the condition of being sick and in pain. The discourse taken up below distinguishes the body and the mind as related but not necessarily conjoined components of the experience of being in pain. In the present instance the Buddha teaches this distinction to an ageing lay disciple. According to this teaching, even though the body is sick, the mind need not be sick as well. Consequently one should make an effort to avoid as much as possible that the mind suffers along with the body.

This provides a practical application of the curative perspective afforded by right view, discussed in the last chapter, and at the same time is where much of what comes in subsequent chapters of this book falls into place. In addition to looking after the body with the help of modern or traditional forms of medical care, there is considerable scope for training the mind so that it will not also fall sick. Such training not only alleviates any mental distress, but also stands considerable chance of supporting physical recovery.

The discourse translated below stems from the *Saṃyukta-āgama*, with counterparts in the *Saṃyutta-nikāya* and in the *Ekottarika-*

āgama.[1] The three versions agree that, after the Buddha had delivered the enigmatic instruction that one should prevent the mind from becoming sick along with the body, a chief disciple of the Buddha by the name of Sāriputta gave a more detailed explanation of this statement.

Elsewhere the early discourses assign to Sāriputta the role of keeping the wheel of Dharma rolling that had been set in motion by the Buddha.[2] The idea of rolling the wheel of Dharma refers back to the Buddha's first teaching of the four noble truths, mentioned in the previous chapter. The present instance provides a fitting illustration of Sāriputta's role in keeping the wheel of the Buddha's instruction rolling, since he skilfully expands on what the Buddha had taught in brief, showing how this can be applied to the predicament of being in physical pain. The one who receives the brief instruction by the Buddha and its detailed exegesis by Sāriputta is the ageing lay disciple Nakula, known in Pāli discourses as "father Nakula", Nakulapitā. According to the Pāli commentarial tradition he had been the Buddha's father in many past lives.[3]

II.2 TRANSLATION[4]

> Thus have I heard. At one time the Buddha was staying among the Bhaggas at Suṃsumāragira in the Deer Park, the Bhesakaḷā Grove. At that time the householder Nakula was one hundred and twenty years old, and his faculties were ripe with age. [Although] being weak and suffering from disease, he still wished to meet the Blessed One and the senior and esteemed monastics who were his good friends.[5] He approached the Buddha, paid respect with his head at the Buddha's feet, withdrew to sit to one side, and said to the Buddha:

1 SN 22.1 at SN III 1,1 (translated Bodhi 2000: 853) and EĀ 13.4 at T II 573a1.

2 Sn 557, a qualification found also in the *Divyāvadāna*, Cowell and Neil 1886: 394,23.

3 Mp I 400,16; see in more detail Malalasekera 1938/1998: 3f as well as Nyanaponika and Hecker 1997: 375–8.

4 The translated discourse is SĀ 107 at T II 33a6 to 33b27, which I already translated in Anālayo 2014h: 27–31.

5 The introductory narrations in SN 22.1 and EĀ 13.4 do not provide information about the householder's age and his wish to meet the Buddha and the monastics.

"Blessed One, I am feeble from old age, I am weak and suffer from disease, [yet] with my own strength I make the effort to meet the Blessed One and the senior and esteemed monastics who are my good friends. May the Blessed One give me a teaching so that it will be for my peace for a long time."[6]

At that time the Blessed One said to the householder Nakula: "It is well, householder. You are really ripe with age, weak and suffering from disease, yet you are able with your own strength to meet the Tathāgata and the other senior and esteemed monastics who are your good friends.

"Householder you should know,[7] [when] the body is suffering from disease, you should constantly train so that the ⟨mind⟩ does not suffer from disease."[8]

At that time the Blessed One, having ⟨instructed⟩,[9] taught, illuminated, and delighted the householder Nakula, remained silent. The householder Nakula, hearing what the Buddha had said, rejoiced in it and was delighted. He paid respect to the Buddha and left. The venerable Sāriputta was then seated under a tree not far from the Buddha.[10] The householder Nakula approached the venerable Sāriputta, paid respect with his head at [Sāriputta's] feet, and withdrew to sit to one side.

Then the venerable Sāriputta asked the householder: "Your faculties are now joyfully relaxed, the colour of your complexion is bright. Have you been able to hear a profound teaching from the Blessed One?"

---

6 In SN 22.1 at SN III 1,8 he instead points out that he does not always get a chance to come for a visit.

7 SN 22.1 at SN III 1,14 and EĀ 13.4 at T II 573a8 precede this injunction with a reference to fools who claim to be healthy for a moment (SN 22.1) or who rely on the body to be happy for a moment (EĀ 13.4).

8 My rendering here and in the next passage is based on emending "body" to "mind". This emendation is based on the formulation used by Sāriputta in his explanation later in SĀ 107 and by the context. SN 22.1 at SN III 1,16 confirms that it is the mind which should not be sick; see also the *Vastusaṃgrahaṇī*, T 1579 at T XXX 799a7. A comparable error appears to have occurred in EĀ 13.4 at T II 573a9, in that, just as SĀ 107 erroneously speaks of the body in both cases, EĀ 13.4 has the mind for both cases, although with a variant reading preserving the correct reference to the body for the first instance.

9 My rendering follows an emendation suggested by Yìnshùn 1983a: 195 note 2.

10 Whereas SN 22.1 does not provide such an indication, EĀ 13.4 at T II 573a13 also reports that Sāriputta was seated close by.

The householder Nakula said to Sāriputta: "Today the Blessed One has given me a teaching, instructing, teaching, illuminating, and delighting me [as if] anointing my body and mind with the ambrosia of the Dharma. For this reason my faculties are now joyfully relaxed and my complexion is bright."

The venerable Sāriputta asked the householder: "How has the Blessed One taught you the Dharma, instructing, teaching, illuminating, and delighting you [as if] anointing you with ambrosia?"

The householder Nakula said to Sāriputta: "I approached the Blessed One and said to the Blessed One: 'I am feeble from old age, weak, and suffer from disease, yet with my own strength I come to meet the Blessed One and the senior and esteemed monastics who are my good friends.'

"The Buddha said to me: 'It is well, householder. You are really ripe with age, weak and suffering from disease, yet you are able with your own strength to approach me and the senior and esteemed monastics. Now that your body is suffering from disease, you should constantly train so that your ⟨mind⟩ does not suffer from disease.' Giving me a teaching in this way, the Blessed One has instructed, taught, illuminated, and delighted me [as if] anointing me with ambrosia."

The venerable Sāriputta asked the householder: "Did you not proceed to ask the Blessed One again: 'How does the body suffer from disease and the mind [also] suffer from disease? How does the body suffer from disease and the mind not suffer from disease?'"

The householder replied: "I have approached the venerable one because of the meaning [of this]. May he explain to me in brief the import of the teaching."[11]

The venerable Sāriputta said to the householder: "It is well, householder. Now listen to what I shall tell you.

---

11 In SĀ 107 Nakula seems to have come on purpose to receive a more detailed explanation from Sāriputta. SN 22.1 at SN III 3,1 instead gives the impression that he had at first not thought of the possibility of receiving further explanations, but, once Sāriputta mentioned this possibility, he happily took up the opportunity, stating that he would come a long way to get such explanations. EĀ 13.4 at T II 573a12, however, explicitly records the householder reflecting that he would now approach Sāriputta to ask about this matter.

"A foolish unlearned worldling does not understand as it really is the arising of bodily form, the cessation of bodily form, the gratification in bodily form,[12] the danger in bodily form, and the escape from bodily form.[13] Because of not understanding it as it really is, [the worldling] craves with delight for bodily form, declaring bodily form to be the self or to belong to the self, clinging and taking hold of it.

"If bodily form is ruined, if it becomes otherwise, [the foolish unlearned worldling's] mind and consciousness follow it in turn, giving rise to vexation and pain. Vexation and pain having arisen, [the foolish unlearned worldling] is frightened, obstructed, worried, distressed, and passionately bound.

"A foolish unlearned worldling does not understand as it really is the arising of feeling, *the cessation of feeling, the gratification in feeling, the danger in feeling, and the escape from feeling. Because of not understanding it as it really is, the foolish unlearned worldling craves with delight for feeling, declaring feeling to be the self or to belong to the self, clinging and taking hold of it.*

"If feeling is ruined, if it becomes otherwise, the foolish unlearned worldling's mind and consciousness follow it in turn, giving rise to vexation and pain. Vexation and pain having arisen, the foolish unlearned worldling is frightened, obstructed, worried, distressed, and passionately bound.

"A foolish unlearned worldling does not understand as it really is the arising of perception, *the cessation of perception, the gratification in perception, the danger in perception, and the escape from perception. Because of not understanding it as it really is, the foolish unlearned worldling craves with delight for perception, declaring perception to be the self or to belong to the self, clinging and taking hold of it.*

"If perception is ruined, if it becomes otherwise, the foolish unlearned worldling's mind and consciousness follow it in turn, giving rise to vexation and pain. Vexation and pain having arisen, the foolish

---

12 In the original text, the danger comes before the gratification. I have adjusted this to keep in line with the standard formulation, which is also found in SĀ 107 when it comes to expounding the case of the learned noble disciple.

13 In SN 22.1 at SN III 3,15 and EĀ 13.4 at T II 573b10 the worldling's lack of insight manifests in construing a self according to the twenty modes of identity view (*sakkāyadiṭṭhi*), on which see below p. 88.

unlearned worldling is frightened, obstructed, worried, distressed, and passionately bound.

"A foolish unlearned worldling does not understand as it really is the arising of formations, *the cessation of formations, the gratification in formations, the danger in formations, and the escape from formations. Because of not understanding them as they really are, the foolish unlearned worldling craves with delight for formations, declaring formations to be the self or to belong to the self, clinging and taking hold of them.*

"If formations are ruined, if they become otherwise, the foolish unlearned worldling's mind and consciousness follow them in turn, giving rise to vexation and pain. Vexation and pain having arisen, the foolish unlearned worldling is frightened, obstructed, worried, distressed, and passionately bound.

"A foolish unlearned worldling does not understand as it really is the arising of consciousness, *the cessation of consciousness, the gratification in consciousness, the danger in consciousness, and the escape from consciousness. Because of not understanding it as it really is, the foolish unlearned worldling craves with delight for consciousness, declaring consciousness to be the self or to belong to the self, clinging and taking hold of it.*

"If consciousness is ruined, if it becomes otherwise, the foolish unlearned worldling's mind and consciousness follow it in turn, giving rise to vexation and pain.[14] *Vexation and pain having arisen, the foolish unlearned worldling is frightened, obstructed, worried, distressed, and passionately bound.*

"This is called body and mind suffering from disease. How does the body suffer from disease and the mind not suffer from disease?

"A learned noble disciple understands as it really is the arising of bodily form, the cessation of bodily form, the gratification in bodily form, the danger in bodily form, and the escape from bodily form. Having understood it as it really is, [the learned noble disciple] does not give rise to craving with delight, seeing bodily form as the self or as belonging to the self.

"If bodily form changes, if it becomes otherwise, [the learned noble disciple's] mind does not follow it in turn, giving rise to

---

14 I take it that this refers to one's present mind experiencing vexation in relation to past states of consciousness.

vexation and pain. The mind not having followed it in turn and given rise to vexation and pain, [the learned noble disciple] does not get frightened, obstructed, worried, [distressed], and passionately bound.

"A learned noble disciple understands as it really is the arising of feeling, *the cessation of feeling, the gratification in feeling, the danger in feeling, and the escape from feeling. Having understood it as it really is, the learned noble disciple does not give rise to craving with delight, seeing feeling as the self or as belonging to the self.*

"If feeling changes, if it becomes otherwise, the learned noble disciple's mind does not follow it in turn, giving rise to vexation and pain. The mind not having followed it in turn and given rise to vexation and pain, the learned noble disciple does not get frightened, obstructed, worried, distressed, and passionately bound.

"A learned noble disciple understands as it really is the arising of perception, *the cessation of perception, the gratification in perception, the danger in perception, and the escape from perception. Having understood it as it really is, the learned noble disciple does not give rise to craving with delight, seeing perception as the self or as belonging to the self.*

"If perception changes, if it becomes otherwise, the learned noble disciple's mind does not follow it in turn, giving rise to vexation and pain. The mind not having followed it in turn and given rise to vexation and pain, the learned noble disciple does not get frightened, obstructed, worried, distressed, and passionately bound.

"A learned noble disciple understands as it really is the arising of formations, *the cessation of formations, the gratification in formations, the danger in formations, and the escape from formations. Having understood them as they really are, the learned noble disciple does not give rise to craving with delight, seeing formations as the self or as belonging to the self.*

"If formations change, if they become otherwise, the learned noble disciple's mind does not follow them in turn, giving rise to vexation and pain. The mind not having followed them in turn and given rise to vexation and pain, the learned noble disciple does not get frightened, obstructed, worried, distressed, and passionately bound.

"A learned noble disciple understands as it really is the arising of consciousness, *the cessation of consciousness, the gratification in consciousness, the danger in consciousness, and the escape from*

consciousness. Having understood it as it really is, the learned noble disciple does not give rise to craving with delight, seeing consciousness as the self or as belonging to the self.

"If consciousness changes, if it becomes otherwise, the learned noble disciple's mind does not follow it in turn, giving rise to vexation and pain. The mind not having followed it in turn and given rise to vexation and pain, the learned noble disciple does not get frightened, obstructed, worried, distressed, and passionately bound.

"This is called the body suffering from disease and the mind not suffering from disease."

When the venerable Sāriputta spoke this teaching, the householder Nakula attained the pure eye of Dharma.[15] At that time the householder Nakula saw the Dharma, attained the Dharma, understood the Dharma, entered the Dharma, crossing beyond all doubt, not needing to rely on others, and his mind attained fearlessness in the right Dharma.

He rose from his seat, adjusted his clothes, paid respect, and, with his palms held together [in respect] towards the venerable Sāriputta, said:

"I have gone beyond, I have crossed over. I now take refuge in the jewels of the Buddha, the Dharma, and the Saṅgha as a lay disciple. Be my witness that from today until the end of my life I take refuge in the three jewels."[16]

At that time the householder Nakula, hearing what Sāriputta had said, rejoiced in it and was delighted. He paid respect and left.

II.3 DISCUSSION

The three versions disagree regarding the outcome of this instruction. Only the *Saṃyukta-āgama* discourse translated above reports that Nakula attained the eye of Dharma, an expression referring to the attainment of stream-entry. This is the first of the four levels of awakening recognized in early Buddhist thought, to which I will come back in Chapter 8.

---

15 SN 22.1 and EĀ 13.4 do not report any attainment

16 SN 22.1 and EĀ 13.4 do not report that he took refuge. For him to take refuge in the way described in SĀ 107 does in fact not fit the narrative context too well: the way he acts before suggests he must already have done so earlier.

Whatever the final outcome of the instruction Nakula received, the explanation given by Sāriputta in the present discourse and its parallels involves the "five aggregates of clinging", which are:

- bodily form,
- feeling,
- perception,
- formations,
- consciousness.

These five aggregates of clinging represent the different components of what one tends to cling to as "I" or "myself". In addition to the physical *body* as the location of "where I am", *feeling* pleasant, painful, or neutral sensations is responsible for "how I am". *Perceptions* as different cognitions, combining the input of sense data with recognition based on past experiences and one's accumulated knowledge, make up a considerable part of "what I am". *Formations* represent volitions and intentions, the way one reacts to what happens now based on one's conditioning from the past, and thereby provide the "why I am" acting in a certain way. Finally *consciousness* represents the act of experiencing and being conscious, which furnishes the "whereby I am".

Clinging to the sense of "I am", which so naturally arises in relation to each of these five aggregates, is bound to lead to frustration and conflict as soon as things do not go the way one wants. Undeniably there is pleasure to be derived from this sense of "I am" when the body is healthy, feelings are pleasant, perceptions are welcome and interesting, formations result in accomplishing what one wants, and consciousness knows agreeable experiences. This is what the early discourses reckon the "gratification" (*assāda*) that can be found in relation to each of these five aggregates.

Yet this "gratification" comes together with a "danger" (*ādīnava*). This danger is based on the simple fact that everything is bound to change. Things arise and sooner or later cease again; they are impermanent. When what is pleasant and agreeable ceases, what arises next will be different, and the chances are that it will be less pleasant and less agreeable. To the extent to which one has been clinging to the five aggregates when they were gratifying, to that extent one will be upset and suffer when they change and become otherwise.

To emerge from this predicament calls for an understanding of each of these five aggregates as it really is. This is the basic contrast described in the discourse above between the foolish unlearned worldling and the learned noble disciple. Worldlings are unlearned in so far as they have no acquaintance with liberating teachings of the type provided in the present discourse. Lacking such directives, and thereby the means to acquire true wisdom, they remain immersed in ignorance and consequently react foolishly when confronted with the vicissitudes of life.

In contrast, disciples who have become learned through receiving instructions, comparable to those given in the present case to Nakula, are able to ennoble themselves by cultivating wisdom and emerging from the foolishness caused by ignorance. In particular they learn to see clearly that body, feeling, perception, formations, and consciousness are impermanent phenomena. Therefore the gratification they can provide comes inexorably bound to the danger of clinging and attachment, resulting in *dukkha* once conditions change and become otherwise. The resultant understanding is the fertile soil within which freedom from attachment and a lessening of identification can grow, leading to the ability to remain with a healthily non-attached mind even when experiencing strong pain and serious disease.

In practical terms, when strong pain arises, instead of succumbing to the natural tendency to own this as "mine", giving rise to all sorts of apprehensions about what this pain is doing to "me" now and going to do to "my" future, one might try just to be aware of the fluctuating physical sensations of pain. By remaining in present-moment awareness of painful sensations, without appropriating them as "mine" and reacting to them mentally, much of the mental affliction caused by physical pain can be avoided. This is how the mind can gradually learn not to suffer along with the body.

III

THE ARROW OF PAIN

III.1 INTRODUCTION

This chapter continues the theme broached in the discourse in the last chapter, which made it clear that the mind can avoid being sick when the body is afflicted by disease. In that discourse a succinct instruction by the Buddha on this topic led to an exposition of the five aggregates by Sāriputta.

The second of these five aggregates, feeling, is of particular relevance to learning how to avoid bodily pain affecting the mind. This is the theme of the discourse taken up in the present chapter, which illustrates this task with the help of a simile that describes being shot by one or two arrows.

The discourse translated below stems from the *Saṃyukta-āgama*, which has a parallel in the *Saṃyutta-nikāya*.[1] Both versions show how physical pain can lead on to defilements that obstruct the path to mental freedom. These defilements are presented in terms of three underlying tendencies, *anusaya*. Early Buddhist thought recognizes seven such underlying tendencies, which are proclivities of the mind to be influenced in a way that is usually not consciously noted. These hidden driving forces in the mind tend to trigger the arising of the following defiled mental conditions:

1 SN 36.6 at SN IV 207,22 (translated Bodhi 2000: 1263).

- sensual passion,
- aversion,
- speculative views,
- doubt,
- conceit,
- craving for existence,
- ignorance.

The present discourse takes up three of these: the underlying tendencies to sensual passion, aversion, and ignorance. These three directly relate to the three types of feeling. Pleasant feeling can activate the tendency to sensual passion, painful feeling the tendency to aversion, and neutral feeling the tendency to ignorance. The resultant correlations are as follows:

- pleasant – sensual passion,
- painful – aversion,
- neutral – ignorance.

The chief task in relation to the experience of feeling is therefore to avoid the activation of these underlying tendencies.

III.2 TRANSLATION[2]

Thus have I heard. At one time the Buddha was staying at Rājagaha in the Bamboo Grove, the Squirrels' Feeding Ground.[3] At that time the Blessed One said to the monastics: "To a foolish unlearned worldling painful feelings,[4] pleasant feelings, and neutral feelings arise. To a learned noble disciple painful feelings, pleasant feelings, and neutral feelings also arise. Monastics, what is the difference between the worldling and the noble person?"

The monastics said to the Buddha: "The Blessed One is the root of the Dharma, the eye of Dharma, the foundation of the Dharma. It would be well if the Blessed One were to explain it in detail. Having heard it, the monastics will receive it respectfully."

2 The translated discourse is SĀ 470 at T II 119c28 to 120b14; for two extracts from this discourse see Anālayo 2013b: 120.
3 SN 36.6 does not mention the location where the Buddha was staying.
4 The translation is based on adopting a variant that adds "feeling" to the reference "painful".

The Buddha said to the monastics: "Listen and give proper attention to what I shall tell you.[5] Monastics, to a foolish unlearned worldling through bodily contact feelings arise that are increasingly painful, even leading to the ending of life. [The worldling] is worried and complains by crying and wailing, with the mind giving rise to disorder and derangement. At that time two feelings arise, bodily feeling and mental feeling.[6]

"It is just like a person whose body has been afflicted by two poisonous arrows and extremely painful feelings arise.[7]

"The foolish unlearned worldling is also just like this, giving rise to two feelings [when] extremely painful feelings arise, bodily feeling and mental feeling. Why is that? It is because that foolish unlearned worldling lacks understanding.

"Being contacted by pleasant feeling arisen from the five [strands] of sensuality, [the worldling] clings to the pleasure of the five [strands] of sensuality. Because of clinging to the pleasure of the five [strands] of sensuality, [the worldling] is affected by the underlying tendency to passion.

"Because of being contacted by pain, [the worldling] then gives rise to aversion. Because of giving rise to aversion, [the worldling] is affected by the underlying tendency to aversion.[8]

"In relation to these two feelings [the worldling] does not understand as it really is their arising, their cessation, their gratification, their danger, and the escape from them. Because of not understanding it as it really is, when neutral feelings arise [the worldling] is affected by the underlying tendency to ignorance.

---

5 The translation follows the suggestion by Yìnshùn 1983b: 197 note 4 to delete a redundant sentence that seems to be the result of a textual error.

6 The parallel SN 36.6 at SN IV 208,7 only indicates that the feeling is painful, without mentioning that it is oppressive and leads to the ending of life. Nevertheless SN 36.6 does convey a sense of the severity of the condition as it depicts the worldling beating his (or her) breast.

7 In SN 36.6 at SN IV 208,11 the arrow is not poisoned.

8 SN 36.6 has this part in the opposite order, proceeding from the worldling's experience of pain to the experience of pleasure. This fits the context well, since by beginning with pain the exposition links directly to the previous exposition and the arrow simile, which were concerned with the experience of pain. Moreover, in its transition from pain to pleasure SN 36.6 at SN IV 208,20 offers the significant indication that, being touched by pain, the worldling then seeks sensual pleasure because of knowing no other alternative to the experience of pain.

"[The worldling] is bound by pleasant feeling, not freed from it, bound by painful feeling, not freed from it, and bound by neutral feeling, not freed from it. By what is [the worldling] bound? That is, [the worldling] is bound by passion, aversion, and ignorance, and is bound by birth, old age, disease, death, worry, sorrow, vexation, and pain.

"To a learned noble disciple through bodily contact painful feeling arises that is greatly painful and oppressive, even leading to the ending of life. [The noble disciple] does not give rise to worry or complain by crying and wailing, and the mind does not become disordered or deranged. At that time only one feeling arises, namely bodily feeling; mental feeling does not arise.

"It is just like a person who is afflicted by one poisonous arrow, not being afflicted by a second poisonous arrow. [For the learned noble disciple] at that time only one feeling arises, namely bodily feeling; mental feeling does not arise.

"Being contacted by pleasant feeling, [the noble disciple] is not defiled by the pleasure of sensuality. Because of not being defiled by the pleasure of sensuality, in relation to pleasant feeling [the noble disciple] is not affected by the underlying tendency to passion.

"Being contacted by painful feeling, [the noble disciple] does not give rise to aversion. Because of not giving rise to aversion, [the noble disciple] is not affected by the underlying tendency to aversion.

"In relation to these two ⟨feelings⟩,[9] [the noble disciple] understands as it really is their arising, their cessation, their ⟨gratification⟩,[10] their danger, and the escape from them. Because of understanding it as it really is, with neutral feelings [the noble disciple] is not affected by the underlying tendency to ignorance.

"[The noble disciple] is liberated from pleasant feeling, not bound by it, liberated from painful feeling, *not bound by it, liberated from* neutral feeling, not bound by it. By what is [the noble disciple] not bound? That is, [the noble disciple] is not bound by passion, aversion, and ignorance, and not bound

9 The translation is based on emending a reference to "underlying tendency" to read "feeling".

10 The translation "gratification" is based on an emendation suggested in the CBETA edition.

by birth, old age, disease, death, worry, sorrow, vexation, and pain."[11]

At that time the Blessed One spoke this poem:[12]

"The learned [noble disciple] does not feel
Pain and pleasure without acute understanding,
Which for a foolish person
Truly are a great ⟨obstruction⟩.[13]
"Being without negligence with pleasant feeling,
And not giving rise to worry when touched by pain,
Being with equanimity in relation to both pain and pleasure
[The noble disciple] neither succumbs to them nor opposes
them.
"A monastic with diligent effort
And with right comprehension will not be perturbed
By all of these feelings,
Being able to understand them with wisdom.
"Because of understanding feelings,
[The noble disciple] here and now eradicates the influxes,
And with the death of the body is no [longer subject to]
reckoning,
Forever abiding in Nirvāṇa."

When the Buddha had spoken this discourse, hearing what the Buddha had said the monastics were delighted and received it respectfully.

III.3 DISCUSSION

The discourse translated above and its parallel in the *Saṃyutta-nikāya* illustrate the situation of one whose mind suffers along with bodily pain with the example of a person who is shot by two arrows. In contrast, remaining unshaken by bodily pain is comparable to being shot by only a single arrow.

11 In SN 36.6 at SN IV 210,6 the Buddha sums up that this is the difference between the worldling and the noble disciple.
12 The stanzas in SN 36.6 take up similar themes, but differ considerably in the way they express these.
13 The translation "obstruction" follows an emendation suggested by Yìnshùn 1983b: 197 note 5.

The *Saṃuykta-āgama* version additionally qualifies the arrows to be poisoned. Since with a poisonous arrow the main problem of being poisoned arises on being hit by even a single arrow, this results in a less apt presentation. When the question at stake is just the pain of being hurt by a poison-free arrow, as is the case in the *Saṃyutta-nikāya* version, then there is indeed quite a difference between being hit by one arrow or by two arrows. In this respect, the *Saṃyutta-nikāya* discourse has clearly preserved the preferable presentation.

The point vividly illustrated with the simile of the two arrows is that grief and resistance, worry and dejection, as well as any other negative attitude towards physical pain, will simply increase the suffering one experiences. Although this is easily said, it is less easily carried out. Fortunately the discourse does not stop short at highlighting this basic principle, but also shows how to put it into practice.

A decisive difference between the worldling who suffers with the pain and the noble disciple who does not suffer can be found in their respective understanding. The additional arrow can be avoided by cultivating a proper understanding of feelings. Crucial here is the understanding that, just as they arise, so are they bound to cease. This helps to counter a natural tendency of the mind to perceive feelings, in particular painful feelings at a time of sickness, as if they were solid and never-ending. Instead, feelings are a changing process.

Every time one reacts to pain with irritation, this activates the underlying tendency, *anusaya*, to aversion in the mind. The more this underlying tendency is activated, the stronger it becomes, and therefore the more readily a future arising of aversion will be triggered. Conversely every single instance of not reacting to pain weakens the underlying tendency to aversion and promotes the growth of liberating understanding. In this way pain is not only a taxing challenge, it also affords a powerful opportunity to make progress on the path to freedom.

This holds not only for countering the habit of reacting with aversion. The experience of pain easily leads to the pursuit of sensual pleasure, a point made with particular clarity in the *Saṃyutta-nikāya* version. According to its presentation, on being touched by pain, the worldling seeks an alternative to the experience of pain in some form of sensual pleasure. The Pāli discourse explains that this is because the worldling does not know any other way to escape from pain, except for indulging in sensual pleasure. To the common mind the only alternative to the painful reality of a sick body is to distract oneself with some form of sensual enjoyment. Such a strategy does not solve the problem and instead leads to activating and strengthening of the underlying tendency to sensual passion.

The more one yields to the gratification feelings can provide, the more one will be affected by their inherent danger. This danger is in particular that, the more one clings to pleasant feelings, the more one will be affected by their changing nature, especially when this change is a return to the experience of pain after a brief interlude of having enjoyed some sensual distraction. In this way the strategy of recompensing oneself for the experience of pain by indulging in sensual pleasure provides momentary relief at the cost of long-term deterioration, comparable to scratching an infected wound, whereby the itch briefly disappears but the wound gets even more infected. The net result of resorting to sensual distraction when in pain is a vicious circle of being ever more subject to unwise reactions to feelings and thereby subject to the activation of the underlying tendencies.

Lack of understanding remains a problem even when feelings are neutral, as their bland nature is so easily ignored, which activates the underlying tendency to ignorance. This manifests in particular in the desire for some sort of diversion from what is perceived as a boring experience.

In contrast, by approaching with mindful understanding the experience of feelings in general, and of pain in particular, this experience can become a powerful source of insight. All it takes is to remain aware, in the present moment, of the changing process of feelings as it is, without reacting. The discourse translated above proclaims that one who goes beyond being afflicted by the second arrow can similarly go beyond the whole host of problems that according to the first noble truth make up *dukkha*. In this way, from the perspective of early Buddhist thought there is considerable potential in the experience of being in physical pain, if such a situation can be approached with mindfulness and wisdom.

Although the early discourses clearly give prominence to meditative wisdom, they also take into account other qualities that are of help when experiencing sickness. In addition to being able to bear with pain, the passages taken up in the next chapter present a set of commendable qualities of a patient as well as of a nurse that will ensure swift recovery. These passages give due recognition to ordinary aspects of the situation of being ill, alongside the recurrent emphasis on how to approach such a situation from a meditative perspective. They thereby implicitly clarify that the meditative approach to disease is not meant to replace proper medical care, but rather serves to supplement it. Expressed in terms of the simile of the two arrows, the idea is not that one should just endure any pain without doing anything about it at all. Instead, one properly takes care of what has led to the first arrow with whatever reasonable and appropriate medical means are at one's disposal, and alongside that one trains the mind in such a way as to avoid the second arrow.

IV

QUALITIES OF A PATIENT AND A NURSE

IV.1 INTRODUCTION

The present chapter approaches the situation of being ill from two complementary perspectives: what are commendable qualities for a patient and for a nurse? These commendable qualities are described in two consecutive discourses from the *Ekottarika-āgama*, translated below. These show some variations when compared to their two parallels found in the *Aṅguttara-nikāya*.[1]

One of the commendable qualities for a patient according to the *Ekottarika-āgama* discourse is *mettā*, a term often translated as "loving-kindness", although I think a preferable translation would be "benevolence". Just as with *dukkha*, however, it seems best to me to retain the original word in Pāli. This quality of *mettā* constitutes the first of four divine abodes, *brahmavihāra*, which are:

- *mettā*,
- compassion,
- sympathetic joy,
- equanimity.

---

1 AN 5.123 at AN III 143,19 (translated Bodhi 2012: 741) and AN 5.124 at AN III 144,14 (translated Bodhi 2012: 741); on qualities of a nurse according to the ancient Indian medical treatises *Carakasaṃhitā* and *Suśrutasaṃhitā* see Leslie and Wujastyk 1991.

These four divine abodes are the ideal attitudes towards others recommended in early Buddhist thought and mental training.[2] The term "divine abode" not only reflects the notion that successful practice will lead to a heavenly rebirth, but can also be interpreted in the sense that dwelling in any of these is akin to experiencing heaven on earth.

The first of these four, *mettā*, refers to an attitude of kindness and well-wishing towards others, which by its nature is directly opposed to aversion, irritation, and ill will. The second, compassion, will be a recurrent theme throughout this book, in particular in the form of the altruistic wish to ease the suffering of others and provide them with guidance in how to face disease and death. By nature compassion is the opposite of the intention to harm others. Sympathetic joy is the opposite of envy, jealousy, and discontent. The fourth divine abode rounds off the whole set, offering the option of equanimity for situations in which the other attitudes would not be appropriate. I will come back to the four *brahmavihāra*s as a meditation practice at the time of passing away in Chapter 15.

IV.2 TRANSLATION (1)[3]

Thus have I heard. At one time the Buddha was staying at Sāvatthī in Jeta's Grove, Anāthapiṇḍika's Park.[4] At that time the Blessed One said to the monastics:

"A patient who is endowed with five qualities will not gain timely recovery and will remain bedridden.[5] What are the five?

"Here a patient does not discern what to drink and eat, does not eat at the proper time, does not take the medicine, grieves too much and enjoys being irritable, and does not arouse a mental attitude of *mettā* towards the nurse.[6] Monastics, these are

2 On these four see in more detail Anālayo 2015b: 5–49.
3 The translated discourse is EĀ 32.8 at T II 680b19 to 680c2.
4 AN 5.123 does not mention the location where the Buddha was staying.
5 AN 5.123 at AN III 143,19 instead introduces its set of five qualities in terms of what makes it difficult to take care of such a person.
6 The five qualities listed in AN 5.123 at AN III 143,21 are: 1) doing what is not appropriate, 2) not knowing moderation with what is appropriate, 3) not taking the medicine, 4) not disclosing as it really is if the affliction is becoming worse or better, and 5) being unable to endure painful feelings.

reckoned to be the five qualities, endowed with which a patient will not gain timely recovery.

"Again, if a patient is endowed with five qualities, [the patient] will gain timely recovery. What are the five?

"Here a patient discerns what to [drink and] eat, eats at the proper time, takes the medicine, does not cherish grieving, and fully arouses a mental attitude of *mettā* towards the nurse. Monastics, these are reckoned to be the five qualities, endowed with which a patient will gain timely recovery in turn.

"Monastics, in this way you should mindfully discard the former five qualities, and you should together respectfully uphold the latter five qualities. Monastics, you should train in this way."[7]

At that time, hearing what the Buddha had said, the monastics were delighted and received it respectfully.

IV.3 TRANSLATION (2)[8]

Thus have I heard. At one time the Buddha was staying at Sāvatthī in Jeta's Grove, Anāthapiṇḍika's Park.[9] At that time the Blessed One said to the monastics:

"If a nurse is endowed with five qualities, [the patient] will not gain timely recovery and remain bedridden.[10] What are the five?

"Here a nurse does not discern when administering medicine, is negligent and has a mental attitude that lacks energy, regularly enjoys getting irritated and is exceedingly drowsy, nurses the patient out of greed for food, not because of reverence for the Dharma, and does not come back to converse with the patient.[11]

7 AN 5.123 records no injunction addressed to the monastics.

8 The translated discourse is EĀ 32.9 at T II 680c3 to 680c17.

9 AN 5.124 does not mention the location where the Buddha was staying.

10 AN 5.124 at AN III 144,14 instead introduces its set of five qualities as what disqualifies a nurse from taking care of a patient.

11 The five qualities listed in AN 5.124 at AN III 144,16 are: 1) the nurse is unable to prepare medicine, 2) due to not knowing what is appropriate and what is not appropriate, the nurse gives the patient what is not appropriate and withholds what is appropriate, 3) the nurse looks after the patient for the sake of worldly gains, not out of *mettā*, 4) the nurse feels disgusted when having to remove faeces, urine, vomit, and spittle, 5) the nurse is unable to instruct and gladden the patient from time to time with a talk on the Dharma.

Monastics, these are reckoned to be the five qualities; if a nurse is endowed with them, [the patient] will not gain timely recovery.

"Again, monastics, if a nurse is endowed with five qualities, [the patient] will gain timely recovery in turn and will not remain bedridden. What are the five?

"Here a nurse discerns when administering medicine, is not negligent, being the first to rise and the last to lie down, constantly enjoys conversing and has little drowsiness, [nurses] out of reverence for the Dharma and not out of greed for food and drink, and is capable of teaching the Dharma to the patient. Monastics, these are reckoned to be the five qualities; [if] a nurse is endowed with them, [the patient] will gain timely recovery.

"Therefore, monastics, when you are nursing, you should [mindfully] discard the former five qualities, and undertake the latter five qualities. Monastics, you should train in this way."[12]

At that time, hearing what the Buddha had said, the monastics were delighted and received it respectfully.

IV.4 DISCUSSION

According to the first *Ekottarika-āgama* discourse, a patient who does not discern in regard to the appropriate type of food and drinks and the proper time for consuming these will deteriorate, and the same holds if the patient does not take the medicine. The *Aṅguttara-nikāya* presentation formulates the same basic advice in a more general way. The sickness will become worse if the patient does not do what is appropriate and, in relation to what is appropriate, knows no moderation. Here, too, the same holds if the patient does not take the medicine.

Other qualities that prevent a patient's recovery in the *Ekottarika-āgama* discourse are being irritable and lacking *mettā* towards the nurse. The *Aṅguttara-nikāya* version instead describes a patient who does not disclose a worsening or improvement of the condition and who is unable to endure pain.

The *Ekottarika-āgama* discourse and its *Aṅguttara-nikāya* parallel agree in continuing their presentation by listing

12 AN 5.124 records no injunction addressed to the monastics.

the opposite five qualities as the means for quick recovery. Combining the two versions and presenting the result in a summary fashion, the qualities that will enable a patient's speedy recovery are:

- to take only the appropriate food and drink,
- to take these at the right time and in moderation,
- to take the prescribed medicine,
- to disclose one's condition truthfully and not get irritated,
- to cultivate *mettā* towards the nurse and patiently endure pain.

Regarding the qualities of a nurse in the second *Ekottarika-āgama* discourse translated above, both versions take up a nurse's lack of ability or powers of judgement when administering medicine. The *Aṅguttara-nikāya* discourse presents this problem in terms of two qualities, where a nurse lacks ability to prepare the medicine and lacks judgement as to when something should be administered and when it should better be withheld. The second quality in the *Ekottarika-āgama* version is instead negligence, which would also adversely affect the providing of adequate medication and health care.

A quality only mentioned in the *Ekottarika-āgama* version combines the enjoyment a nurse may find in displaying irritation with becoming exceedingly drowsy. The next quality in the *Ekottarika-āgama* discourse and its counterpart in the Pāli parallel turns to the issue of nursing for the sake of material gains. In the ancient Indian setting monastics had to look after each other, as a result of which some of them took up the office of nursing those who were sick and in need of care. Once provisions offered by the laity for the sick and those who looked after them became abundant, undertaking the task of caring for those who were ill could be motivated by the wish for material gains, and for an easy supply of food. Instead, as pointed out explicitly in the *Aṅguttara-nikāya* version, one should care for the sick out of altruism, being motivated by *mettā*.

A quality found only in the *Aṅguttara-nikāya* discourse is the disgust a nurse might feel when having to remove faeces, urine, vomit, and spittle. The last quality in both versions highlights the importance of conversing with the patient. The *Ekottarika-āgama* version makes it clear that, if a nurse does not come back to converse with the patient, this will run counter to the patient's recovery. The *Aṅguttara-nikāya* parallel more specifically speaks of a nurse's inability to instruct and gladden the patient with a talk on the Dharma.

The need to take care of the mental condition of a patient and provide a source of comfort through conversation and instruction will be a recurrent topic in the next chapters, which regularly show the Buddha and his disciples compassionately visiting the sick and dying to offer support by teaching the Dharma. As explained by de Silva in relation to the present discourse:[13]

> It is noteworthy that the nurse [is] expected to be efficient not only in taking care of the body by giving proper food and medicine, but ... is also expected to take care of the patient's mental condition. It is well known that the kindness of doctors and nurses is almost as efficient as medicine for the patient's morale and recovery. When one is desperately ill or helpless, a kind word or a gentle act becomes the source of comfort and hope.

The *Ekottarika-āgama* discourse and its *Aṅguttara-nikāya* parallel continue their exposition by listing the opposite five qualities of a nurse that will lead to a patient's quick recovery. Combining their presentation in a summary fashion and focusing on what seem to be the essential points, the following are the main qualities of a nurse that will facilitate a patient's recovery:

- to give proper medication,
- to be attentive to the needs of the patient,
- to cope with one's own disgust,
- to be willing to converse with the patient,
- to maintain an altruistic motivation and avoid getting irritated.

The coverage given to these sets of qualities shows that the early Buddhist teachings related to disease are not only concerned with what falls directly within the domain of

13 This and the next quote below are both from de Silva 1993: 29.

progress to awakening. Although this is clearly a prominent concern, alongside this overall orientation towards awakening, proper room is given to ordinary aspects of the situation of someone who is sick.

Such giving of room appears to have been not merely a question of verbal teachings; in fact in the *Vinaya* the Buddha himself is on record for setting an inspiring example for the willingness to nurse those who are sick. The episode in question is directly related to the lists of qualities in the two discourses translated above, since the account of this event in the Pāli *Vinaya* continues by listing the same five qualities of a patient and of a nurse as found in the *Aṅguttara-nikāya*, thereby setting a narrative context for the teachings discussed in this chapter. Other *Vinaya*s similarly relate this episode to comparable listings of qualities.

According to this narrative context, in the way it has been recorded in the Pāli *Vinaya*, the Buddha had chanced upon a sick monastic left lying in his own excrement by his companions. Aided by his personal attendant Ānanda, the Buddha is on record for himself washing the monastic. Afterwards he admonished the other monastics, explaining that it was their duty to look after a sick fellow monastic, which they should consider to be just as if they were looking after the Buddha himself.[14] As noted by de Silva:

> The Buddha not only advocated the importance of looking after the sick, he also set a noble example by himself administering to the helplessly sick.

Besides throwing into relief the Buddha's compassion, even to the extent that he becomes personally involved in cleaning one of his disciples, another remarkable aspect of the same event is the lack of concern of the other monastics. The episode gives the impression that to take care of one's companions in the monastic life was not necessarily seen as a self-evident duty, otherwise the monastics would not have needed to be told that they should look after the sick. The Buddha apparently had to set an example to inspire in his monastic disciples the

---

14 Vin I 302,3 (translated Horner 1951/1982: 431); for a study of the parallel versions see Demiéville 1974: 236–8.

compassionate attitude that makes it natural to be willing to nurse another, independent of whether the patient will be able to recompense in some way the care received. This makes such a compassionate attitude in nursing an integral and even characteristic aspect of the Buddha's teaching.

The importance of compassion also emerges from the listings of qualities of a nurse and a patient, where due room is given to the beneficial repercussions of an attitude of *mettā* and empathy, free from irritability and carelessness. This is perhaps the most salient aspect to be taken away from this chapter, in that a sincere attitude of altruism and benevolence aids speedy recovery, an attitude to be cultivated by both patient and nurse.

The two sets of qualities that are detrimental or beneficial for a patient's recovery have a counterpart in two sets of qualities that are detrimental or beneficial for a meditator's progress on the path to mental health, the path to awakening. These two sets of qualities are the hindrances and the awakening factors, which are the theme of the next chapter.

V

THE HEALING POTENTIAL OF THE AWAKENING FACTORS

V.1 INTRODUCTION

In the early discourses the Buddha recurrently sets an example in nursing the sick, in particular in line with the last quality mentioned in the *Aṅguttara-nikāya* discourse in the previous chapter, namely instructing and gladdening a patient with a talk on the Dharma. The compassionate motivation to help someone who is sick usually takes the form of providing the appropriate dosage of the medicine of Dharma. Such a type of nursing will be a continuous theme in this and the next chapters. In this chapter's discourse, the Buddha undertakes such nursing in relation to one of his eminent disciples by the name of Mahākassapa.

The early discourses present Mahākassapa as outstanding among the Buddha's disciples for his stern and ascetic conduct.[1] In relation to the present discourse this is significant in so far as his admitting to being seriously sick gives the impression that he must be ill indeed and is not just being squeamish.

The teaching Mahākassapa receives concerns the seven awakening factors, seven mental qualities that have been

1 The listings of outstanding disciples, AN 1.14 at AN I 23,19 (translated Bodhi 2012: 109) and EĀ 4.2 at T II 557b8, reckon Mahākassapa as outstanding among male monastics in regard to ascetic practices; see also the *Divyāvadāna*, Cowell and Neil 1886: 395,23, and the *Mahāvastu*, Senart 1882: 64,14 (the translation in Jones 1949/1973: 53 does not do full justice to the original). For biographical sketches of Mahākassapa see Malalasekera 1938/1998: 476–83 and Nyanaponika and Hecker 1997: 109–36.

singled out in early Buddhist meditation theory for their propensity to awaken the mind. These are regularly shown to stand in direct contrast to five qualities of the mind known as the hindrances. By analogy with the qualities of a patient and a nurse discussed in the previous chapter, early Buddhist meditation theory approaches the situation of being mentally sick with defilements by listing qualities that are detrimental to one's mental health, the five hindrances, and qualities that promote mental health, the seven awakening factors.[2] The five hindrances are:

- sensual desire,
- aversion,
- sloth-and-torpor,
- restlessness-and-worry,
- doubt.

These five quite literally "hinder" the proper functioning of the mind. They lead in the direction opposite to awakening and even mundane tasks such as properly learning something are rendered difficult as a result. The listing of five actually covers seven mental states, where in the case of sloth and torpor as well as in the case of restlessness and worry two states have been combined, presumably due to their similar effect and character.

Since the hindrances in actuality cover seven distinct mental states, they in a way correspond in number to the set of seven awakening factors that have instead a healthy effect on the mind. In this way, just as the previous chapter opposed five detrimental qualities to five beneficial qualities in the case of a nurse and a patient, the present contrast is between seven detrimental qualities and seven beneficial qualities. The seven mental factors of awakening that lead in the opposite direction of the hindrances are:

- mindfulness,
- investigation-of-dharmas,

2 On the five hindrances see in more detail Anālayo 2003: 186–200 and 2013b: 177–94, and on the seven awakening factors Anālayo 2003: 233–42 and 2013b: 195–226.

- energy,
- joy,
- tranquillity,
- concentration,
- equanimity.

The potential of these awakening factors is not restricted to mental health, as they also can lead to physical recovery. This is the theme of three consecutive discourses in the *Saṃyutta-nikāya*. One of these, in which the Buddha himself recovers health on hearing a monastic recite the seven awakening factors for him, has a parallel in the *Saṃyukta-āgama*.[3] I will return to this discourse in the discussion below. Another two discourses feature the monastics Mahāmoggallāna and Mahākassapa recovering from disease when the Buddha recites the awakening factors for them. Whereas in the case of the discourse featuring Mahāmoggallāna no parallel is known,[4] in the case of the discourse which has Mahākassapa as its protagonist a parallel has been preserved in Tibetan.[5] It is this version that I translate below, the original of which was apparently brought to Tibet by a Sri Lankan monastic and thus stems from a Theravāda lineage of transmission,[6] although clearly showing some variations when compared to its Pāli parallel.

V.2 TRANSLATION[7]

Thus have I heard. At one time [the Blessed One] was dwelling at Rājagaha in the Bamboo Grove, the Squirrels' Feeding Ground. On that occasion, at that time, the venerable Mahākassapa, who

3 SĀ 727 at T II 195b29 to 196a11 (partial translation Anālayo 2013b: 212–14) and its parallel SN 46.16 at SN V 81,1 (translated Bodhi 2000: 1581).

4 SN 46.15 at SN V 80,19 (translated Bodhi 2000: 1581). Another related instance can be found in EĀ 39.6 at T II 731a22, however, where the Buddha visits a sick monastic (Cunda?) and commends that he himself should recite the seven awakening factors. The sick monastic recites them and recovers from his disease.

5 The Pāli version is SN 46.14 at SN V 79,17 (translated Bodhi 2000: 1580).

6 See in more detail Skilling 1993.

7 The translated part is found in D 40 *ka* 281b2 to 282a6 or Q 756 *tsi* 298b1 to 299a8; the part I have translated is preceded by the title "Discourse to Mahākassapa". This discourse has already been translated into French by Feer 1883: 150–2.

was dwelling in the Pipphali Cave, was suffering, being afflicted by a serious disease.

Towards evening the Blessed One, who had been seated [in meditation] and considering it all,[8] approached the whereabouts of the venerable Mahākassapa. Having approached him,[9] the Blessed One sat down on a prepared seat. Having sat down, he said to the venerable Mahākassapa:

"Kassapa, how is your appetite for food and drink?[10] Are you in pain or are you at ease? The means for alleviating [the disease] do not alleviate it, is it not so?"[11]

Then the venerable Mahākassapa said: "Venerable Sir, I have no appetite for food and drink; I am afflicted by a serious disease. The means for alleviating it do not alleviate it. Please provide me with a means to alleviate it."[12]

[The Buddha said]: "I expounded the seven awakening factors, which on being cultivated and made much of lead to direct knowledge, awakening, and Nirvāṇa. What are the seven?

"The awakening factor of mindfulness, Kassapa, I expounded as an awakening factor, which on being cultivated and made much of leads to direct knowledge, awakening, and Nirvāṇa.

"Kassapa, I expounded the awakening factor of investigation-of-dharmas, which on being cultivated and made much of leads to direct knowledge, awakening, and Nirvāṇa.

"Kassapa, I expounded the awakening factor of energy, which on being cultivated and made much of leads to direct knowledge, awakening, and Nirvāṇa.

"Kassapa, I expounded the awakening factor of joy, which on being cultivated and made much of leads to direct knowledge, awakening, and Nirvāṇa.

---

8 The parallel SN 46.14 at SN V 79,22 only notes that the Buddha had been in seclusion, presumably also meditating. SN 46.14 does not mention that the Buddha had been considering it all, which I take to mean that he considered the circumstances of Mahākassapa's affliction.

9 Q 756 *tsi* 298b3 does not repeat the indication that the Buddha had approached him.

10 SN 46.14 at SN V 79,26 does not refer to appetite for food or drink, hence it later also has no such reference in Mahākassapa's reply.

11 SN 46.14 has no counterpart to a reference to means for alleviating the pain. The same is consequently also not found in Mahākassapa's reply.

12 In SN 46.14 Mahākassapa makes no request of any type and additionally notes that he has strong pain.

"Kassapa, I expounded the awakening factor of tranquillity, which on being cultivated and made much of leads to direct knowledge, awakening, and Nirvāṇa.

"Kassapa, I expounded the awakening factor of concentration, which on being cultivated and made much of leads to direct knowledge, awakening, and Nirvāṇa.

"Kassapa, I expounded the awakening factor of equanimity, which on being cultivated and made much of leads to direct knowledge, awakening, and Nirvāṇa.

"Kassapa, I expounded these seven awakening factors, which on being cultivated and made much of lead to direct knowledge, awakening, and Nirvāṇa."

[Mahākassapa said]: "The Blessed One, the Well-gone One has [indeed] expounded the awakening factors in which one should train."[13]

This is what the Blessed One said. The venerable Mahākassapa delighted in what the Blessed One had said. The venerable Mahākassapa right away recovered from the disease. Being recovered from the disease, the venerable Mahākassapa rose up.[14]

V.3 DISCUSSION

Together with the other discourses that similarly report the healing potential of the awakening factors, the Tibetan discourse translated above shows these seven qualities of the mind to be of considerable assistance in the case of disease. The *Saṃyukta-āgama* discourse mentioned above in the introduction, which shows the healing effect a recitation of these seven awakening factors had in the case of the Buddha himself, continues with a set of stanzas spoken by an unnamed monastic. According to one of these stanzas, on hearing the seven awakening factors being recited, the Buddha re-experienced the taste of full awakening.[15]

---

13 In SN 46.14 at SN V 80,14 Mahākassapa does not refer to a need to train in the awakening factors, but instead repeats that they are indeed the awakening factors.

14 SN 46.14 does not report that Mahākassapa rose up.

15 SĀ 727 at T II 195c23; see also a Sanskrit parallel in Waldschmidt 1967: 244 and an Uighur parallel in von Gabain 1954: 13.

For the mere recitation of the awakening factors to have such a healing effect, the patient should ideally be one who has already made full use of the awakening potential of these seven qualities, as had been the case for the Buddha and his two arahant disciples, Mahāmoggallāna and Mahākassapa. This does not mean, however, that the present discourse is only of relevance for arahants. Recitation of the present discourse, as well as mental recollection of its import, can function as a source of joy for anyone who feels inspired by the goal of awakening in general or more specifically by the Buddha's awakening and his teaching of the path to liberation. The present discourse in fact forms part of several texts used in a traditional Theravāda setting as a *paritta*, whose recitation is believed to have protective and healing power.[16] Thus a recitation or recollection of the teaching given in the discourse translated above can certainly serve as a powerful source of inspiration, the beneficial effects of which are not confined to those who are proficient in cultivating the awakening factors.

The *Saṃyukta-āgama* discourse that reports the Buddha's recovery highlights energy as the awakening factor whose cultivation made the Buddha reach full awakening.[17] Although this is not mentioned in the Pāli parallel, it does concord with the traditional account of the Buddha's prolonged quest for awakening. This highlight on energy seems to imply that, according to personal character and inclination, one or the other of the awakening factors may be of particular significance for one's personal progress to awakening. At the same time, in the three Pāli versions as well as in the Tibetan discourse translated above, the whole set of seven awakening factors is responsible for successful healing, making it clear that the healing potential is not confined to energy alone.

An attempt to appreciate this healing potential requires taking a closer look at how these awakening factors are to be cultivated. The early discourses describe two main dynamics in cultivating the seven awakening factors.[18] One of these involves a sequential building up, the other requires balancing the seven factors.

---

16 See, e.g., Suvimalee 2012.

17 SĀ 727 at T II 195c14.

18 See in more detail Anālayo 2013b: 201–5 and 215–17.

In the first of these two, the sequential building up, mindfulness serves as a foundation. Based on being well established in mindfulness one then investigates, corresponding to the second awakening factor. While investigating one also needs to make an effort in order to avoid distraction, and the activity of investigation in turn yields a momentum that arouses further energy. In combination this results in the full establishment of the third awakening factor of energy.

The form of energized investigation undertaken in this way sooner or later should lead to the arising of wholesome forms of joy, the next awakening factor. For this to happen, practice needs to be monitored in such a way that investigation and energy do not result in the arising of tension and agitation, which can happen when practice becomes too pushy. Instead, investigation and energy are at their best when only taken up to the point of a continuous and sustained interest in the present moment's experience. Out of this sustained interest, joy can arise, and this joy in turn is of a type that results in calmness of body and mind. Calmness of body and mind can then become manifestations of the awakening factor of tranquillity.

In one who dwells with bodily and mental tranquillity, the next awakening factor of concentration arises when the mind remains collected and aloof from distraction. With the mind finely balanced in this way, one reaches equipoise or equanimity, the seventh of the awakening factors.

The other of the two main dynamics described in the early discourses, concerned with balancing the awakening factors, distinguishes those that energize from those that calm. Investigation, energy, and joy are energizing factors, whereas tranquillity, concentration, and equanimity are calming factors. Whereas the other six awakening factors require balancing, mindfulness is useful in any situation.

In actual practice, once the sequential build-up has established the other awakening factors based on a foundation in mindfulness, if one finds that the mind has become a little sluggish, one gives emphasis to investigation, energy, and joy in order to energize the practice. If instead the mind has become slightly agitated, one gives emphasis to the qualities of tranquillity, concentration, and equipoise. By navigating in this way through whatever fluctuations occur, the seven factors of awakening become increasingly well established in the mind and can eventually fulfil their purpose in providing the mental condition in which awakening can take place.

From the viewpoint of these two main dynamics of cultivating the seven awakening factors, mindfulness stands out as the foundation for the sequential building up as well as being the one factor that is always required in relation to balancing. The eminent role of mindfulness that emerges in this respect is not only of relevance for those who are fully awakened, but can unfold its potential in the case of anyone who seriously engages in cultivating this quality. This potential concerns not only healing on the physical level, as mindfulness also constitutes the commendable attitude for facing the pain of disease. In the next three chapters I will continue to explore this role of mindfulness, a role to which I return again in relation to the topic of facing death in later chapters in this book.

VI

MINDFUL PAIN REDUCTION

VI.1 INTRODUCTION

The protagonist in this chapter's discourse is another eminent disciple of the Buddha by the name of Anuruddha. In the early discourses Anuruddha features as an accomplished meditator, in particular outstanding among the Buddha's disciples in the exercise of a supernormal ability called the divine eye.[1] The divine eye, necessarily based on a high degree of concentrative accomplishment, refers to the ability to see what is far away, including in other realms of existence recognized in Buddhist cosmology.

The *Naḷakapāna-sutta* and its parallels feature an occasion when the recently ordained Anuruddha is in the company of the monastics Nandiya and Kimbila,[2] who are also with him on an occasion reported in the *Upakkilesa-sutta*, when they receive detailed instructions from the Buddha on how to deepen their concentration.[3] This gives the impression that during the

1 AN 1.14 at AN I 23,20 (translated Bodhi 2012: 109) and EĀ 4.2 at T II 557b9; for biographical sketches of Anuruddha see Malalasekera 1937/1995: 85–90 as well as Nyanaponika and Hecker 1997: 185–210.

2 MN 68 at MN I 462,26 (translated Ñāṇamoli 1995/2005: 566) and its parallel MĀ 77 at T I 544b24.

3 MN 128 at MN III 157,20 (translated Ñāṇamoli 1995/2005: 1012) and its parallels MĀ 72 at T I 536c11 and D 4094 *ju* 275b7 or Q 5595 *thu* 19b8.

early years of his monastic life Anuruddha was staying in the company of Nandiya and Kimbila.

The *Cūḷagosinga-sutta* and its parallels report another occasion on which these three stay together. At this time Anuruddha is able to proclaim in front of the Buddha the success of the whole group in gaining deep concentrative attainments leading up to an attainment known as the "cessation of perception and feeling".[4] This attainment implies the ability to dwell in a state that is completely devoid of the experience of any feelings.[5]

On the present occasion Anuruddha is no longer in the company of Nandiya and Kimbila. Moreover, he is visited by a group of many monastics, which gives the impression that by now he has become sufficiently well known to merit such attention. This makes it highly probable that the present episode should be located at a later time in his monastic life, when he has already acquired the concentrative abilities described in the *Cūḷagosinga-sutta* and its parallels.[6]

Anuruddha's ability to dwell in the cessation of perception and feeling is significant in so far as the discourse below shows that, when being subjected to painful bodily feelings, Anuruddha does not resort to this ability. His approach is not to try to block off pain by withdrawing into an attainment that would have enabled him to stop the experience of feelings. Instead he decides to face pain with mindfulness.

This is exemplary of the proper attitude to pain, namely just to face it with mindfulness. Facing pain with mindfulness is possible for anyone with some minimal degree of training and does not require the previous acquisition of deep concentrative abilities. Therefore the exemplary mode of being with pain that emerges from the present discourse is of general relevance and not the domain of highly accomplished practitioners only.

---

4 MN 31 at MN I 209,22 (translated Ñāṇamoli 1995/2005: 304) and its parallel EĀ 24.8 at T II 629b25. Another parallel, MĀ 185 at T I 730b28, instead lists the six supernormal knowledges.

5 On the attainment of cessation see, e.g., the monograph study by Griffiths 1986/1991.

6 That Anuruddha developed his concentrative abilities soon after going forth is also reflected in Mp I 191,22, according to which he cultivated the divine eye, which requires the ability to attain the fourth absorption, already during the first rains retreat after his ordination.

A record of Anuruddha enduring pain with mindfulness is found in a discourse in the *Saṃyutta-nikāya*.[7] This discourse has two consecutive parallels in the *Saṃyukta-āgama*, one of which takes place when Anuruddha is still sick, whereas in the other he has already recovered from his disease.[8] In what follows I translate the first of these two.

The description given by Anuruddha of the condition of his disease in the discourse below is a standard account of a serious sickness. This is so much the case that the *Saṃyukta-āgama* collection provides this description only once in relation to a discourse that features another monastic by the name of Khemaka, translated below in Chapter 11, and on other occurrences simply abbreviates and refers back to that occurrence for supplementation.

The vivid similes given in this standard description are best understood as depicting the condition of the disease and not as expressions of any anguish on the part of the patient. This is clearly the case for their usage in the present instance by Anuruddha, as the whole point of the discourse is precisely that he was not overwhelmed by the pain he experienced.

VI.2 TRANSLATION[9]

Thus have I heard. At one time the Buddha was staying at Sāvatthī in Jeta's Grove, Anāthapiṇḍika's Park.[10] At that time the venerable Anuruddha was staying at Sāvatthī in a dwelling in a pine forest and his body had come to be sick and in pain.

Then a group of many monastics approached the venerable Anuruddha. Having exchanged polite and friendly greetings, they stood to one side and said to the venerable Anuruddha: "Venerable Anuruddha, is your affliction

---

7 SN 52.10 at SN V 302,11 (translated Bodhi 2000: 1757).

8 SĀ 541 at T II 140c13 (translated Anālayo 2015c: 26f).

9 The translated discourse is SĀ 540 at T II 140b26 to 140c12.

10 SN 52.10 at SN V 302,11, which does not mention the Buddha's whereabouts, reports that Anuruddha was staying in the Blind Men's Grove, also located at Sāvatthī.

increasing or decreasing? Is it endurable? Is the force of the disease gradually decreasing and not in turn increasing?"[11]

The venerable Anuruddha said: "My disease is not becoming appeased and it is difficult to endure. The pains in the body are gradually increasing and not decreasing.[12] *It is just as if many strong men were to take hold of a weak man, put a rope around his head and with both hands pull it tight, so that he is in extreme pain. My pain now exceeds that.*

"It is just as if a cow butcher with a sharp knife were to cut open a living cow's belly to take its internal organs. How could that cow endure the pains in its belly? My belly is now more painful than that cow's.

"It is just as if two strong men were to grab one weak person and hang him over a fire, roasting both his feet. The heat of both my feet now exceeds that. The pain of my disease is increasing and not decreasing.

"Even though my body has come to be in such pain, I shall just endure it with right mindfulness and clear comprehension."

The monastics asked the venerable Anuruddha: "In what is your mind dwelling that you are able to endure such great pain in this way with right mindfulness and clear comprehension?"

The venerable Anuruddha said to the monastics: "Dwelling in the four establishments of mindfulness I am able to endure the pains arising in the body on my own with right mindfulness and clear comprehension.[13] What are the four establishments of mindfulness?

"That is, the establishment of mindfulness by contemplating the body as a body internally,[14] *with energetic effort, right mindfulness, and clear comprehension, overcoming desire and*

---

11 In SN 52.10 at SN V 302,15 the visiting monastics directly ask him about his (meditative) dwelling, which enables him to dwell without his mind being afflicted by the pain, without any preceding enquiry about his present condition, wherefore in this version he does not describe his sick condition.

12 SĀ 540 abbreviates what comes next and indicates that this should be supplemented with the description in the discourse by Khemaka. This is SĀ 103 (see below p. 91) and the section to be supplemented is found at T II 29c15; for a survey of such references to the discourse by Khemaka see Anālayo 2010b: 6 note 10.

13 SN 52.10 SN V 302,18 specifies that his way of dwelling in the four *satipaṭṭhānas* was with the "mind well established" in them and that this led to the bodily pain not overwhelming his mind.

14 The corresponding part in SN 52.10 at SN V 302,21 does not bring in the distinction between internal and external *satipaṭṭhāna* practice.

discontent in the world. The establishment of mindfulness by contemplating the body as a body externally, with energetic effort, right mindfulness, and clear comprehension, overcoming desire and discontent in the world. The establishment of mindfulness by contemplating the body as a body internally-and-externally, with energetic effort, right mindfulness, and clear comprehension, overcoming desire and discontent in the world.

"The establishment of mindfulness by contemplating feelings *as feelings internally, with energetic effort, right mindfulness, and clear comprehension, overcoming desire and discontent in the world. The establishment of mindfulness by contemplating feelings as feelings externally, with energetic effort, right mindfulness, and clear comprehension, overcoming desire and discontent in the world. The establishment of mindfulness by contemplating feelings as feelings internally-and-externally, with energetic effort, right mindfulness, and clear comprehension, overcoming desire and discontent in the world.*

"The establishment of mindfulness by contemplating the mind *as mind internally, with energetic effort, right mindfulness, and clear comprehension, overcoming desire and discontent in the world. The establishment of mindfulness by contemplating the mind as mind externally, with energetic effort, right mindfulness, and clear comprehension, overcoming desire and discontent in the world. The establishment of mindfulness by contemplating the mind as mind internally-and-externally, with energetic effort, right mindfulness, and clear comprehension, overcoming desire and discontent in the world.*

"The establishment of mindfulness by contemplating dharmas *as dharmas internally, with energetic effort, right mindfulness, and clear comprehension, overcoming desire and discontent in the world. The establishment of mindfulness by contemplating dharmas as dharmas externally, with energetic effort, right mindfulness, and clear comprehension, overcoming desire and discontent in the world. The establishment of mindfulness by contemplating dharmas as dharmas internally-and-externally, with energetic effort, right mindfulness, and clear comprehension, overcoming desire and discontent in the world.*

"This is called being established in the four establishments of mindfulness, which enables me to endure the pains in the body on my own with right mindfulness and clear comprehension."

Then these worthy ones, having discussed this matter together, rejoiced in it and were delighted. They each rose from their seats and left.

VI.3 DISCUSSION

In agreement with its Pāli parallel, the discourse translated above highlights Anuruddha's practice of the four establishments of mindfulness, *satipaṭṭhāna*:

- contemplation of the body,
- contemplation of feelings,
- contemplation of the mind,
- contemplation of *dharma*s.

The term *dharma* can have a wide variety of meanings. Two prominent meanings are the Dharma as the teaching given by the Buddha and *dharma*s as phenomena in general. Because both meanings seem relevant to the fourth *satipaṭṭhāna*, I find it preferable to retain the Indic term.

For a better appreciation of the significance of *dharma* in the context of the fourth *satipaṭṭhāna*, a comparative study of the *Satipaṭṭhāna-sutta* and its Chinese *Āgama* parallels provides helpful perspectives. From the viewpoint of such comparison, the main thrust of this fourth *satipaṭṭhāna* seems to be the cultivation of the mental condition within which awakening can take place.[15] In this way the fourth *satipaṭṭhāna* provides a direct link to the topic of the previous chapter. In fact the awakening factors are the one exercise common to the exposition of contemplation of *dharma*s in the *Satipaṭṭhāna-sutta* and its parallels.

The same type of comparative study of the *Satipaṭṭhāna-sutta* and its Chinese *Āgama* parallels also provides a perspective on the first *satipaṭṭhāna*. According to this perspective, contemplation of the body appears to be predominantly concerned with cultivating an understanding of the body's true nature, in particular its lack of inherent beauty, its empty material constitution, and its inevitable passing away and falling apart.[16]

---

15 Anālayo 2013b: 176.
16 Anālayo 2013b: 53f.

In this way an understanding of the true nature of the body, awareness of the nature of feelings and of the mind, and cultivating the mental condition within which awakening can take place appear to be central themes underlying the four *satipaṭṭhānas*. According to the present discourse, these four together provide a vantage point for facing pain with mindfulness and clear comprehension. In terms of these central themes underlying the four *satipaṭṭhānas*, facing disease with mindfulness can reveal the limitations inherent in having a body, whose nature is to be subject to falling sick. The same mindful facing of disease clearly discloses the changing and ultimately unsatisfactory nature of feelings, and it even more clearly exposes the quality of one's own mind when confronted with the most unwanted of all experiences: strong physical pain. In this way even serious illness can become an opportunity to cultivate qualities and insights related to awakening, all of which build on and converge on mindfulness.

As mentioned earlier, the central role taken by mindfulness is particularly remarkable in the case of Anuruddha. The example he provides implies that to dwell in mindfulness is a preferable option over the possibility of entering an attainment that would have cut him off completely from any feeling. The discourse above makes it clear that the painful feelings Anuruddha is experiencing are not only difficult to endure, but that they are moreover increasing, a situation that one would expect to lead naturally to the wish to cut off the experience of such feelings. Yet this is not Anuruddha's reaction.

The significance of this aspect of the above discourse emerges also from the question that the other monastics pose. In both versions they naturally want to know what type of mental dwelling he employs to handle the situation of intense pain. In the *Saṃyutta-nikāya* version they ask this question right away on meeting him.[17] Such a question is natural when meeting someone who is able to handle well the situation of being seriously sick. Anuruddha himself asks the same question when visiting a lay disciple in the discourse translated below in Chapter 8. The present episode, given that Anuruddha

17 See above note 11.

would have been renowned among his monastic companions for his meditative abilities, gives the impression that the other monastics wanted to know which of the various attainments at his disposal he employed in this situation. For Anuruddha to opt for *satipaṭṭhāna* practice reveals the power of mindfulness in being with pain, fully aware of the present moment of pain just as it is. I will continue exploring this role of mindfulness in relation to pain in the next two chapters.

Central in all this is the power aspect of mindfulness when cultivated as a form of bare attention to whatever manifests in the present moment, instead of immediately reacting to it. The venerable Nyanaponika explains this power aspect in the following manner:[18]

> Just as certain reflex movements automatically protect the body, similarly the mind needs spontaneous spiritual and moral self-protection. The practice of bare attention will provide this vital function ...
>
> Grave consequences issue from that fundamental perceptual situation: our rush into hasty or habitual reactions after receiving the first few signals from our perceptions. But if we muster the restraining forces of mindfulness and pause for bare attention, the material and mental processes ... [are] no longer dragged at once into the whirlpool of self-reference, [but] allowed to unfold themselves before the watchful eye of mindfulness ...
>
> By developing the habit of pausing for bare attention, it becomes increasingly easier ... to forgo useless reactions ...
>
> By refraining from busying ourselves unnecessarily, external frictions will be reduced and the inner tensions they bring will loosen up.

18 The quotations are taken from Nyanaponika 1968/1986: 35, 34, 30, and 31.

VII

ENDURING PAIN WITH MINDFULNESS

VII.1 INTRODUCTION

The discourse translated in the present chapter reports an occasion when the Buddha's foot had been injured and he was subject to strong pain. Besides the Buddha, the discourse also features *devas*, celestial beings, who comment on the exemplary way in which he faces the pain.

The occurrence of such celestial beings is a regular feature of the early discourses, which often report that the Buddha and some of his eminent disciples are in conversation with various *devas*. Contrary to a mode of interpretation sometimes advocated nowadays, such occurrences of *devas* cannot invariably be reduced to mere impersonations of personal reflections or inner uncertainties of the human protagonist in question.[1] Instead, a proper understanding of the thought-world of the early discourses requires an acknowledgement that, as far as the texts allow us to judge, the Buddha and his disciples believed in and affirmed the existence of such celestial beings.[2]

This does not mean that one needs to believe in the existence of *devas* oneself so as to be able to benefit from a discourse in which they feature. It does mean, however, that, in order to understand properly the message given in the discourse in

1 See in more detail Anālayo 2014b: 116–19.
2 See in more detail Anālayo 2015a.

question, it is best to consider a statement made by a *deva* in the same way as one would consider a statement made by a human protagonist who features in the events depicted.

In the present instance, the comments made by the *deva*s on the Buddha's endurance of pain are therefore ideally read in the same way as one would read the statement made in the *Saṃyukta-āgama* discourse mentioned briefly in Chapter 5 by an unnamed monastic, who comments on the effect of a recitation of the awakening factors on the Buddha's illness, explaining that their recitation made the Buddha re-experience the taste of awakening. Similarly in the present discourse information on how the Buddha handled the pain of his injury is provided by other onlookers, who just happen to be celestial beings instead of human beings.

The discourse translated below stems from a *Saṃyukta-āgama* collection that has been preserved only partially in Chinese translation. Parallels are extant in the *Saṃyutta-nikāya* as well as in the other *Saṃyukta-āgama* collection that has been preserved almost completely in Chinese,[3] and which is also the source of most of the translations in this book.

VII.2 TRANSLATION[4]

> Thus have I heard. At one time the Buddha was dwelling at Rājagaha in the Sattapaṇṇi Cave by the side of Mount Vebhāra.[5] Then the Buddha's foot had been pierced by a [piece] of acacia wood,[6] and he was in extreme pain. The Tathāgata

3 SN 1.38 at SN I 27,12 (translated Bodhi 2000: 116) and its parallel in SĀ 1289 at T II 355a19.

4 The translated text is SĀ² 287 at T II 473c27 to 474a18; for a translation of an excerpt from this discourse see Anālayo 2015c: 26.

5 The location in SN 1.38 at SN I 27,12 is the Maddakucchi Deer Park at Rājagaha.

6 According to SN 1.38 at SN I 27,14, the Buddha's feet had been pierced by a stone splinter, which the commentary explains to have been the result of an attempt by Devadatta to kill the Buddha; see Spk I 78,1. For comparative studies of this episode, reported in a range of sources, see, e.g., Frauwallner 1956: 119, Mukherjee 1966: 67–70, Bareau 1991: 119, and Ray 1994: 167f; for depictions in art see, e.g., Deeg 1999: 203 note 12. Although SĀ² 287 does not provide any explicit reference to Devadatta, some degree of defensiveness or apprehension seems to express itself in the recurrent reference to those who are foolish enough to slander the Buddha; see also below note 11.

silently endured it. He required nothing even with recurrent pain.[7]

At that time there were eight devas of beautiful complexion who approached the Buddha.[8] One deva among them said: "The recluse Gotama is truly a lion among brave men.[9] Even though he experiences pain, he does not relinquish the awakening [factor] of mindfulness and his mind is not troubled or altered.[10]

"If there should still be a person who gives rise to slander of Gotama, the great lion, it should be understood that this person is very much deluded."[11]

Besides, the second deva said: "The recluse Gotama is a brave elephant. Even though he experiences pain, he does not relinquish the awakening [factor] of mindfulness and his mind is not troubled or altered.

"If there should still be a person who gives rise to slander of Gotama, the [brave] elephant, it should be understood that this person is very much deluded."

Again, the third deva said: "The recluse Gotama is like a skilled riding bull. *Even though he experiences pain, he does not relinquish the awakening factor of mindfulness and his mind is not troubled or altered.*

"If there should still be a person who gives rise to slander of Gotama, the skilled riding bull, it should be understood that this person is very much deluded."

Again, the fourth deva said: "The recluse Gotama is like a skilled riding horse. *Even though he experiences pain, he does not relinquish the awakening factor of mindfulness and his mind is not troubled or altered.*

"If there should still be a person who gives rise to slander of Gotama, the skilled riding horse, it should be understood that this person is very

7 In SN 1.38 the Buddha lies down.

8 SN 1.38 at SN I 27,22 reports that 700 *deva*s had arrived, that their visit took place at night, and that they paid respect to the Buddha.

9 The comparisons employed in SN 1.38 differ in sequence; the lion features as second, for example.

10 SN 1.38 at SN I 28,2 notes that the Buddha bears the pain, which appears to be rather strong, with mindfulness and clear comprehension, and without becoming distressed.

11 A to some extent comparable remark about someone who tries to act contrary to the Buddha is made in SN 1.38 at SN I 29,2 by the eighth *deva* and in SĀ 1289 at T II 355b11 by the fourth *deva*.

much deluded."

Again, the fifth deva said: "The recluse Gotama is just like a king of bulls. *Even though he experiences pain, he does not relinquish the awakening factor of mindfulness and his mind is not troubled or altered.*

"If there should still be a person who gives rise to slander of Gotama, the king of bulls, it should be understood that this person is very much deluded."

Again, the sixth deva said: "The recluse Gotama is supremely brave. *Even though he experiences pain, he does not relinquish the awakening factor of mindfulness and his mind is not troubled or altered.*

"If there should still be a person who gives rise to slander of the supremely brave Gotama, it should be understood that this person is very much deluded."

Again, the seventh deva said: "The recluse Gotama is a lotus among men.[12] *Even though he experiences pain, he does not relinquish the awakening factor of mindfulness and his mind is not troubled or altered.*

"If there should still be a person who gives rise to slander of Gotama, the lotus among men, it should be understood that this person is very much deluded."

Again, the eighth deva said: "The recluse Gotama is just like a white lotus (*puṇḍarīka*). Observe his meditative equanimity, supremely well concentrated, entirely without arrogance and also without baseness. Because of being calm he is liberated, and because of being liberated he is calm."

Then the eighth deva spoke this poem:

> "One does not have a purified mind
> Even if one has completed a hundred years
> In being well versed in the five [branches of the] Vedas.
> "On account of being entangled in clinging to moral
>   observances

---

12 The lotus does not feature among the comparisons employed by the *deva*s in SN 1.38.

And of being immersed in the sea of sensual craving,
One will be unable to cross over to the other shore."[13]

At that time, when the eight devas had spoken these poems, they paid respect with their heads at the feet of the Buddha and returned to their abode.

VII.3 DISCUSSION

The eight *deva*s in the discourse above are so inspired by the Buddha's ability to bear with pain that they employ various comparisons. These involve animals, which in ancient Indian thought can embody exemplary good qualities, and the lotus, which conveys the idea of rising above attachment and desire. The last *deva* compares the Buddha's composure favourably to what among brahmins was considered the acme of achievements, namely being well versed in their sacred scriptures, the *Veda*s.

Besides these comparisons, another topic that the *deva*s bring up is the foolishness of slandering someone who is as accomplished as the Buddha. This in a way builds on the comparisons employed by the *deva*s, in the sense that the Buddha's composure in facing strong pain shows him to be such a highly accomplished practitioner that it would indeed be rather silly to speak badly about him.

The eulogies by the *deva*s all throw into relief the Buddha's reliance on mindfulness. The two parallel versions agree that, when his foot had been hurt, the Buddha endured the strong pains by relying on mindfulness. They do not explicitly specify that this was the awakening factor of mindfulness, but just mention mindfulness and clear comprehension.[14] In spite of this minor variation, what is common to the three versions is the spotlight they provide on the potential of mindfulness in bearing with pain. This is evidently considered to be of such significance that a whole host of *deva*s comes to eulogize the Buddha's exemplary attitude in facing pain with mindfulness.

---

13 In SN 1.38 at SN I 29,10 the eighth *deva* continues with another two stanzas.
14 SN 1.38 at SN I 28,8 and SĀ 1289 at T II 355a21.

The Buddha's bearing with pain in the present discourse complements the record of his recovery from disease on hearing a recitation of the awakening factors, mentioned briefly in Chapter 5. The same episode also complements Anuruddha's apparent preference for mindfulness over the cessation of perception and feeling when face to face with pain, discussed in Chapter 6. In the case of Anuruddha, and even more so in the case of the Buddha, given their meditative expertise it can safely be ruled out that they are just unable to enter concentration. In fact the Buddha is on record for effortlessly entering the cessation of perception and feeling even on the verge of his passing away.[15]

Moreover, in the discourse translated above, the eighth *deva* explicitly notes that the Buddha, in spite of being in pain, is "supremely well concentrated". Similarly, in the *Saṃyutta-nikāya* parallel the eighth *deva* states that the Buddha is with well-developed concentration, and in the other *Saṃyukta-āgama* version it is the fifth *deva* who proclaims that the Buddha is concentrated.[16] Thus the Buddha's concentrated condition on this occasion is common ground among the parallels.

The circumstance that the Buddha and Anuruddha opt for mindfulness instead of entering the cessation of perception and feeling, which would have cut them off from any pain, conveys the impression that even highly accomplished practitioners consider it appropriate just to face the experience of strong pain with mindfulness.

Facing pain with mindfulness offers a powerful option that is open to anyone willing to try, without needing to have developed a high level of meditative expertise, unlike the attainment of the cessation of perception and feeling. A discourse in the *Saṃyutta-nikāya* and its *Saṃyukta-āgama* parallel record the Buddha's explicit instruction that newly ordained monastics should right away be trained in the four *satipaṭṭhānas*.[17] This makes it clear that the practice of *satipaṭṭhāna* was not considered the domain of accomplished practitioners

---

15 See below p. 195.
16 SN 1.38 at SN I 28,31 and SĀ 1289 at T II 355b15.
17 SN 47.4 at SN V 144,15 (translated Bodhi 2000: 1630) and its parallel SĀ 621 at T II 173c16.

only, but was rather seen as commendable even for those who have just embarked on the gradual path of training.

The potential of mindfulness in aiding even those with relatively little meditative training to face physical and mental pain has received major exposure in recent times, in particular through the development of Mindfulness-Based Stress Reduction. Here is how Kabat-Zinn describes the main principles of how mindfulness can reduce stress and help to face pain:[18]

> Pain is a natural part of the experience of life. Suffering is one of many possible responses to pain ... it is not always the pain per se but the way we see it and react to it that determines the degree of suffering we will experience. And it is the suffering that we fear most, not the pain ...
>
> Several classic laboratory experiments with acute pain showed that *tuning in* to sensations is a more effective way of reducing the level of pain experienced when the pain is intense and prolonged than is distracting yourself ... the sensory, the emotional, and the cognitive/conceptual dimensions of the pain experience can be *uncoupled* from one another, meaning that they can be held in awareness as independent aspects of experience ... this phenomenon of uncoupling can give us new degrees of freedom in resting in awareness and holding whatever arises in any or all of these three domains in an entirely different way, and dramatically reduce the suffering experienced.

18 The quotations are taken from Kabat-Zinn 1990/2013: 364 and 374.

VIII

MINDFULLY FACING DISEASE

VIII.1 INTRODUCTION

In this chapter I continue with the topic of facing pain with mindfulness. Whereas in Chapter 6 Anuruddha faced his own pain by being established in the four *satipaṭṭhānas*, in the present instance he visits a sick lay disciple by the name of Mānadiṇṇa, who engages in the same practice of the four *satipaṭṭhānas* for the same purpose.

The present discourse is one of several examples that document the practice of *satipaṭṭhāna* undertaken by lay disciples. Contrary to an assumption sometimes found in modern writings, it is not correct to suppose that in ancient times only monastics practised mindfulness.[1] Such a suggestion ignores the textual evidence at our disposal. In fact the present instance features a lay disciple with a high degree of proficiency in *satipaṭṭhāna* practice, as can be seen in the

1 E.g. Wilson 2014: 21 comments on the *Satipaṭṭhāna-sutta* that "in this classic presentation mindfulness is taught to monks, not the general Buddhist community." As I have already shown in Anālayo 2003: 275f, the discourses clearly document the practice of *satipaṭṭhāna* by lay disciples. Moreover, the term "monk" as a form of address used in the early discourses does not imply a restriction of the instructions to male monastics only; see in more detail Collett and Anālayo 2014.

discourse translated below from the *Saṃyukta-āgama* and in its parallel in the *Saṃyutta-nikāya*.[2]

VIII.2 TRANSLATION[3]

Thus have I heard. At one time the Buddha was staying in the country of Campā, by the side of the Gaggarā Pond. At that time the householder Mānadiṇṇa had just recovered from being sick.[4]

Then the householder Mānadiṇṇa said to one person: "Good man, approach the venerable Anuruddha, pay respect at Anuruddha's feet on my behalf, and enquire about his bodily health: 'Are you dwelling at ease?'

"I hope he will accept an invitation for tomorrow with a whole body of four men. If he accepts the invitation, further tell him on my behalf: 'We ordinary people have many tasks in relation to the king's household; we are not able to approach and meet him respectfully ourselves. May the venerable one arrive in time, coming with a whole body of four men to attend to my invitation, out of compassion.'"[5]

Then that man, having received the instructions from the householder [Mānadiṇṇa], approached the venerable Anuruddha, paid respect at his feet, and said to the venerable one: "The householder Mānadiṇṇa pays his respect and enquires: 'Do you have little disease and little worry? Regarding your bodily health, are you dwelling at ease? May the venerable one out of compassion accept my invitation for tomorrow midday with a whole body of four men.'" Then the venerable Anuruddha accepted the invitation by [remaining] silent.

---

2 SN 47.30 at SN V 178,1 (translated Bodhi 2000: 1655). Mānadiṇṇa seems to appear only in this particular discourse, leaving little scope to give further information about him; see also Malalasekera 1938/1998: 606.

3 The translated discourse is SĀ 1038 at T II 270c15 to 271a29.

4 In SN 47.30 at SN V 178,3 he appears to be still sick at the time of the discourse.

5 The introductory narration in SN 47.30 is abbreviated, referring to the preceding discourse for supplementation. In SN 47.29 at SN V 176,16 the householder protagonist of this discourse sends a messenger to invite Ānanda to come for a visit, not for a meal. Thus the introductory narrations in SN 47.30 and SĀ 1038 differ considerably.

Then that man further said to the venerable Anuruddha, on behalf of the householder Mānadiṇṇa: "We ordinary people have many tasks in relation to the king's household; we are not able to meet him respectfully ourselves. May the venerable one with a whole body of four men compassionately accept my invitation for tomorrow at midday, out of compassion."

The venerable Anuruddha said: "For now you can be at ease. I know myself the time tomorrow for approaching the house with a whole body of four men."

Then that man, having received the venerable Anuruddha's instruction, returned to the householder [Mānadiṇṇa and said]: "Noble one, please know that I have approached the venerable Anuruddha and fully explained the honourable one's intentions. The venerable Anuruddha said: 'For now you can be at ease. I know myself the time.'"

During the night the householder Mānadiṇṇa had clean and delicious food and drink prepared. In the morning he again said to that man: "Approach the venerable Anuruddha and tell him: 'The time has come.'"

Then that man, having received the instruction, approached the venerable Anuruddha, paid respect at his feet, and said: "The supplies have been completely prepared. Please know that it is time."

Then the venerable Anuruddha put on his robe, took his bowl, and with a whole body of four men approached the house of the householder [Mānadiṇṇa].

Then the householder Mānadiṇṇa was standing to the left of the inner entrance, surrounded by the women [of his household]. On seeing the venerable Anuruddha, he paid respect with his whole body at [the venerable Anuruddha's] feet and led him to take a seat. Having paid respect to each [of the monastics] separately and enquired about their health, he withdrew to sit to one side.[6]

The venerable Anuruddha asked the householder [Mānadiṇṇa]: "Are you enduring and dwelling at ease?"

The householder [Mānadiṇṇa] said: "It is like this, venerable sir, I endure and dwell at ease. Earlier I encountered a disease

---

6 SN 47.30 (to be supplemented from SN 47.29) does not report how the monastics were received.

and was right away thrown down by being seriously ill. Now I have come to recover."

The venerable Anuruddha asked the householder [Mānadiṇṇa]: "Dwelling in what [meditative] dwelling were you able to recover from the affliction at the time of being sick?"

The householder [Mānadiṇṇa] said: "Venerable Anuruddha, because I dwelled in the four establishments of mindfulness, being focused on cultivating collected mindfulness, at that time the bodily affliction came to be appeased. What are the four?

"That is, dwelling in mindfulness by contemplating the body as a body internally, with energetic effort, right mindfulness, and clear comprehension, overcoming desire and discontent in the world.[7] *Dwelling in mindfulness by contemplating the body* as a body externally, *with energetic effort, right mindfulness, and clear comprehension, overcoming desire and discontent in the world. Dwelling in mindfulness by contemplating the body* as a body internally-and-externally, *with energetic effort, right mindfulness, and clear comprehension, overcoming desire and discontent in the world.*

"Dwelling in mindfulness by contemplating feelings as feelings internally, *with energetic effort, right mindfulness, and clear comprehension, overcoming desire and discontent in the world. Dwelling in mindfulness by contemplating feelings* as feelings externally, *with energetic effort, right mindfulness, and clear comprehension, overcoming desire and discontent in the world. Dwelling in mindfulness by contemplating feelings* as feelings internally-and-externally, *with energetic effort, right mindfulness, and clear comprehension, overcoming desire and discontent in the world.*

"Dwelling in mindfulness by contemplating the mind as mind internally, *with energetic effort, right mindfulness, and clear comprehension, overcoming desire and discontent in the world. Dwelling in mindfulness by contemplating the mind* as mind externally, *with energetic effort, right mindfulness, and clear comprehension, overcoming desire and discontent in the world. Dwelling in mindfulness by contemplating the mind* as mind internally-and-externally, *with energetic effort, right mindfulness, and clear comprehension, overcoming desire and discontent in the world.*

7 SN 47.30 at SN V 178,7 does not distinguish between internal and external practice of *satipaṭṭhāna*.

"Dwelling in mindfulness by contemplating dharmas as dharmas internally, *with energetic effort, right mindfulness, and clear comprehension, overcoming desire and discontent in the world. Dwelling in mindfulness by contemplating dharmas* as dharmas externally, *with energetic effort, right mindfulness, and clear comprehension, overcoming desire and discontent in the world.* Dwelling in mindfulness by contemplating dharmas as dharmas internally-and-externally, with energetic effort, right mindfulness, and clear comprehension, overcoming desire and discontent in the world.

"Venerable Anuruddha, because in this way I dwelled in the four establishments of mindfulness with a collected mind, at that time the bodily afflictions came to be appeased. Venerable Anuruddha, it is because of that dwelling that the bodily afflictions came to be appeased at that time."[8]

The venerable Anuruddha said to the householder [Mānadiṇṇa]: "You have now yourself declared the fruit of non-returning."

Then the householder Mānadiṇṇa with his own hands offered various clean and attractive [kinds of] food and drink, personally offering them [until the monastics] were sated.[9] The meal being over and the washing concluded, the householder Mānadiṇṇa again sat on a low seat to listen to the sublime Dharma being taught.[10] The venerable Anuruddha in various ways taught him the Dharma. Having instructed, taught, illuminated, and delighted [the householder Mānadiṇṇa], he rose from his seat and left.

---

8 Yìnshùn 1983c: 747 note 7 suggests that this repetition is redundant and has left it out of his edition of SĀ 1038. I have decided to follow the original, since such repetition could be understood to give additional emphasis to his reply. Nevertheless, I think Yìnshùn is probably correct in assuming that some textual error has occurred at the present juncture, which I assume could have led to a loss of the type of statement found in SN 47.30 at SN V 178,11, where Mānadiṇṇa informs Anuruddha that he has overcome the five lower fetters. This information is required by the context, since without it Anuruddha would not have sufficient grounds for coming to the conclusion that Mānadiṇṇa had made a declaration of non-return.

9 SN 47.30 does not report a meal offering.

10 The addition of "sublime" follows a variant reading.

VIII.3 DISCUSSION

The *Saṃyutta-nikāya* version agrees with the discourse translated above that Anuruddha drew the conclusion that Mānadiṇṇa had reached non-return, differing in so far as the householder had concluded his description of dwelling in the four *satipaṭṭhāna*s by declaring that he had overcome the five lower fetters. An indication of this type would indeed be required, since, however impressive Mānadiṇṇa's description of his dwelling in the four *satipaṭṭhāna*s when sick may have been, in itself this does not suffice to draw the conclusion that he must be a non-returner. Such dwelling in the four *satipaṭṭhāna*s and consequently overcoming a disease could also take place if a practitioner has not yet reached such a high level on the path to liberation. Thus for Anuruddha to come to the conclusion that Mānadiṇṇa had declared himself to be a non-returner, a reference to his having overcome the five lower fetters is required. This makes it likely that some such reference has been lost in the *Saṃyukta-āgama* version translated above.

The high level of liberation reached according to both versions by Mānadiṇṇa, the attainment of non-return, is one of the four stages of awakening recognized in early Buddhism:

- stream-entry,
- once-return,
- non-return,
- full awakening.

Progress through these stages of awakening takes place by way of eradication of fetters (*saṃyojana*). These are ten in total. The five lower fetters whose removal corresponds to the attainment of non-return are:

- personality view,
- doubt,
- dogmatic clinging to rules and observances,
- sensual desire,
- aversion.

Here "personality view" refers to belief in a substantial and permanent self. Doubt is in particular concerned with substantial doubts about the efficacy of the early Buddhist teachings on the path to awakening. Dogmatic clinging to rules and observances appears to imply clinging to these as self-sufficient for reaching awakening.

These three fetters are overcome with the first experience of Nirvāṇa at stream-entry, to which I turn in more detail in the next chapter. The fact that this experience comes as the result of implementing the early Buddhist teachings on virtue, concentration, and wisdom makes it impossible for the stream-enterer to entertain any further doubt about the efficacy of these teachings to lead to the goal of awakening. It also makes it evident that, however much morality is an indispensable basis for progress on the path, the mere observance of rules does not suffice to bring about liberation on its own.

The two fetters of sensual desire and aversion are diminished substantially with the next breakthrough, the attainment of once-return. When non-return is reached, all sensual desire and aversion or ill will in any form are eradicated and have no more scope to manifest in the mind of one who has reached this third level of awakening. As the present discourse clearly documents, this rather high degree of mental freedom was considered within the range of householders still living at home with their family. This is quite evident in the *Saṃyukta-āgama* discourse translated above, which depicts Mānadiṇṇa surrounded by the women of his household when waiting for Anuruddha to arrive. Although as a non-returner he would no longer have had amorous relations with any of them, he nevertheless lived as a lay disciple. Within the setting of this type of lifestyle he had been able to reach such lofty heights of liberation.

This is perhaps the most salient point to be taken away from this chapter, in that since ancient times Buddhist lay practitioners have been on record for fully engaging in formal meditation practice, for successfully facing pain with mindfulness, and for having reached even high levels of awakening, such as the attainment of non-return in the present case.

The attainment of non-return features in the concluding section of the *Satipaṭṭhāna-sutta* and its *Madhyama-āgama* parallel as one of two fruits to be expected from sustained practice of the four *satipaṭṭhānas*, the other fruit being full awakening.[11] The two discourses thereby agree in presenting the potential of practice of the four *satipaṭṭhānas* in terms of the complete removal of sensual desire and aversion from the mind.

Alongside the potential of mindfulness to enable one to endure the pain of disease, as documented in the present and preceding chapters, the *Satipaṭṭhāna-sutta* and its *Madhyama-āgama* parallel point towards what early Buddhist thought considers to be supreme mental health: freedom from desire and aversion, eventually also culminating in freedom from delusion with the attainment of full awakening.

The path to such supreme mental health requires a threefold training, which covers the following:

- virtue,
- concentration,
- wisdom.

These three trainings, which build on and enhance each other, provide the context within which mindfulness practice takes place in early Buddhism. Having covered the relationship between mindfulness and facing pain in three chapters, in the next three chapters I turn to these three topics of virtue, concentration, and wisdom, in particular from the perspective of their relation to the time of falling sick.

---

11 MN 10 at MN I 62,34 (translated Ñāṇamoli 1995/2005: 155) and MĀ 98 at T I 584b16 (translated Anālayo 2013b: 283).

IX

FEARLESSNESS WHEN SICK

IX.1 INTRODUCTION

The present chapter offers a close-up of the qualities that result from the attainment of stream-entry, the first level of awakening, in particular in relation to virtue. The sick protagonist of the discourse translated below is the householder Anāthapiṇḍika, who receives a visit from Ānanda, the personal attendant of the Buddha.[1] In Chapter 16 I turn to another occasion when Ānanda (who on this occasion comes in the company of Sāriputta) pays a visit to Anāthapiṇḍika because the latter is sick, which differs from the present episode inasmuch as, due to that other illness, Anāthapiṇḍika passes away.

In the early discourses in general the householder Anāthapiṇḍika features as an exemplary supporter of the Buddha and his disciples. In fact Jeta's Grove at Sāvatthī, where the Buddha and his monastic disciples regularly stay, is repeatedly referred to as "Anāthapiṇḍika's Park", conveying the sense that it was bought by Anāthapiṇḍika from Prince Jeta and donated to the Buddhist monastic Community.

A discourse in the *Saṃyutta-nikāya* and its parallels depict Anāthapiṇḍika being thrilled when he first heard the news that

1 For biographical sketches of Ānanda and Anāthapiṇḍika see Malalasekera 1937/1995: 249–68 and 67–72 as well as Nyanaponika and Hecker 1997: 139–82 and 337–62.

a Buddha had arisen in the world. He could not sleep the whole night and set out to visit the Buddha when it was still dark. At that time the Buddha was staying in the Cool Grove by the charnel grounds of Rājagaha. Thus the terrain through which Anāthapiṇḍika had to pass in the dark to meet the Buddha was frightening, and he almost turned back.[2] During the ensuing meeting with the Buddha, Anāthapiṇḍika received a teaching on the four noble truths that led to his stream-entry.[3] The two themes of fear and stream-entry recur in the present discourse, found in the *Saṃyukta-āgama* and in a parallel in the *Saṃyutta-nikāya*.[4]

IX.2 TRANSLATION[5]

Thus have I heard. At one time the Buddha was staying at Sāvatthī in Jeta's Grove, Anāthapiṇḍika's Park. Then the venerable Ānanda heard that the householder Anāthapiṇḍika's body had become afflicted.[6] He approached [Anāthapiṇḍika's] house.

On seeing Ānanda from afar, the householder Anāthapiṇḍika wanted to get up, supporting himself on the bed.[7] *Having seen this, Ānanda said to him: "Householder, do not get up, your affliction will increase."*

---

2 SN 10.8 at SN I 211,10 (translated Bodhi 2000: 311), corresponding to Vin II 155,38 (translated Horner 1952/1975: 218), and its parallels SĀ 592 at T II 157c20 and SĀ² 186 at T II 440c1; see also MĀ 28 at T I 460a14 (translated Bingenheimer et al. 2013: 195).

3 Vin II 157,3 (SN 10.8 does not cover this part of their encounter) and its parallels SĀ 592 at T II 158b6 (which differs on what the Buddha taught him) and SĀ² 186 at T II 441a17; see also MĀ 28 at T I 460b29.

4 SN 55.27 at SN V 385,12 (translated Bodhi 2000: 1819).

5 The translated discourse is SĀ 1031 at T II 269b19 to 269c7.

6 In SN 55.27 at SN V 385,16 Anāthapiṇḍika sends a messenger asking Ānanda to come.

7 SN 55.27 does not report that Anāthapiṇḍika tried to get up. SĀ 1031 continues after reporting this by indicating that the remainder of the introductory narration should be supplemented from the discourse by Khemaka (translated below in Chapter 11). Since the discourse by Khemaka does not have the standard reply to one who tries to get up from the bed, I supplement this from the discourse that precedes SĀ 1031 in the *Saṃyukta-āgama*, SĀ 1030 at T II 269b5 to 269b7, where the Buddha visits the sick Anāthapiṇḍika.

Ānanda sat down and said to the householder [Anāthapiṇḍika]: "How is it, householder, is the disease bearable? Is the affliction of the body increasing or is it decreasing?"

The householder Anāthapiṇḍika said to Ānanda: "I have not recovered from the illness and my body is not at ease; the pains keep increasing and there is no relief. It is just as if many strong men were to take hold of a weak man, put a rope around his head and with both hands pull it tight, so that he is in extreme pain. My pain now exceeds that.

"It is just as if a cow butcher with a sharp knife were to cut open a living [cow's] belly to take its internal organs. How could that cow endure the pains in its belly? My belly is now more painful than that cow's.

"It is just as if two strong men were to grab one weak person and hang him over a fire, roasting both his feet. The heat of both my feet now exceeds that.[8] The affliction is still increasing and not decreasing."

Then the venerable Ānanda said to the householder [Anāthapiṇḍika]: "Do not be afraid. If a foolish unlearned worldling has no confidence in the Buddha, *no confidence* in the Dharma, no confidence in the Community, and is not endowed with noble virtue, there is reason to be afraid, to have fear of death as well as of suffering in the next life.[9] You have now already eliminated lack of confidence, you already have come to know and are endowed with pure confidence in the Buddha, *endowed with pure confidence* in the Dharma, endowed with pure confidence in the Community, and you are accomplished in noble virtue."[10]

The householder [Anāthapiṇḍika] said to the venerable Ānanda: "How could I now be afraid? When I met the Blessed One for the first time among the charnel grounds in the Cool Grove by the city of Rājagaha,[11] I at once gained unshakeable confidence in the Buddha, *unshakeable confidence* in the Dharma,

8 In SN 55.27 Anāthapiṇḍika does not employ similes to illustrate his condition.

9 SN 55.27 at SN V 386,5 more specifically indicates that fear arises when the worldling reflects on the fact of being without confidence.

10 SN 55.27 additionally offers a description of the qualities of each of the three jewels and qualifies noble virtue as conducive to concentration.

11 SN 55.27 has no reference to the first meeting between Anāthapiṇḍika and the Buddha or to the consequences of that meeting.

unshakeable confidence in the Community, and became accomplished in noble virtue. From then onwards the wealth in my house has all been for the support of the Buddha and his disciples, shared out among the male monastics, the female monastics, the male lay disciples, and the female lay disciples."

The venerable Ānanda said: "It is well, householder, you have yourself declared the fruit of stream-entry."

The householder [Anāthapiṇḍika] said to the venerable Ānanda: "You may take your meal here."[12] The venerable Ānanda accepted the invitation by [remaining] silent.

Various types of clean and delicious food and drink were promptly prepared and offered to the venerable Ānanda. After the meal was over, he further taught the Dharma in various ways to the householder [Anāthapiṇḍika]. Having instructed, taught, illuminated, and delighted [the householder Anāthapiṇḍika], he rose from his seat and left.

IX.3 DISCUSSION

The above discourse presents the four limbs of stream-entry (*sotāpattiyaṅga*) as a source of fearlessness when sick. These four are:

- firm confidence in the Buddha,
- firm confidence in the Dharma,
- firm confidence in the Community,
- being accomplished in noble virtue.

These are mentioned recurrently in the discourses as the characteristic marks of a stream-enterer. The first three limbs of stream-entry reflect the inner certainty the stream-enterer has gained that the Buddha indeed teaches a viable path to awakening, that the Dharma he teaches does lead to this aim, and that the Community of those who practise accordingly are indeed practising the path to liberation; the fourth limb points to the virtuous conduct that becomes natural for one who has reached stream-entry.

---

12 Such an invitation and its acceptance are not recorded in SN 55.27, which concludes with Ānanda's remark that Anāthapiṇḍika had declared the fruit of stream-entry.

Reports of the actual event of stream-entry speak of the arising of the eye of Dharma, such as in the case of the householder Nakula in Chapter 2, who "saw the Dharma, attained the Dharma, understood the Dharma, entered the Dharma, crossing beyond all doubt, not needing to rely on others, ... his mind [had] attained fearlessness in the right Dharma."

Such descriptions clearly refer to a distinct experience, where with the first realization of Nirvāṇa one comes to see, attain, understand, and in a way plunge into the very essence of the Dharma. The resultant removal of doubt as one of the fetters left behind with stream-entry, discussed in the previous chapter, results in becoming independent of the guidance of others. Such self-reliance can in turn provide a source of fearlessness.

When it comes to assessing stream-entry, the early discourses focus on the qualities that this experience of the "eye of Dharma" engenders. In this way the emphasis is less on closely scrutinizing the actual experience of stream-entry in order to determine if this can be considered genuine, as is the case in some modern-day meditation circles, but more on the inner change that the stream-enterer must have undergone. This is in line with a general tendency underlying early Buddhist thought, which appears to reflect clear awareness of the dangers of the reification of a particular experience. Instead, emphasis should be given to the shared characteristics of all experience as merely empty processes and in the case of meditative experiences what matters is their transformative effect.

In early Buddhist thought, meditative practice requires a firm foundation in moral conduct, the first of the three trainings mentioned in the previous chapter and the fourth limb of stream-entry listed in the discourse translated above. In the case of stream-entry such noble virtue comes as a result of the insight gained into the nature of reality and especially into the four noble truths. This makes it impossible for a stream-enterer to commit a major breach of the five precepts. These require refraining from the following activities:

- killing living beings,
- theft,
- sexual misconduct,

- falsehood,
- using intoxicants.

A stream-enterer can still commit minor breaches of morality – after all the main springs of unwholesome action in sensual desire and aversion have not yet been removed from the mind. Nevertheless, major breaches are no longer possible.

Anyone who abstains from killing thereby gives others a gift of fearlessness, inasmuch as they need not fear that this person will try to take their life. The same holds for theft, sexual misconduct, and falsehood, which are likewise sources of dread for others. Intoxication features in the same category, since those who are drunk or under the influence of drugs can easily evoke fright, as one cannot be sure what they might do next.

In this way the conduct of one who observes the five precepts has a direct relation to fearlessness, and such a gift of fearlessness can be made by anyone who keeps the precepts, regardless of whether one has already reached stream-entry. This invests the teaching on fearlessness given in the present discourse with direct relevance to building the indispensable moral foundation for one's own practice. Building such a moral foundation as a gift to others and a source of fearlessness throws into relief the altruistic dimension of keeping the precepts.

Having made an offering of fearlessness to others through one's moral conduct by keeping the precepts, one in turn gains fearlessness oneself at the time of sickness. The importance of freedom from regret can be seen, for example, in a standard enquiry made by the Buddha when visiting a sick monastic (as is the case for the discourse to be taken up in the next chapter). On hearing that the patient has regrets, the Buddha immediately turns to the issue of breaches of the precepts. Moral blamelessness is indeed a major asset in times of sickness and can serve as a fountain of fearlessness, a topic to which I return in Chapter 20. Thus virtue as the first of the three trainings can offer considerable support in the face of sickness.

In the discourse translated above, Ānanda's comment leads Anāthapiṇḍika to recollect his own virtues and qualities as a source of fearlessness. Following the example set in this way, when ministering to the sick one might encourage patients to think of their own good qualities and bring to mind the wholesome deeds they have done in their life. This can diminish fear and help the ailing person to face the condition of sickness with a positive state of mind.

X

THE MEDICINE OF INSIGHT

X.1 INTRODUCTION

The discourse below offers an additional perspective on how to face disease, namely by way of insight. This insight perspective comes together with a warning against excessive reliance on one's concentrative experiences. When evaluating this warning, it needs to be kept in mind that in early Buddhist thought the attainment of deep states of concentration forms an integral part of the path to liberation and for this reason has its position as the second of the three trainings, alongside virtue and wisdom. The point to be taken home from the present discourse is therefore not a wholesale rejection of concentration. That would be a sad misunderstanding. The point is only to show the limits of concentration attainments when not supplemented and rounded off by the cultivation of insight. This holds in particular when experiencing sickness.

The discourse translated below is found in the *Saṃyukta-āgama* and has a parallel in the *Saṃyutta-nikāya*.[1] The main protagonist of the discourse is a monastic by the name of Assaji, who appears to be different from the monastic by the same

1 SN 22.88 at SN III 124,14 (translated Bodhi 2000: 941).

name who was one of the first five disciples of the Buddha.[2] The monastic who attends on Assaji is called Puṇṇiya. Similarly to the Assaji of the present episode, he is not a prominent disciple in the early discourses, so no additional information seems available to provide some background to the present episode.[3]

X.2 TRANSLATION[4]

Thus have I heard. At one time the Buddha was staying at Sāvatthī in Jeta's Grove, Anāthapiṇḍika's Park. At that time the venerable Assaji was dwelling in the Eastern Park, the Hall of Migāra's Mother.[5] His body had become sick in a serious way; an extreme affliction had arisen. The venerable Puṇṇiya was looking after him.[6]

Then Assaji said to Puṇṇiya:[7] *"Could you approach the Blessed One, pay respect in my name with your head at the Blessed One's feet and*

2 *Pace* Malalasekera 1937/1995: 225, who considers the Assaji of the present discourse to be one of the first five disciples of the Buddha. This seems to me unconvincing, since that Assaji had at a very early stage in the Buddha's teaching career become an arahant; see SN 22.59 at SN III 68,27 (translated Bodhi 2000: 903), corresponding to Vin I 14,34 (translated Horner 1951/1982: 21) and SĀ 34 at T II 8a2 (translated Anālayo 2014g: 5; for further parallels see Anālayo 2014g: 5 note 3). As an arahant he would have been beyond attachment, whereas the Assaji who is the protagonist of the present discourse clearly is attached to his concentration experiences and needs the Buddha's help to let go of this mistaken attitude. In fact in SĀ 1024 he becomes an arahant at the end of the Buddha's instruction, which thereby clearly differs from the attainment of arahantship of the first five disciples reported in SĀ 34. Even though SN 22.88 does not report such an outcome of the present instruction, its depiction of Assaji would also not fit an arahant. The name Assaji itself appears to have been a common name; another monastic under the same name is part of the infamous "group of six", a gang of monastics responsible for all kinds of mischief. On the group of six see also Anālayo 2012b: 417f.

3 On Puṇṇiya see Malalasekera 1938/1998: 229.

4 The translated discourse is SĀ 1024 at T II 267b5 to 267c6.

5 According to SN 22.88 at SN III 124,16, he stayed at Kassapaka's Park and the Buddha was in the Bamboo Grove at Rājagaha.

6 SĀ 1024 indicates that the remainder of the introductory narration should be supplemented from the discourse on Vakkali. This is SĀ 1265 and the relevant section is found at T II 346b9 to 346b28; for a full translation of this discourse see Anālayo 2011d.

7 In SN 22.88 at SN III 124,18 Assaji asks unnamed attendants to convey a comparable message to the Buddha.

enquire if the Blessed One dwells at ease and is in good health, with little affliction and little vexation? Say: 'Assaji, who is staying in the Eastern Park, is seriously ill and confined to bed. He wishes to see the Blessed One. Being ill and afflicted, he has no strength and is not in a position to come. May the Blessed One condescend to come to the Eastern Park, out of compassion.'"

Then, having received the words of Assaji, Puṇṇiya approached the Blessed One, paid respect with his head at the Buddha's feet, and withdrew to stand to one side. He said to the Buddha: "Blessed One, the venerable Assaji pays respect at the Blessed One's feet and enquires if the Blessed One dwells at ease and is in good health, with little affliction and little vexation?" The Blessed One replied: "May he be at ease."

Puṇṇiya said to the Buddha: "Blessed One, the venerable Assaji, who is staying in the Eastern Park, is seriously ill and confined to bed. He wishes to see the Blessed One. He does not have the bodily strength to come and call on the Blessed One. It would be well if the Blessed One could come to the Eastern Park, out of compassion."

Then the Blessed One assented by remaining silent. Then, knowing that the Blessed One had assented, Puṇṇiya paid respect at the Buddha's feet and left.

Then, in the afternoon, the Blessed One rose from his meditation and went to the Eastern Park. He arrived at Assaji's hut. On seeing the Blessed One from afar, the monastic Assaji tried to get up from his bed. The Buddha told Assaji: "Just stop, do not get up!"

The Blessed One sat on another bed and said to Assaji: "Is your mind able to bear the suffering of this disease? Is the affliction of your body increasing or decreasing?"

The venerable Assaji said: "My disease is not becoming appeased and it is difficult to endure. The pains in the body are gradually increasing and not decreasing. It is just as if many strong men were to take hold of a weak man, put a rope around his head and with both hands pull it tight, so that he is in extreme pain. My pain now exceeds that.

"It is just as if a cow butcher with a sharp knife were to cut open a living cow's belly to take its internal organs. How could that cow endure the pains in its belly? My belly is now more painful than that cow's.

"It is just as if two strong men were to grab one weak person and hang him over a fire, roasting both his feet. The heat of both my feet now

exceeds that. The pain of my disease is increasing and not decreasing."[8]

The Buddha said to Assaji: "Do you have nothing to regret?" Assaji said to the Buddha: "Blessed One, I truly have something to regret."

The Buddha said to Assaji: "Do you gain being without breaches of the precepts?" Assaji said to the Buddha: "Blessed One, I have not broken the precepts."

The Buddha said to Assaji: "If you have not broken the precepts, what is it that you regret?" Assaji said to the Buddha: "Blessed One, earlier, when I was not yet sick, I gained the attainment of tranquillizing the body, which I cultivated much.[9] Now I am no longer able to enter that concentration. I have this thought: 'Am I not falling back, losing this concentration?'"

The Buddha said to Assaji: "I will now question you, answer me according to your understanding. Assaji, do you see bodily form as the self, as distinct from the self [in the sense of being owned by it], as existing [within the self, or a self] existing [within bodily form]?"[10] Assaji said to the Buddha: "No, Blessed One."

[The Buddha] asked again: "Do you see feeling *as the self, as distinct from the self in the sense of being owned by it, as existing within the self, or a self existing within feeling?" Assaji said to the Buddha: "No, Blessed One."*

The Buddha asked again: "Do you see perception *as the self, as distinct from the self in the sense of being owned by it, as existing within the self, or a self existing within perception?" Assaji said to the Buddha: "No, Blessed One."*

The Buddha asked again: "Do you see formations *as the self, as distinct from the self in the sense of being owned by it, as existing*

---

8 SN 22.88 does not have similes with which Assaji illustrates his painful condition.

9 According to SN 22.88 at SN III 125,22, when he was sick earlier he had been able to dwell having tranquillized the bodily formations, which according to the commentary Spk II 315,15 implies the attainment of the fourth absorption.

10 This type of contemplation is regularly presented in the *Saṃyukta-āgama* with a rather cryptic description, wherefore my rendering is necessarily somewhat cumbersome; see also Anālayo 2012d: 40 note 114. Instead of directly setting in with contemplation of not-self, the insight instructions in SN 22.88 at SN III 125,30 begin with the impermanent nature of the five aggregates of clinging, leading on to *dukkha* and not-self.

within the self, or a self existing within formations?" Assaji said to the Buddha: "No, Blessed One."

The Buddha asked again: "Do you see consciousness as the self, as distinct from the self [in the sense of being owned by it], as existing [within the self, or a self] existing [within consciousness]?" Assaji said to the Buddha: "No, Blessed One."

The Buddha said to Assaji: "Since you do not see bodily form as the self, as distinct from the self [in the sense of being owned by it], as existing [within the self, or a self] existing [within bodily form], *you do not see* feeling *as the self, as distinct from the self in the sense of being owned by it, as existing within the self, or a self existing within feeling, you do not see* perception *as the self, as distinct from the self in the sense of being owned by it, as existing within the self, or a self existing within perception, you do not see* formations *as the self, as distinct from the self in the sense of being owned by it, as existing within the self, or a self existing within formations,* you do not see consciousness *as the self, as distinct from the self in the sense of being owned by it, as existing within the self, or a self existing within consciousness*, then for what reason are you worried?"

Assaji said to the Buddha: "Blessed One, it is because I have been giving improper attention."

The Buddha said to Assaji: "Suppose recluses and brahmins [consider] concentration as the essence, concentration as the completeness [of their achievement]. If they do not get to enter that concentration, still they should not think: 'I am falling back with the diminishing of concentration.'[11]

"Suppose a noble disciple in turn does not see bodily form as the self, as distinct from the self [in the sense of being owned by it], as existing [within the self, or a self] existing [within bodily form], *does not see* feeling *as the self, as distinct from the self in the sense of being owned by it, as existing within the self, or a self existing within feeling, does not see* perception *as the self, as distinct from the self in the sense of being owned by it, as existing within the self, or a self existing within perception, does not see* formations *as the self, as distinct from the self in the sense of being owned by it, as existing within the self, or a self existing within formations,* does not see

11 In SN 22.88 at SN III 125,27 a similar remark comes at the outset of the Buddha's instruction and instead notes that recluses and brahmins do have such thoughts. This seems to be a more meaningful presentation.

consciousness as the self, as distinct from the self [in the sense of being owned by it], as existing [within the self, or a self] existing [within consciousness], [that noble disciple] should still come to realize:[12]

"Passionate desire is to be forever eradicated without remainder, ill will *is to be forever eradicated without remainder*, delusion is to be forever eradicated without remainder. Passionate [desire], ill will, and delusion being forever eradicated without remainder, all influxes are eradicated. With the absence of the influxes, being liberated in the mind and liberated by wisdom, one here and now personally knows and realizes: 'Birth for me has been eradicated, the holy life has been established, what had to be done has been done, I myself know that there will be no receiving of any further existence.'"

When the Buddha gave this teaching, the venerable Assaji by not clinging attained liberation of the mind from the influxes.[13] He rejoiced and was delighted. Because of rejoicing and being delighted, his body was rid of the sickness.[14]

When the Buddha had spoken this discourse, causing the venerable Assaji to rejoice and be delighted, he got up from his seat and left.

X.3 DISCUSSION

The actual encounter between the Buddha and the sick Assaji begins with the monastic trying to get up on seeing the Buddha arrive. This is a standard occurrence in such situations, whereby the sick person expresses respect and appreciation of the fact that the Buddha has personally come to visit. The usual reaction by the Buddha or other eminent monastics when visiting the sick is to express their compassion by telling the patient to stay where they are, thereby preventing them from acting out of

---

12 In SN 22.88 at SN III 126,4 the Buddha instead gives Assaji a teaching on feeling.

13 The part translated as "not clinging" would more literally be "not giving rise to", a Chinese rendering that appears to be due to a misunderstanding of an underlying Indic expression that refers to the absence of clinging; see Anālayo 2014g: 8 note 17 and below p. 155 note 15.

14 SN 22.88 does not report any attainment by Assaji or any improvement in his condition.

respect in a way that could be detrimental to their diseased condition. This exemplifies an attitude where compassionate concern for those who are suffering takes priority over minor aspects of external conduct.

In the discourse translated above, the Buddha begins the conversation by enquiring if Assaji's afflictions are bearable. This directly targets a main problem of sickness, namely having to endure pain. In terms of the discourse in Chapter 3, the enquiry is about the arrow of physical pain and its potential to lead on to the other arrow of mental pain. In terms of the discourses in Chapters 6, 7, and 8, the same enquiry is also about the patient's ability to bear the pain, which should ideally be with mindfulness.

On being informed of the seriousness of the disease, the Buddha's next enquiry is whether Assaji experiences any regret. Given that he admits to having regret, the Buddha naturally turns to the problem of breaches of morality. This is clearly something that has to be taken up. The burden of breaches of morality can become heavy at the time of disease, and even more so at the time of death. As discussed in the previous chapter, having maintained morality in turn provides a source of fearlessness. Assaji clarifies that this applies to his case; he is not burdened by moral misconduct.

The discourse next puts a spotlight on the problem of attachment to concentration experiences. Instead of yielding to such attachment, the task is to avoid identifying with these or any other aspect of experience. This lessening of identification is not only the proper approach to disease, but also the way to full mental health through awakening. Although the two versions differ, in so far as the *Saṃyutta-nikāya* discourse does not report that Assaji reached full awakening or that he recovered his health, the basic message remains the same. Relinquishing all identification and attachment is the key to true peace and tranquillity, which are no longer in danger of being lost again.

The way the discourse presents the theme of relinquishing all identification is somewhat cryptic in the Chinese original, wherefore I had to add material in square brackets for it to make sense. Underlying its presentation is a standard approach in the early discourses which applies the following pattern to each of the five aggregates of bodily form, feeling, perception, formations, and consciousness:

- viewing the aggregate as the self,
- viewing the aggregate as distinct from the self,
- viewing the aggregate as existing within the self,
- viewing the self as existing within the aggregate.

This fourfold pattern, when applied to each of the five aggregates, results in twenty types of "personality view" (*sakkāyadiṭṭhi*). Such personality view in the form of the belief in a substantial and permanent self is one of the fetters to be overcome with stream-entry. The experience of Nirvāṇa at stream-entry makes it indubitably part of direct experience that no permanent self could exist anywhere. This is simply by dint of having had an experience utterly devoid of any self-reference or anything that could be identified with. Although at this point the upholding of a fully fledged view regarding the existence of a self has become impossible, the task of realizing not-self has not yet been completed, since conceit and a sense of ego still remain. These will be overcome only with the realization of full awakening, a topic to which I return in the next chapter.

The freedom of the mind gained with the realization of full awakening implies that the influxes have been forever eradicated. Such influxes (*āsava*) exert their influence on one's apperceptions and reactions, thereby leading one to act in unwholesome and detrimental ways.[15] Early Buddhist thought recognizes three such influxes:

- the influx of sensuality,
- the influx of becoming,
- the influx of ignorance.

To this list of three, a fourth influx has at times been added, the influx of views. The complete eradication of all influxes is a standard reference in the early discourses used to designate full awakening, with which one has accomplished what according to early Buddhist thought should be done by one who has embarked on the "holy life", that is, on a life of celibacy as a Buddhist

---

15 On the influxes see in more detail Anālayo 2012e: 80–3.

monastic. For reaching this final consummation of the holy life, concentration offers an important support. Nevertheless, the cultivation of concentration has potential drawbacks, as highlighted in the present discourse. Concentrative experience can be immensely gratifying, even exhilarating. Since all such experiences are impermanent and bound to change, clinging to them and investing one's sense of identity in them will sooner or later lead to frustration and worry. Hence concentration is at its best when cultivated in combination with wisdom, thereby functioning as an aspect of the threefold training without being allowed to overshadow other aspects and become a building block for a sense of identity, as evidently had been the case with Assaji.

In practical terms, a central message to be taken from the present discourse is the potential of non-identification. Assaji had identified with his concentration attainment, which had caused him to become agitated when he fell sick. Although he was free of the burden of regret on account of moral breaches, he was not free of the burden of clinging to his meditative experiences. Taking the medicine of insight he was able to let go of that unnecessary burden; in fact in the discourse translated above he was able to let go of all unnecessary burdens by reaching the supreme mental health of awakening.

Applied to one's own situation, the time of falling ill can be turned into an occasion to take stock of one's sense of identity: is there any unnecessary burden in the form of clinging that one carries along and which could do with a dose of the medicine of non-identification?

XI

LIBERATING TEACHINGS FROM A PATIENT

XI.1 INTRODUCTION

The finer distinction mentioned in the last chapter between the realization of not-self reached with stream-entry and the full integration of this realization into one's mental continuum reached with full awakening is the theme of the discourse translated in the present chapter.

The doctrine of not-self (*anattā*) is not understood easily. In fact the present discourse shows a group of monastics who appear to be not entirely clear regarding the difference between the realization with stream-entry that there is no permanent self to be found anywhere in experience and the total freedom from conceit and ego that comes with the completion of the training in wisdom that will be reached with full awakening.

The realization that all aspects of personal experience are merely changing processes is in itself already rather profound, yet to implement fully the consequences of this realization requires more. In the discourse translated below from the *Saṃyukta-āgama* and in its *Saṃyutta-nikāya* parallel, the monastic Khemaka successfully explains this difference, offering illustrative similes to clarify the issue.[1]

1 SN 22.89 at SN III 126,29 (translated Bodhi 2000: 942). Khemaka seems to feature only in this discourse, so that no further information on him appears to be available; see also Malalasekera 1937/1995: 726.

XI.2 TRANSLATION[2]

Thus have I heard. At one time a group of many elder monastics were staying at Kosambī in Ghosita's Park. At that time the monastic Khemaka was dwelling at Kosambī in the Jujube Tree Park. His body had become seriously ill. At that time the monastic Dāsaka was looking after the sick.[3]

Then the monastic Dāsaka approached the elder monastics, paid respect at the feet of the elder monastics, and stood to one side. The elder monastics said to the monastic Dāsaka: "Approach the monastic Khemaka and say: 'The elder monastics ask you: is your body recovering a little and at ease, is the severity of your painful affliction not increasing?'"

Then the monastic Dāsaka, having received the instructions from the elder monastics, approached the monastic Khemaka. He said to the monastic Khemaka: "The elder monastics ask you: 'Are you gradually recovering from your painful affliction? Is the multitude of pains not increasing?'"

The monastic Khemaka said to the monastic Dāsaka: "I have not recovered from the illness and my body is not at ease; the pains keep increasing and there is no relief. It is just as if many strong men were to take hold of a weak man, put a rope around his head and with both hands pull it tight, so that he is in extreme pain. My pain now exceeds that.

"It is just as if a cow butcher with a sharp knife were to cut open a living [cow's] belly to take its internal organs. How could that cow endure the pains in its belly? My belly is now more painful than that cow's.

"It is just as if two strong men were to grab one weak person and hang him over a fire, roasting both his feet. The heat of both my feet now exceeds that."[4]

Then the monastic Dāsaka returned to the elders. He told the elders all that the monastic Khemaka had said about the condition of his illness. Then the elders sent the monastic Dāsaka

2 The translated discourse is SĀ 103 at T II 29c6 to 30c11, already translated in Anālayo 2014h: 4–10 (the footnotes to that translation also cover relevant Sanskrit fragments).
3 SN 22.89 does not indicate that Dāsaka was looking after the sick.
4 In SN 22.89 Khemaka does not use any simile to illustrate the severity of his condition.

back to approach the monastic Khemaka, to say to the monastic Khemaka:

"There are five aggregates of clinging taught by the Blessed One. What are the five? They are the bodily form aggregate of clinging, the feeling *aggregate of clinging*, the perception *aggregate of clinging*, the formations *aggregate of clinging*, and the consciousness aggregate of clinging. Khemaka, are you just able to examine these five aggregates of clinging as not-self and not belonging to the self?"

Then the monastic Dāsaka, having received the instructions from the elder monastics, approached the monastic Khemaka and said: "The elders say to you: 'The Blessed One has taught the five aggregates of clinging. Are you just able to examine them as not-self and not belonging to the self?'"

The monastic Khemaka said to Dāsaka: "I am able to examine these five aggregates of clinging as not-self and not belonging to the self."

The monastic Dāsaka returned and said to the elders: "The monastic Khemaka says: 'I am able to examine these five aggregates of clinging as not-self and not belonging to the self.'"

The elders again sent the monastic Dāsaka to say to the monastic Khemaka: "Being able to examine these five aggregates of clinging as not-self and not belonging to the self, are you thus an arahant, with influxes eradicated?"

Then the monastic Dāsaka, having received the instructions from the elder monastics, approached the monastic Khemaka. He said to Khemaka: "A monastic who is able to contemplate the five aggregates of clinging in this way, is he thus an arahant, with the influxes eradicated?"

The monastic Khemaka said to the monastic Dāsaka: "I contemplate the five aggregates of clinging as not-self and not belonging to the self, [yet] I am not an arahant, with the influxes eradicated."[5]

Then the monastic Dāsaka returned to the elders. He said to the elders: "The monastic Khemaka says: 'I contemplate the five

5 At this juncture in SN 22.89 at SN III 128,33 Khemaka adds that he has not yet abandoned the conceit "I am" in relation to the five aggregates of clinging.

aggregates of clinging as not-self and not belonging to the self, yet I am not an arahant, with the influxes eradicated.'"

Then the elders said to the monastic Dāsaka: "Return again to say to the monastic Khemaka: 'You say: I contemplate the five aggregates as not-self and not belonging to the self, yet I am not an arahant, with the influxes eradicated.' The former and the latter [statement] contradict each other."

Then the monastic Dāsaka, having received the instructions from the elder monastics, approached the monastic Khemaka and said: "You say: 'I contemplate the five aggregates of clinging as not-self and not belonging to the self, yet I am not an arahant, with the influxes eradicated.' The former and the latter [statement] contradict each other."

The monastic Khemaka said to the monastic Dāsaka: "I examine these five aggregates of clinging as not-self and not belonging to the self, yet I am not an arahant, [with the influxes eradicated]. I have not yet abandoned the 'I am' conceit, the desire [related to the notion] 'I am', and the underlying tendency towards 'I am', have not yet [fully] understood it, not yet become separated from it, not yet vomited it out."[6]

The monastic Dāsaka returned to the elders. He said to the elders: "The monastic Khemaka says: 'I examine these five aggregates of clinging as not-self and not belonging to the self, yet I am not an arahant, with the influxes eradicated. I have not yet abandoned the "I am" conceit in relation to the five aggregates of clinging, the desire [related to the notion] "I am", and the underlying tendency towards "I am", have not yet [fully] understood it, not yet become separated from it, not yet vomited it out.'"

The elders again sent the monastic Dāsaka to say to the monastic Khemaka: "You [seem] to affirm that there is a self. Where is that self? Is bodily form the self? Or is the self distinct from bodily form? Is feeling *the self? Or is the self distinct from feeling*? Is perception *the self? Or is the self distinct from perception*? Are formations *the self? Or is the self distinct from formations*? Is consciousness the self? Or is the self distinct from consciousness?"

6 Since in SN 22.89 at SN III 128,33 Khemaka had already during the previous exchange mentioned the conceit "I am", the present exchange is without a parallel in SN 22.89.

The monastic Khemaka said to the monastic Dāsaka:[7] "I do not say that bodily form is the self, or that the self is distinct from bodily form; that feeling *is the self, or that the self is distinct from feeling*; that perception *is the self, or that the self is distinct from perception*; that formations *are the self, or that the self is distinct from formations*; that consciousness is the self, or that the self is distinct from consciousness. Yet in relation to these five aggregates of clinging I have not yet abandoned the 'I am' conceit, the desire [related to the notion] 'I am', and the underlying tendency towards 'I am', have not yet [fully] understood it, not yet become separated from it, not yet vomited it out."

The monastic Khemaka said to the monastic Dāsaka: "Why trouble you now, making you run back and forth? Bring my walking stick. Supporting myself with the walking stick, I will approach the elders. I wish you to give me the walking stick for my use."

The monastic Khemaka, supporting himself with the walking stick, approached the elders. Then the elders saw from afar that the monastic Khemaka was coming, supported by a walking stick. They themselves prepared a seat for him and set up a footrest. They came forward themselves to welcome him, took his robe and bowl, and told him to sit down right away.[8] They exchanged polite greetings with one another. Having exchanged polite greetings, the [elders] said to the monastic Khemaka:

"You speak of the conceit 'I am'. Where do you see a self? Is bodily form the self? Or is the self distinct from bodily form? Is feeling *the self? Or is the self distinct from feeling*? Is perception *the self? Or is the self distinct from perception*? Are formations *the self? Or is the self distinct from formations*? Is consciousness the self? Or is the self distinct from consciousness?"

The monastic Khemaka said: "Bodily form is not-self and there is no self that is distinct from bodily form. Feeling *is not-self and there is no self that is distinct from feeling*. Perception *is not-self and there is no self that is distinct from perception*. Formations *are not-self and there is no self that is distinct from formations*. Consciousness is not-self, and there is no self that is distinct from consciousness.

7 In SN 22.89 at SN III 129,27 Khemaka replies by directly saying that he will approach the elders himself.

8 SN 22.89 does not report that the elders prepared a seat, etc.

"⟨However⟩,[9] in relation to these five aggregates of clinging I have not yet abandoned the 'I am' conceit, the desire [related to the notion] 'I am', and the underlying tendency towards 'I am', have not yet [fully] understood it, not yet become separated from it, not yet vomited it out.

"It is just like the fragrance of uppala lotuses, paduma lotuses, kumuda lotuses, puṇḍarīka lotuses.[10] Is the fragrance in the roots? Is the fragrance distinct from the roots? Is the fragrance in the stalks, the leaves, the stamen, its finer and coarser parts? Or is it distinct from [the stalks, the leaves, the stamen,] its finer and coarser parts? Is this correctly spoken?"

The elders replied: "No, monastic Khemaka. The fragrance is not in the roots of uppala lotuses, paduma lotuses, kumuda lotuses, puṇḍarīka lotuses, nor is the fragrance distinct from the roots. The fragrance is also not in the stalks, the leaves, the stamen, its finer and coarser parts, and the fragrance is also not distinct from [the stalks, the leaves, the stamen,] its finer and coarser parts."

The monastic Khemaka asked again: "Where is the fragrance?" The elders replied: "The fragrance is in the flower."

The monastic Khemaka said again: "With me it is in the same way. Bodily form is not-self and there is no self distinct from bodily form. Feeling *is not-self and there is no self that is distinct from feeling*. Perception *is not-self and there is no self that is distinct from perception*. Formations *are not-self and there is no self that is distinct from formations*. Consciousness is not-self, and there is no self distinct from consciousness.

"Although in relation to these five aggregates of clinging I see no self and nothing belonging to the self, still I have not yet abandoned the 'I am' conceit, the desire [related to the notion] 'I am', and the underlying tendency towards 'I am', have not yet [fully] understood it, not yet become separated from it, not yet vomited it out.

"Elders, allow me to speak a simile. Wise ones usually gain understanding because of a comparison through a simile. It is

9 The translation "however" follows an emendation suggested by Yìnshùn 1983a: 183 note 5.

10 SN 22.89 at SN III 130,13 lists three type of lotuses and then distinguishes three parts of each plant.

just like a wet-nurse who gives a cloth [used as a nappy] to the launderer. With various kinds of lye and soap he washes out the dirt, yet there is still a remainder of smell. By mixing it with various kinds of fragrance he makes that disappear.[11]

"In the same way, ⟨although⟩ the learned noble disciple rightly contemplates these five aggregates of clinging as not-self and not belonging to a self,[12] ⟨still⟩ [the noble disciple] has not yet abandoned the 'I am' conceit in relation to these five aggregates of clinging,[13] the desire [related to the notion] 'I am', and the underlying tendency towards 'I am', has not yet [fully] understood it, not yet become separated from it, not yet vomited it out.

"Yet at a later time [the noble disciple] progresses in giving attention to these five aggregates of clinging by examining their rise and fall: this is bodily form, this is the arising of bodily form, this is the cessation of bodily form; this is feeling, *this is the arising of feeling, this is the cessation of feeling*; this is perception, *this is the arising of perception, this is the cessation of perception*; these are formations, *this is the arising of formations, this is the cessation of formations*; this is consciousness, this is the arising of consciousness, this is the cessation of consciousness.

"Having contemplated the rise and fall of these five aggregates of clinging in this way, [the noble disciple] completely relinquishes all 'I am' conceit, desire [related to the notion] 'I am', and the underlying tendency towards 'I am'. This is called truly and rightly contemplating."

When the monastic Khemaka spoke this teaching, the elders attained the pure eye of Dharma that is remote from [mental] stains and free from [mental] dust, and the monastic Khemaka by

11 According to the simile in SN 22.89 at SN III 131,8, which just speaks of a cloth being dirty, this cloth still smells of the washing materials. To get rid of the smell the owners then put it into a scented casket. Another difference is that SN 22.89 has the exposition of how to cultivate insight, which in SĀ 103 comes after the simile, already before the simile and then again after it. Regarding the translation "not clinging" see p. 86 note 13.

12 The translation "although" follows an emendation suggested by Yìnshùn 1983a: 183 note 6.

13 The translation "still" follows an emendation suggested by Yìnshùn 1983a: 184 note 7.

not clinging attained liberation of the mind from the influxes.[14] Because of the benefit of the joy of Dharma, his body got completely rid of the illness.

Then the elder monastics said to the monastic Khemaka: "When we heard what [our] friend said for the first time, we already understood and already delighted in it, what to say of hearing him again and again.[15] When asking [further] we wished for [our] friend to manifest his refined eloquence. Not to harass you, [but] for you to be willing and able to teach in detail the Dharma of the Tathāgata, the arahant, the fully awakened one."

Then the elders, hearing what the monastic Khemaka had said, were delighted and received it respectfully.

XI.3 DISCUSSION

The explanation and in particular the similes used by Khemaka were apparently exactly what the elders needed to reach realization. This is even more evident in the case of the Pāli parallel. Whereas in the discourse translated above they reach stream-entry, referred to as attaining "the eye of Dharma", according to the *Saṃyutta-nikāya* account they even reached full awakening.

The teaching given by Khemaka makes it clear that, even though one may no longer be able to pinpoint anything as a self, the tendency to identify still pervades one's experience like fragrance pervades a flower. Although one's cultivation of insight has already washed out the dirt of fully fledged self-notions, further practice is required to get rid of the remaining smell. The practice required is deceptively simple: to direct mindfulness to the impermanent nature of all aspects of experience. Such contemplation of the rise and fall of the five aggregates often features in the early discourses as a powerful mode of practice for reaching full liberation. This type of meditation practice also features in the next chapter,

---

14 According to SN 22.89 at SN III 132,10, not only Khemaka but also the sixty elders with whom he had the discussion attained full awakening. SN 22.89 does not mention that Khemaka recovered from his disease.

15 Such an indication is not given in SN 22.89 at SN III 132,1, where the elders simply state that they wanted him to explain the teachings.

and instructions on how to implement it can be found in the conclusion to the present book.

Besides the actual teaching, another remarkable feature of this discourse is Khemaka's compassion. Even though he is seriously ill, on realizing that the other monastics have not fully grasped the subtle but important difference between the realization that there is no permanent self and complete freedom from any conceit, he pulls himself together and with the support of a stick walks over to meet them in order to clarify the issue. The example set by Khemaka in this way can serve as a source of inspiration to act similarly, to be willing to give priority to helping others improve their understanding over personal discomfort. In the discourse translated above this act of compassion has its immediate recompense, since Khemaka recovers from his illness (an outcome not recorded in the Pāli parallel) and attains full awakening (reported in both versions).

Another significant indication offered by the present discourse in relation to this book's overall theme is that the one who delivers a rather profound teaching is the patient himself. In this way the discourse by Khemaka can be read as an invitation to be receptive to what one can learn from a sick person, and also as an encouragement to the sick to speak the truth they have on their mind. Such opening on both sides can have a considerable transformative effect.

With the next chapter I turn to a series of meditation practices. Similar to the teaching by Khemaka in the discourse translated above, the successful implementation of this meditation programme can result in the physical recovery of the patient and carries with it the seeds of insight that can lead to total mental health through full awakening.

XII

A CURATIVE MEDITATION PROGRAMME

XII.1 INTRODUCTION

The discourse in this chapter presents a whole programme of different meditation practices, whose recitation the Buddha prescribed for a sick monastic by the name of Girimānanda.[1] In the present case the Buddha does not go himself to visit the sick and instead sends Ānanda to convey instructions to Girimānanda. Since Girimānanda recovers upon hearing Ānanda report the Buddha's teaching, the implication seems to be that the curative effect of this teaching does not require the Buddha's personal presence. Instead, even someone who has not yet reached full awakening, like Ānanda during the time he served as the Buddha's attendant, can successfully guide a patient through this series of meditations.

The case of Girimānanda is similar to the recitation of the awakening factors to Mahākassapa discussed in Chapter 5, in so far as in both cases recitation of the respective text, doubtlessly functioning as a form of guided meditation, led to

---

1 Besides featuring in the present discourse, Girimānanda seems to appear only as the speaker of a set of stanzas in the *Theragāthā*, Th 325–9 (translated Norman 1969: 36f), from which it emerges that by the time of speaking these he had become an arahant; see also Malalasekera 1937/1995: 770f.

recovery. Like the text translated in Chapter 5, the translation of the present text is based on a Tibetan original apparently brought to Tibet by a Sri Lankan monastic.[2] Besides this Tibetan version, another version can be found among the Tens of the *Aṅguttara-nikāya*.[3]

XII.2 TRANSLATION[4]

Thus have I heard. At one time the Buddha was staying at Sāvatthī in Jeta's Grove, Anāthapiṇḍika's Park. At that time, on that occasion the venerable Girimānanda was seriously sick and oppressed by pain. Then the venerable Ānanda approached the Blessed One. Having approached him, he paid respect to the Blessed One and sat to one side. Having sat to one side, the venerable Ānanda said to the Blessed One:

"Venerable sir, the venerable Girimānanda is seriously sick and oppressed by pain. Venerable sir, it would be good if the Blessed One could please approach the venerable monastic Girimānanda, approaching him out of compassion."

Then the Blessed One said to the venerable Ānanda: "Then, Ānanda, go straightaway to the monastic Girimānanda and announce to him ten perceptions, recite them to him clearly. Furthermore the monastic Girimānanda, on hearing the ten perceptions, will become fully aware of these dwellings [for one who is] oppressed by sickness.[5]

"What are the ten? [They are] the perception of impermanence

---

2 See in more detail Skilling 1993.

3 AN 10.60 at AN V 108,17 (translated Bodhi 2012: 1411); on the meditative perceptions described in AN 10.60 cf. also Gunaratana 2014.

4 The translated part of the discourse is taken from D 38 *ka* 276a6 to 279a1 or Q 754 *tsi* 293a1 to 295b7; the part I have translated is preceded by the title "Discourse to Girimānanda". In the translation I have numbered the perceptions to facilitate discussion; the numbers are not found in the original. Feer 1883: 145–50 supposedly translates the Tibetan version, yet his rendering at times differs so substantially from the Tibetan version that it cannot be a translation properly speaking. Glass 2007: 149 notes the existence of a Mongolian translation based on the Tibetan version.

5 In AN 10.60 at AN V 108,28 the Buddha points out that, on hearing the ten perceptions spoken by Ānanda, the affliction of Girimānanda might right away subside.

(1), the perception of not-self (2), the perception of impurity (3),[6] the perception of impediments (4),[7] the perception of abandoning (5), the perception of dispassion (6), the perception of cessation (7), the perception of not delighting in the whole world (8), the perception of impermanence in all formations (9), and the perception of mindfulness of breathing (10).[8]

1. "[Ānanda], what is the perception of impermanence? Here, Ānanda, having gone to a forest, under a tree, or in an empty hut, a venerable one should attend distinctly in this way: 'Bodily form is impermanent, feeling is impermanent, perception is impermanent, formations are impermanent, consciousness is impermanent.' One should contemplate these five aggregates of clinging as impermanent. [Ānanda], teach the perception of impermanence in this way.[9]

2. "Ānanda, what is the perception of not-self? Here, Ānanda, having gone to a forest, under a tree, or in an empty hut, a monastic should attend distinctly in this way: 'The eye is not-self and forms are not-self, the ear is not-self and sounds are not-self, the nose is not-self and odours are not-self, the tongue is not-self and tastes are not-self, the body is not-self and tangibles are not-self, the mind is not-self and mind-objects are not-self. These six internal and six external sense-spheres are not-self. One should see and contemplate not-self. Ānanda, teach this [perception of] not-self.

3. "Ānanda, as for the perception of impurity: here, Ānanda, a monastic should reflect distinctly on this body from the top of

---

6 AN 10.60 at AN V 109,1 instead speaks of the perception of lack of beauty, *asubha*.

7 AN 10.60 at AN V 109,1 instead speaks of the perception of danger, *ādīnava*.

8 The qualification of mindfulness of breathing as a "perception" is not used in the full exposition given later of this topic. In AN 10.60 at AN V 109,3 already the introductory listing just refers to mindfulness of breathing, *ānāpānasati*, without qualifying this as a perception (even though the introductory statement announces ten perceptions).

9 Here and below AN 10.60 does not have comparable injunctions to Ānanda that he should teach these perceptions. Instead AN 10.60 consistently concludes the exposition of any of these perceptions with a statement by the Buddha that this is called the so-and-so perception. In the case of the first four perceptions, this is preceded by a short summary of the respective practice.

the head down to the soles of the feet, covered by skin, full of many impurities: 'In this body there are head hairs, body hairs, nails, teeth, skin, flesh, sinews, bones, bone marrow, kidneys, heart, spleen, lungs, mesentery, stomach, bowels, colon, bladder, faeces, bile, phlegm, pus, blood, sweat, fat, tears, grease, spittle, snot, puss, urine, and brain.[10] These are the thirty-two impurities. One should contemplate this body as impure. Ānanda, teach this [perception] of impurity.

4. "Ānanda, what is [the perception] of impediments? Here, Ānanda, having gone to a forest, under a tree, or in an empty hut, a monastic should reflect distinctly in this way: 'This body has much pain and many impediments. In this body many diseases arise, such as eye-disease, [external] ear-disease, nose-disease, tongue-disease, body-disease, head-disease, inner ear-disease, mouth-disease, tooth-disease, cough, asthma, catarrh, fever, stomach-disease, fainting, dysentery, colic, cholera, leprosy, furuncles, pox, consumption, epilepsy, scab, itch, ringworm, chickenpox, scabies, haemorrhage, diabetes, haemorrhoids, cancer, fistula, disease due to an imbalance of bile, disease due to an imbalance of phlegm, disease due to an imbalance of wind, disease due to a combination [of these], disease at the time of not getting food, disease of being disturbed due to unbalanced [behaviour], spasmodic disease, disease due to the ripening of karma, cold, heat, hunger, thirst, defecation, and urination.'[11] One should contemplate these diseases in the body as impediments. Ānanda, you should teach this [perception] of impediments.

5. "Ānanda, what are the perceptions of abandoning? Here, Ānanda, a monastic does not dwell in arisen sensual desire but removes it, eliminates it, does not become habituated to it, and does not cultivate it.

---

10 The brain is not part of the listing of anatomical parts in AN 10.60, which also does not have a summary statement giving the overall count of parts (which in its presentation would be only thirty-one); see also Anālayo 2011a: 82f note 281.

11 The listing of diseases in the Tibetan original is not always clear and several of the translated terms are uncertain, while others are not translated but transcribed phonetically from the Pāli. Whatever the exact implication of the single terms, the main point is a long list of different possible ailments to illustrate the nature of the body to become sick.

["A monastic does not dwell in arisen ill will but removes it, eliminates it, does not become habituated to it, and does not cultivate it.][12]

"[A monastic] does not dwell in arisen harmfulness but removes it, eliminates it, does not become habituated to it, and does not cultivate it.

"[A monastic] does not dwell in arisen evil and unwholesome qualities but removes them, eliminates them, does not become habituated to them, and does not cultivate them. Ānanda, this is the perception of abandoning.[13]

6. "Ānanda, what is the perception of dispassion?[14] [Here, Ānanda, having gone to a forest, under a tree, or in an empty hut, a monastic reflects distinctly in this way: 'This is peaceful, this is sublime, namely the calming of all formations, the transformation of what has arisen, the extinguishing of craving, dispassion, Nirvāṇa. Ānanda, this is the perception of dispassion.]

[7. "Ānanda, what is the perception of cessation?] Here, Ānanda, having gone to a forest, under a tree, or in an empty hut, a monastic reflects distinctly in this way: 'This is peaceful, this is sublime, namely the calming of all formations, the transformation of what has arisen, the extinguishing of craving, cessation, Nirvāṇa. Ānanda, this is the perception of cessation.

8. "Ānanda, what is the perception of not delighting in the whole world? Here, Ānanda, a monastic abandons whatever has manifested of worldly knowledge, thoughts, positions, and underlying tendencies and does not delight in them. Ānanda, you should teach this perception of not delighting in the whole world.

9. "Ānanda, what is the perception of impermanence in all formations? Here, Ānanda, a monastic has no attachment in relation to all formations, abandons them, and is disgusted

12 D 38 *ka* 277b2 and Q 754 *tsi* 249a7 proceed directly from sensual desire to harming and thus seem to have lost the case of ill will, which in the early discourses is always mentioned together with sensual desire and harming in the standard reference to unwholesome types of thought.

13 D 38 *ka* 277b4 and Q 754 *tsi* 294b1 here use the singular "perception", even though the introductory statement employs the plural "perceptions".

14 D 38 *ka* 277b4 and Q 754 *tsi* 294b1 seem to have conflated the two perceptions of dispassion and cessation, mentioned separately in the introductory part of the Buddha's exposition, probably the result of a copying error caused by the closely similar formulation of these two.

by them.[15] Ānanda, you should teach this perception of impermanence in all formations."

10. "Ānanda, what is mindfulness of breathing? Ānanda, having gone to a forest, under a tree, or in an empty hut, a monastic should sit down cross-legged, keeping the body erect, and dwell with mindfulness [set up] in front ...[16]

"Ānanda, you should go straightaway to Girimānanda and announce to him these ten perceptions. When that has happened, on hearing the ten perceptions the monastic Girimānanda's sickness will completely subside."

Then the venerable Ānanda, having heard it from the Blessed One, approached the venerable Girimānanda and announced to the venerable Girimānanda each of these ten perceptions.

Then, having heard these ten perceptions, the venerable Girimānanda's sickness completely subsided. The sickness having completely subsided, the venerable Girimānanda rose up. The venerable Girimānanda's disease had disappeared.

XII.3 DISCUSSION

The actual instruction on the sixteen steps of mindfulness of breathing in the Tibetan original has suffered from errors in transmission and in its present form is unfortunately no longer apt for translation. I therefore had to leave out this part. In what follows I supplement the corresponding instruction from

---

15 The instruction in AN 10.60 at AN V 111,9 employs three closely similar terms, all of which convey the sense of being disgusted. Bodhi 2012: 1846 note 2078 mentions an alternative reading *anicchā saññā* apparently found in some manuscripts, the adopting of which would result in the title of the present exercise becoming "the perception of wishlessness in all formations". The Tibetan reads *mi rtag pa'i 'du shes* and thus clearly renders an original *aniccasaññā*, "perception of impermanence". Both titles can be considered to converge on the same basic point, in that it is precisely insight into the impermanent nature of all formations that leads to wishlessness towards them, to giving up one's attachment to them, to being willing to abandon them, and even to becoming disgusted with them.

16 The text of the actual instructions is corrupted in the Tibetan original, making it no longer fit for translation unless one were to introduce a number of emendations (for this part I also consulted the Cone and Narthang edition, alongside the Derge and Peking editions, but this has not helped me to resolve the issue).

the *Aṅguttara-nikāya* parallel. After describing the appropriate location and bodily posture for mindfulness of breathing as well as the establishing of mindfulness, this version proceeds as follows:[17]

"One breathes in mindfully and breathes out mindfully.

"Breathing in long, one knows: 'I breathe in long'; breathing out long, one knows: 'I breathe out long.' Breathing in short, one knows: 'I breathe in short'; breathing out short, one knows: 'I breathe out short.' One trains: 'I breathe in experiencing the whole body'; one trains: 'I breathe out experiencing the whole body.' One trains: 'I breathe in calming the bodily activity'; one trains: 'I breathe out calming the bodily activity.'[18]

"One trains: 'I breathe in experiencing joy'; one trains: 'I breathe out experiencing joy.' One trains: 'I breathe in experiencing happiness'; one trains: 'I breathe out experiencing happiness.' One trains: 'I breathe in experiencing the mental activity'; one trains: 'I breathe out experiencing the mental activity.' One trains: 'I breathe in calming the mental activity'; one trains: 'I breathe out calming the mental activity.'

"One trains: 'I breathe in experiencing the mind'; one trains: 'I breathe out experiencing the mind.' One trains: 'I breathe in gladdening the mind'; one trains: 'I breathe out gladdening the mind.' *One trains: 'I breathe in* concentrating the mind'; *one trains: 'I breathe out concentrating the mind.' One trains: 'I breathe in* liberating the mind'; *one trains: 'I breathe out liberating the mind.'*

"One trains: 'I breathe in contemplating impermanence'; one trains: 'I breathe out contemplating impermanence.' One trains: 'I breathe in contemplating dispassion; one trains: 'I breathe out contemplating dispassion.' One trains: 'I breathe in contemplating cessation; one trains: 'I breathe out contemplating cessation.' One trains: 'I breathe in contemplating letting go; one trains: 'I breathe out contemplating letting go.'"

---

17 AN 10.60 at AN V 111,14 to 112,7.

18 With the rendering "activity" for bodily and mental *saṅkhāra* here and below in the conclusion and in the appendix I follow the example of Bodhi 2012: 1414, who has shifted from his earlier use of "formation" to what from a practical perspective seems to me a very apt translation for conveying the import of the present instructions for mindfulness of breathing.

In addition to the above translation, in an appendix to this book I present renderings of two versions of the sixteen steps of mindfulness of breathing preserved in *Vinaya* texts of the Mūlasarvāstivāda and Sarvāstivāda traditions.[19]

For a better appreciation of the meditative dynamics underlying the entire series of meditations in this discourse, the rule of waxing syllables can be consulted. The basic principle behind this rule is that terms in a list tend to be arranged in such a way that words with fewer syllables are followed by words with an equal or a higher number of syllables.[20] Items in longer lists tend to be arranged in subgroups, based on a thematic or formal connection between the members of a subgroup. In the case of the Pāli list of ten perceptions, the following three subgroups emerge:[21]

- the perceptions of impermanence (1), not-self (2), lack of beauty (3), danger (4);
- the perceptions of abandoning (5), dispassion (6), cessation (7), not delighting in the whole world (8), impermanence in all formations (9);
- mindfulness of breathing (10).

The principle of waxing syllables groups together the first four perceptions. This division finds further support in a minor stylistic feature in the *Girimānanda-sutta*, as the Pāli version concludes the first four perceptions with a summary statement that highlights the gist of the respective practice.[22] Such summaries are not found in the rest of the instructions.

Considering the first four perceptions as a group, closer inspection brings to light that this part of the meditative progression described in the *Girimānanda-sutta* and its Tibetan parallel corresponds to a tour through the four distortions

19 See below p. 242. Another two versions, found in the Mahāsāṅghika *Vinaya* and a *Saṃyukta-āgama* discourse, I already translated in Anālayo 2013b: 228–30.

20 See in more detail Anālayo 2009c.

21 The syllable counts are as follows: *aniccasaññā*: 5, *anattasaññā*: 5, *asubhasaññā*: 5, *ādīnavasaññā*: 6, *pahānasaññā*: 5, *virāgasaññā*: 5, *nirodhasaññā*: 5, *sabbaloke anabhiratasaññā*: 11, *sabbasaṅkhāresu aniccāsaññā*: 11, and *ānāpānasati*: 6. The resultant grouping of the whole set then becomes: a) 5+5+5+6, b) 5+5+5+11+11, and c) 6.

22 See above note 9.

(*vipallāsa*). According to a discourse in the *Aṅguttara-nikāya* and its parallel in a partially preserved *Ekottarika-āgama* collection, these four involve the following mistaken projections:[23]

- permanence in what is impermanent (a),
- pleasure in what is *dukkha* (b),
- self in what is not-self (c),
- attractiveness in what is unattractive (d).

The resultant correspondences between the first four perceptions in the *Girimānanda-sutta* and the four distortions are as follows:

perceptions:	distortions:
1) impermanence	a) permanence in what is impermanent
2) not-self	c) self in what is not-self
3) lack of beauty	d) attractiveness in what is unattractive
4) danger	b) pleasure in what is *dukkha*

The sequence of these four perceptions in the instruction to Girimānanda results in a gradually increasing focus on the body, appropriate to the experience of being ill. The body comes in as the first of the five aggregates of clinging taken up in the perception of impermanence (1). The perception of not-self (2) turns to the six senses, of which five are related to the body. The perception of lack of beauty (3) then presents a detailed survey of the anatomical constitution of the body, so that here the entire meditation exercise is concerned with the body. With the perception of danger (4) the focus on the body comes to its culmination point in a manner that is of direct relevance to the case of sickness, namely by way of the different diseases that can afflict the body and cause physical pain.

Among the remaining perceptions in the *Girimānanda-sutta* and its Tibetan parallel another set of four can be identified, namely four perceptions which in complementary ways focus on the final goal, Nirvāṇa. These are the perceptions of dispassion (6), of cessation (7), of not delighting in the whole world (8), and of impermanence in all formations (9). In this way the first set of four perceptions (1 to 4) frees the mind

23 AN 4.49 at AN II 52,3 (translated Bodhi 2012: 437) and its parallel EĀ² 5 at T II 876c21.

from the four distortions (*vipallāsa*), and the second set of four perceptions (6 to 9) inclines the mind towards total freedom.

Each of these two groups of four is followed by a single perception (5 and 10).[24] These single perceptions again involve a basic pattern of four. The perception of abandoning (5) begins with the removal of sensual thoughts (5a), which forms a natural extension of the meditative thrust resulting from the perception of lack of beauty (3) and the perception of danger (4). The perception of abandoning then continues with the removal of ill will (5b), of harmfulness (5c), and of any other evil and unwholesome quality (5d), the last providing a natural lead into the four perceptions (6 to 9) that incline the mind towards Nirvāṇa. The removal of sensual thoughts (5a), of ill will (5b), of harmfulness (5c), and of any other evil and unwholesome quality (5d) taken together come under the heading of the single perception of abandoning, which thereby clearly involves a basic pattern of four.

The meditation programme has its culmination point in the sixteen steps of mindfulness of breathing (10), which the rule of waxing syllables in fact sets apart from the preceding perceptions. Elsewhere the early discourses correlate the sixteen steps with the four *satipaṭṭhāna*s, which underlie the four tetrads that make up the sixteen steps of mindfulness of breathing.[25] In this way, similar to the perception of abandoning, mindfulness of breathing can be considered to involve a basic division into four.

The resultant pattern of fours underlying the entire meditative programme proceeds as follows:

- impermanence (1), not-self (2), lack of beauty (3), danger (4);
- abandoning sensual desire (5a), ill will (5b), harmfulness (5c), unwholesomeness (5d);

24 This division into groups conforms to the principle of waxing syllables, as the resultant grouping of the whole set then becomes: a) 5+5+5+6, b) 5, c) 5+5+5+11+11, and d) 6. On consulting only the principle of waxing syllables, as done earlier, the division now to be made between b) and c) was not yet apparent.

25 See Anālayo 2007a and 2013b: 233–5.

- dispassion (6), cessation (7), not delighting in the whole world (8), impermanence in all formations (9);
- mindfulness of breathing: first tetrad (10a), second tetrad (10b), third tetrad (10c), and fourth tetrad (10d).

In this series of instructions given to the sick Girimānanda, mindfulness of breathing forms the culmination point, rounding off a whole range of meditative approaches. The breath as what sustains life naturally has a close relationship to disease and also to death; in fact a mode of recollection of death to be explored in Chapter 24 employs precisely the breath as its object. Be it mindfulness of breathing or recollection of death, insight into impermanence, cultivated with the help of mindfulness, has a central role to play.

A message to be taken away from this chapter is the need to build up one's own inner resources through meditation practice, in particular by cultivating mindfulness and insight into impermanence. In the conclusion to this book I will return to the *Girimānanda-sutta* and describe in detail how to put these ten perceptions into practice. Before coming to that, however, the second of the two main themes of this book needs to be explored, namely how to face death, one's own and that of others.

XIII

THE INEVITABILITY OF DEATH

XIII.1 INTRODUCTION

My exploration of the early discourses now turns from the topic of disease, covered in the first twelve chapters, to the closely related topic of death, in the remaining twelve chapters. The predicament of death is explicitly taken up in the formulation of the first of the four noble truths, discussed above in Chapter 1 as the foundational framework for the early Buddhist approach to disease and death. This first truth reckons death, together with birth, old age, and disease, as a manifestation of *dukkha*.

The second truth identifies craving as responsible for the arising of *dukkha*. Applied to the case of death, the stronger one's grasping, craving, and attachments are, the more threatening death will appear to be. Fear of death can therefore be seen as a measuring rod of one's degree of attachment to this particular embodied existence.

The third truth regarding the cessation of *dukkha* implies that it is possible to have an attitude towards death and dying that is free from *dukkha*. Letting go of craving and attachment is what leads to increasing degrees of freedom from the fear of death.

The fourth truth delineates the practical path to be undertaken in order to arrive at inner freedom from the fear of death. This practical path combines a foundation in moral conduct with a systematic training of the mind. In this way, the threat posed by death and dying can become a powerful motivating force for dedicating oneself to moral conduct and mental cultivation through meditation.

The way death leads to the arising of *dukkha* has several dimensions, one of which is grief caused by the passing away of loved ones. The discourse translated below reports such a case of grief, which involves the king of Kosala, Pasenadi. King Pasenadi features frequently in the early discourses as an admirer of the Buddha who regularly comes for a visit.[1]

In addition to the *Saṃyukta-āgama* discourse translated below, versions of the present episode can be found in the *Saṃyutta-nikāya*, in a Sanskrit fragment, in a discourse in the other *Saṃyukta-āgama* that has not been fully preserved in Chinese translation, in a discourse in the *Ekottarika-āgama*, and in an individually translated discourse.[2]

XIII.2 TRANSLATION[3]

Thus have I heard. At one time the Buddha was staying at Sāvatthī in Jeta's Grove, Anāthapiṇḍika's Park. At that time King Pasenadi's grandmother, whom he held in very high esteem, had suddenly passed away and was being cremated outside the town.[4] Having finished taking care of her bodily remains,[5] with soiled clothes and dishevelled hair, [King Pasenadi] approached the Buddha, paid respect at the Buddha's feet and withdrew to sit to one side.[6]

---

1 For a biographical sketch of Pasenadi see Malalasekera 1938/1998: 168–74.

2 SN 3.22 at SN I 96,31 (translated Bodhi 2000: 188), SHT VI 1586, Bechert and Wille 1989: 202 (see also Yamada 1972), SĀ² 54 at T II 392a26, EĀ 26.7 at T II 638a2, and T 122 at T II 545a24.

3 The translated discourse is SĀ 1227 at T II 335b9 to 335c16.

4 Thī-a 21,24 (translated Pruitt 1998/1999: 35) reports that Pasenadi's sister Sumanā, even though she wanted to go forth, remained in the royal household to nurse their grandmother. She only went forth after the grandmother had passed away, and still reached full awakening.

5 The text at this juncture uses a term which can mean "body" as well as "relic"; see in more detail Silk 2006. In an attempt to convey both nuances, here and in subsequent chapters I have opted for the rendering "bodily remains".

6 SN 3.22 sets in with Pasenadi approaching the Buddha and does not provide the information given in SĀ 1227 ahead of their meeting.

Then the Blessed One asked King Pasenadi: "Great King, where are you coming from with soiled clothes and dishevelled hair?"

King Pasenadi said to the Buddha: "Blessed One, I lost my grandmother, whom I held in very high esteem. She left me and died.[7] Having finished taking care of her cremation outside the town, I have come to approach the Blessed One."

The Buddha said: "Great King, do you have thoughts of intense love and esteem for your grandparent?"[8]

King Pasenadi said to the Buddha: "Blessed One, I have a very high esteem and love for her. Blessed One, if by giving to someone all the elephants, horses, and seven treasures in this country, even up to the country's dominion, I would be able to save my grandmother's life, I would give it all. Since I am not able to save her from passing away and from the [cycle] of birth and death, I am in grief and despair, not being able to bear it on my own.

"Formerly I heard the Blessed One say: 'All living beings, all insects, all who live, being born, will entirely pass away, none of them will not expire. There is no escape by which those who are born will not die.' Only now I understand what the Blessed One said so well."[9]

The Buddha said: "Great King, it is like this, it is like this. All living beings, all insects, all who live, being born, will entirely pass away and come to expire in the end. Not a single one, being born, will not die."

The Buddha said: "Great King, even those born in a great family of brahmins, a great family of warriors, a great family of merchants will all pass away.[10] None will not die. Even a great head-anointed warrior king, who holds the position of governing

7 Pasenadi's grandmother had been 120 years old according to SN 3.22 at SN I 97,4, her age had been 100 years according to T 122 at T II 545a25, and she had been close to 100 years according to EĀ 26.7 at T II 638a8.

8 SN 3.22 does not report such a question.

9 In SN 3.22 at SN I 97,16 the Buddha makes a statement on the mortality of all living beings and Pasenadi, who in this version appears to hear such a statement for the first time, approves of it as being well said.

10 Instead of listing various types of human beings who are not exempt from death, in SN 3.22 at SN I 97,23 the Buddha illustrates the situation with a simile, according to which all vessels made by a potter are bound to break. The Sanskrit text in Yamada 1972 combines both presentations, as it lists various types of human beings not exempt from death and also has a version of the potter simile (which differs in so far as the exposition is addressed to monastics and not to Pasenadi).

over the four continents and has gained unimpeded power over it, without a [single] hostile country that has not been vanquished [by him], in the final end will reach the ultimate limit and is not beyond passing away.

"Again, Great King, one who is born among devas of long life as their king in the heavenly palace, with unimpeded enjoyment, will in the end also come to exhaustion and is not beyond passing away.

"Again, Great King, arahant monastics who have eradicated the influxes, left behind the heavy burdens, done what is to be done, reached their own benefit, eradicated all the fetters, whose minds are well liberated by right knowledge, they will also in the end come to exhaustion, abandon their bodies, and [attain final] Nirvāṇa.

"Again, Paccekabuddhas, who are well tamed and well pacified, with the exhaustion of their bodies and lives will in the end come to [attain final] Nirvāṇa.

"Buddhas, Blessed Ones who are endowed with the ten powers and the four intrepidities, having roared their supreme lion's roar, will in the end abandon their bodies and attain final Nirvāṇa.

"In the same way as well, Great King, it should be understood that all living beings, all insects, all who live, being born, will entirely pass away and come to be extinguished in the end. They are not beyond passing away."

Then the Blessed One further spoke this poem:

> "All types of living being,
> Being alive will in the end come to die.
> Each following their karmic destiny
> Will receive their own good and evil fruits.
> "Evil doers fall into hell.
> On account of wholesomeness, one ascends to heaven.[11]
> Those who cultivate the most excellent path,
> With influxes eradicated, they [attain] final Nirvāṇa.

---

11 SN 3.22 at SN I 97,32 continues by pointing out that one should do what is good, and by explaining that merits are a support in the afterlife; it has no counterpart to the remainder of the stanzas in SĀ 1227.

"A Tathāgata and a Paccekabuddha
And the disciples of a Buddha
Share in common that they will abandon their bodies and lives.
What to say of ordinary people?"

When the Buddha had spoken this discourse, hearing what the Buddha had said King Pasenadi rejoiced in it and was delighted. He paid homage and left.

XIII.3 DISCUSSION

The discourse translated above highlights that death is inevitable. Even though this is common knowledge, when it happens to those who are close and dear, it can often be difficult to accept it. According to some of the parallel versions, Pasenadi's grandmother was 100 or even 120 years of age. For her to pass away is not that unexpected. Even so, Pasenadi experiences such deep grief that he would give away everything he owns, just to have her back.

The exposition continues by applying the same principle to those from eminent families, listing the three types that make up the higher strata of ancient Indian society: brahmins, warriors, and merchants. Then follows the example of a king governing the whole world, expressed in terms of the four continents recognized in ancient Indian cosmology.

The sweeping power of death is shown to apply to celestial life as well, and to arahants, fully awakened disciples of a Buddha. Early Buddhist thought also recognizes a type of Buddha called Paccekabuddha, who realize full awakening on their own but, unlike a Buddha, do not widely teach their realization to others.[12] Both Paccekabuddhas and arahants have gained supreme mental health through full awakening, but Paccekabuddhas are superior to arahants by dint of having reached the final goal on their own, without having had the benefit of receiving guidance from a Buddha. Even arahants and Paccekabuddhas are bound to die.

---

12 On the notion of Paccekabuddhas see in more detail Anālayo 2010a and 2015d.

The same holds for a Buddha, whose compassionate teaching activity makes him superior to a Paccekabuddha. According to tradition a fully awakened Buddha is endowed with ten exceptional mental powers,[13] in addition to which he is also in the possession of four types of inner intrepidities.[14] These powers and intrepidities enable him to stand his ground in debate with full inner confidence and thereby to teach the Dharma in a fearless way, comparable to a lion's roar.[15] Even someone endowed with these ten exceptional powers and the unshakeable self-confidence of the four intrepidities, in spite of being of such might, will pass away.

The examples given in this way vividly document the all-pervasive power of death. A central message underlying these examples is the need to make mortality something integral to one's own experience, instead of leaving it as just a theoretical acknowledgement that is soon enough again forgotten. A way of putting this into practice during one's everyday activities would be to note from time to time that the person(s) one is just meeting will also die: nobody is exempt from that fate.

A succinct expression that could be used for regular reflection on the mortal nature of all who are born can be found in a stanza in the *Udānavarga*, with parallels in the different *Dharmapada*s and other texts like the *Mahāvastu* and the *Divyāvadāna*. This succinct statement reads as follows:

> Life ends in death.[16]

---

13 The ten powers comprise seven insights into: 1) what is possible and impossible, 2) karma, 3) ways to (rebirth) destinations, 4) the elements in the world, 5) the different inclinations of beings, 6) the faculties of beings, and 7) concentrative attainments. In addition they include the three higher knowledges: 8) recollection of one's own past lives, 9) the divine eye, and 10) the destruction of the influxes.

14 The four intrepidities are the certainty of: 1) being fully awakened, 2) having destroyed all influxes, 3) knowing what are obstructions, and 4) teaching what indeed leads to the destruction of *dukkha*.

15 On the Buddha's lion's roar see Anālayo 2009b.

16 Stanza 1.23b, Bernhard 1965: 103: *maraṇāntaṃ hi jīvitaṃ*, with parallels in Dhp 148d (translated Norman 1997/2004: 22), the Patna *Dharmapada* 259d, Cone 1989: 170 (the relevant line in the Gāndhārī *Dharmapada* 142, Brough 1962/2001: 141, has not been preserved), the *Mahāvastu*, Senart 1890: 66,3 and 424,6 as well as Senart 1897: 152,5 and 183,14 (translated Jones 1952/1976: 63 and 377 as well as Jones 1956/1978: 147 and 179), and the *Divyāvadāna*, Cowell and Neil 1886: 27,30, 100,19, and 486,21 (the first two translated Rotman 2008: 76 and 192); see also Nett 94,20.

As short as this statement is, allowing it to sink fully into one's mind, through repeated recollection, can have a remarkable transformative effect. I will come back to the practice of recollecting one's own mortality in Chapter 24.

Another and more comprehensive reflection by King Pasenadi himself can be found in a discourse in the *Saṃyukta-āgama* and its parallels.[17] Here he reflects on his own on the significance of old age, disease, and death. By way of complementing the discourse already translated in this chapter, I translate the first part of this other discourse.[18]

> Thus have I heard. At one time the Buddha was staying at Sāvatthī in Jeta's Grove, Anāthapiṇḍika's Park. At that time King Pasenadi, who was alone and reflecting in a quiet [place], thought:
>
> "There are these three things which the whole world does not like to think about. What are the three? That is, they are old age, disease, and death. In this way there are these three things which the whole world does not like to think about.[19]
>
> "If there were not these three things in the world that one does not like [to think about], Buddhas, Blessed Ones, would not appear in the world and the world would not come to know the teaching realized by Buddhas, Tathāgatas, being widely taught to people. Because there are these three things in the world that one does not like to think about, that is, old age, disease, and death, therefore Buddhas, Tathāgatas, appear in the world and the world comes to know the teaching realized by Buddhas, Tathāgatas, being widely taught [to people]."

The discourse continues with King Pasenadi reporting his reflection to the Buddha, who expresses his agreement. A comparable presentation can also be found in a discourse in

17 SN 3.3 at SN I 71,1 (translated Bodhi 2000: 167) as well as SĀ² 67 at T II 397a9, EĀ 26.6 at T II 637a18, and T 801 at T XVII 745c15.

18 The translated part is taken from SĀ 1240 at T II 339c19 to 339c27.

19 According to SN 3.3 at SN I 71,3, Pasenadi had approached the Buddha and asked if one who is born could be beyond disease and death. In his reply the Buddha clarified that even those from great and rich families of brahmins, warriors, and merchants, as well as arahants, will grow old and die, an exposition in this respect similar to SĀ 1227 translated earlier in this chapter.

the *Aṅguttara-nikāya* and its parallels, according to which the existence of death, together with old age and disease, is what motivates a Buddha to appear in the world and deliver his teaching.[20]

The *Ariyapariyesanā-sutta* and its *Madhyama-āgama* parallel confirm that death was one of the prominent aspects of *dukkha* motivating the Buddha-to-be to set out on his own quest for awakening. In the words of Amore, for the Buddha

> the decision to "renounce the world" and undertake the life of a wandering ascetic was, then, an attempt to resolve the existential problem of "being toward death" ... his goal was to conquer death within life.[21]

Once awakened and about to share his discovery, according to the *Ariyapariyesanā-sutta* and its *Madhyama-āgama* parallel the Buddha announced that he had attained the "deathless".[22] Having reached the deathless through full awakening, one is no longer affected by the mortality of one's own body or that of others.

---

20 AN 10.76 at AN V 144,9 (translated Bodhi 2012: 1434) and its parallel SĀ 760 at T II 199c28; see also SĀ 346 at T II 95c22 and the Sanskrit fragment parallel, Tripāṭhī 1962: 205,1 (§25.2).

21 Amore 1974: 117; see also Gunaratne 1982 and Walshe 1978.

22 MN 26 at MN I 172,1 (translated Ñāṇamoli 1995/2005: 264) records the Buddha announcing that "the deathless has been reached". The parallel MĀ 204 at T I 777c16 similarly reports the Buddha referring to the deathless at this juncture, which here comes together with affirming that he has reached a condition that is beyond old age etc.

XIV

MINDFUL FREEDOM FROM GRIEF

XIV.1 INTRODUCTION

The discourse in this chapter reports different reactions towards the death of Sāriputta, a chief disciple of the Buddha, renowned for his wisdom.[1] These different reactions involve a contrast between the matter-of-fact attitude of his attendant, the novice Cunda, and the grief experienced by Ānanda. According to the Pāli commentarial tradition, Cunda was a younger brother of Sāriputta and had attained full awakening soon after going forth as a novice.[2] In the present episode he is still a novice and therefore must be fairly young, otherwise he would have already received the higher ordination to become a monastic, as was natural in the early Buddhist period once the required minimum age for higher ordination had been reached.

The discourse translated below from the *Saṃyukta-āgama*, in agreement with a parallel in the *Saṃyutta-nikāya*,[3] reports

1 The listings of outstanding disciples reckon Sāriputta as foremost among male monastics for his wisdom; see AN 1.14 at AN I 23,17 and EĀ 4.2 at T II 557b5; for biographical sketches of Sāriputta see Malalasekera 1938/1998: 1108–18 as well as Nyanaponika and Hecker 1997: 3–66. On Sāriputta as the one who keeps rolling the wheel of Dharma set in motion by the Buddha see above p. 18.

2 Th-a II 18,28; for a biographical sketch and a discussion of the different and perhaps identical Cundas see Malalasekera 1937/1995: 877–9 (no. 2).

3 SN 47.13 at SN V 161,18 (translated Bodhi 2000: 1642).

how Cunda conveyed the news of Sāriputta's passing away to Ānanda, and how Ānanda then expressed his grief in front of the Buddha.

XIV.2 TRANSLATION[4]

Thus have I heard. At one time the Buddha was dwelling at Rājagaha in the Bamboo Grove, the Squirrels' Feeding Ground.[5] At that time the venerable Sāriputta was dwelling in Magadha in Nālakagāma. He was sick and [about to attain final] Nirvāṇa. The novice Cunda was looking after and taking care of him. Then, because of this disease, the venerable Sāriputta [attained final] Nirvāṇa.

Then the novice Cunda, having taken care of the venerable Sāriputta, taking what was left of his bodily remains [after cremation] and carrying [the venerable Sāriputta's] robes and bowl, approached Rājagaha.[6] Having put away his [own] robe and bowl and washed his feet,[7] he approached the venerable Ānanda. Having paid respect at the venerable Ānanda's feet, he withdrew to stand to one side. He said to the venerable Ānanda: "Venerable sir, please know that my preceptor, the venerable Sāriputta, has [attained final] Nirvāṇa. I have come bringing his bodily remains and his robes and bowl."

When the venerable Ānanda had heard what the novice Cunda had said, he approached the Buddha.[8] He said to the Buddha: "Blessed One, now my whole body is [as if it were] falling apart, the four directions are [as if] they had changed their order, the teachings I learned are [as if they were] blocked off, as the novice Cunda has come and told me: 'My preceptor, the

4 The translated discourse is SĀ 638 at T II 176b28 to 177a14.

5 According to SN 47.13 at SN V 161,18, the Buddha was rather staying in Jeta's Grove at Sāvatthī. The two versions agree, however, on the location where Sāriputta had been staying when he passed away.

6 SN 47.13 at SN V 161,26 just reports that he took Sāriputta's robes and bowl; only the commentary Spk III 221,6 notes that he also brought the relics left after cremation.

7 SN 47.13 does not explicitly record him washing his feet and putting away his robes.

8 In SN 47.13 at SN V 162,3 Ānanda suggests to Cunda that they should approach the Buddha together to inform him of this.

venerable Sāriputta, has [attained final] Nirvāṇa. I have come bringing his bodily remains and his robes and bowl.'"

The Buddha said: "How is it, Ānanda, has Sāriputta [attained final] Nirvāṇa and taken [away] the receiving of the aggregate of precepts? *Has he attained final Nirvāṇa and taken away* the aggregate of concentration? *Has he attained final Nirvāṇa and taken away* the aggregate of wisdom? *Has he attained final Nirvāṇa and taken away* the aggregate of liberation? *Has he* [attained final] Nirvāṇa and *taken away* the aggregate of knowledge and vision of liberation?"[9] Ānanda said to the Buddha: "No, Blessed One."

The Buddha said to Ānanda: "The teachings I declare, having myself known them on attaining full awakening, that is, the four establishments of mindfulness, the four right efforts, the four bases for supernormal power, the five faculties, the five powers, the seven factors of awakening, the eightfold path, *has he* [attained final] Nirvāṇa and *taken these away*?"[10]

Ānanda said to the Buddha: "No, Blessed One. Although he has not [attained final] Nirvāṇa and taken [away] the receiving of the aggregate of precepts, *the aggregate of concentration, the aggregate of wisdom, the aggregate of liberation, the aggregate of knowledge and vision of liberation,* the teachings on *the four establishments of mindfulness, the four right efforts, the four bases for supernormal power, the five faculties, the five powers, the seven factors of awakening,* and the eightfold path, yet the venerable Sāriputta was virtuous and learned. He had few wishes and was contented. He continually

9 The Pāli text of SN 47.13 at SN V 162,18 here has the reading *te*, the enclitic of the personal pronoun "you", suggesting the sense of Sāriputta taking away those aggregates from "you", that is, from Ānanda. As pointed out by Bodhi 2000: 1924 note 160, "the ascription to Ānanda of the last two aggregates (liberation, and the knowledge and vision of liberation) seems puzzling, as he is still a trainee and thus not yet fully liberated." No personal pronoun is found in SĀ 638; the Siamese edition of the present passage in SN 47.13 also has no *te*. This makes it probable that the reading *te* is a textual error. Without a personal pronoun, the passage is no longer problematic. When Ānanda in the next passage in SN 47.13 describes how Sāriputta had been his advisor, the use of the personal pronoun *me* is entirely appropriate. Perhaps during oral transmission the same pronoun came to be accidentally applied to the preceding sentence, in which Ānanda speaks of the aggregates.

10 SN 47.13 does not envisage that at the time of his death Sāriputta might also have taken these qualities away.

practised seclusion, with energetic effort and collected mindfulness, dwelling at peace with a unified and concentrated mind. He had swift wisdom, penetratingly sharp wisdom, transcending wisdom, discriminative wisdom, great wisdom, pervasive wisdom, profound wisdom, and incomparable wisdom. He was endowed with the treasure of knowledge and was able to instruct, able to teach, able to illuminate, able to delight, and well able to extol when teaching the Dharma to assemblies. For this reason, Blessed One, because of the Dharma and because of those who receive the Dharma, I am sad and distressed."[11]

The Buddha said to Ānanda: "Do not be sad and distressed. Why do [I say] that? What arises,[12] what occurs, what is constructed, is of a nature to be destroyed. How could it not to be destroyed? Wishing for it not to be destroyed is [wishing] for what is impossible. I have earlier told you, various kinds of things and agreeable matters, everything for which one has thoughts of affection, all of it is entirely of a nature to become separated from one. One cannot keep it forever.

"It is just like a great tree with luxuriant roots, trunk, branches, leaves, flowers, and fruits, whose great branches break first.[13] It is like a great treasure mountain, whose great peak collapses first.[14] In the same way in the great Community of the followers of the Tathāgata the great disciples [attain] Nirvāṇa first.

"In the direction in which Sāriputta dwelled, in that direction I had no concerns. Because of Sāriputta, that direction was certainly not empty for me."[15]

---

11 Ānanda's eulogy of Sāriputta in SN 47.13 at SN V 162,25 is shorter and emphasizes more the assistance Ānanda had received from him.

12 The translation "arises" is based on adopting a variant.

13 In SN 47.13 at SN V 163,4 the Buddha compares the decease of Sāriputta to a great branch breaking off from a tree possessed of heartwood.

14 SN 47.13 does not have the simile of the great mountain.

15 The present reference is without a counterpart in SN 47.13. A to some extent comparable statement can be found in the next discourse, SN 47.14 at SN V 164,1, where the Buddha notes that the assembly seems empty to him after Sāriputta and Mahāmoggallāna have passed away, and that he earlier had no concerns in relation to the direction in which the two were dwelling. The parallel to SN 47.14, SĀ 639 at T II 177a19, also reports the assembly being empty because Sāriputta and Mahāmoggallāna have passed away; it has no counterpart to the Buddha having no concerns in relation to the direction in which the two had been living.

"Now, Ānanda, I earlier on purpose said to you that whatever there is of various agreeable matters for which one has thoughts of affection, all of it is of a nature to become separated from one; it is as I said earlier. Therefore do not be so very sad, Ānanda. You should know that soon the Tathāgata will also be of the past. Therefore, Ānanda, you should have yourself as an island by relying on yourself, you should have the Dharma as an island by relying on the Dharma; you should have no other island, no other reliance."

Ānanda said to the Buddha: "Blessed One, how does one have oneself as an island by relying on oneself? How does one have the Dharma as an island by relying on the Dharma? How does one have no other island, no other reliance?"[16]

The Buddha said to Ānanda: "[This takes place] if a monastic establishes mindfulness by contemplating the body as a body [internally], with energetic effort, right mindfulness, and clear comprehension, overcoming desire and discontent in the world.[17] *One establishes mindfulness by contemplating the body* as a body externally, *with energetic effort, right mindfulness, and clear comprehension, overcoming desire and discontent in the world. One establishes mindfulness by contemplating the body* as a body internally-and-externally, *with energetic effort, right mindfulness, and clear comprehension, overcoming desire and discontent in the world.*

"One establishes mindfulness by contemplating feelings as feelings *internally, with energetic effort, right mindfulness, and clear comprehension, overcoming desire and discontent in the world. One establishes mindfulness by contemplating feelings as feelings externally, with energetic effort, right mindfulness, and clear comprehension, overcoming desire and discontent in the world. One establishes mindfulness by contemplating feelings as feelings*

16 SN 47.13 does not report a query by Ānanda at this point, so that in its presentation the Buddha continues on his own to expound the meaning of his statement regarding having oneself and the Dharma as an island and a refuge.

17 SN 47.13 at SN V 163,14 does not explicitly mention internal, external, and internal-and-external *satipaṭṭhāna* practice. In fact even SĀ 638 does not qualify the first instance of body contemplation as being internal, but, since it then does use the qualifications external as well as internal-and-external, the lack of the qualification internal in the first instance must be a textual loss.

internally-and-externally, with energetic effort, right mindfulness, and clear comprehension, overcoming desire and discontent in the world.

"*One establishes mindfulness by contemplating the mind as* mind *internally, with energetic effort, right mindfulness, and clear comprehension, overcoming desire and discontent in the world. One establishes mindfulness by contemplating the mind as mind externally, with energetic effort, right mindfulness, and clear comprehension, overcoming desire and discontent in the world. One establishes mindfulness by contemplating the mind as mind internally-and-externally, with energetic effort, right mindfulness, and clear comprehension, overcoming desire and discontent in the world.*

"*One establishes mindfulness by contemplating dharmas as dharmas internally, with energetic effort, right mindfulness, and clear comprehension, overcoming desire and discontent in the world. One establishes mindfulness by contemplating dharmas as dharmas externally, with energetic effort, right mindfulness, and clear comprehension, overcoming desire and discontent in the world.* One establishes mindfulness by contemplating dharmas as dharmas *internally-and-externally*, with energetic effort, right mindfulness, and clear comprehension, overcoming desire and discontent in the world.

"Ānanda, this is called having oneself as an island by relying on oneself, having the Dharma as an island by relying on the Dharma, having no other island, no other reliance."[18]

When the Buddha had spoken this discourse, hearing what the Buddha had said the monastics were delighted and received it respectfully.

XIV.3 DISCUSSION

The contrast between the composed manner in which Cunda takes care of things after the death of his older brother and preceptor, and the way in which the same death completely unsettles the mind of Ānanda, reflects their different levels of progress on the path. In spite of his young age Cunda has reached complete liberation of the mind, whereas Ānanda is

18 In SN 47.13 at SN V 163,20 the Buddha adds that those who follow his instruction on dwelling with themselves and the Dharma as an island and a refuge will be foremost among those keen on training.

still "in training" and, with all his vast acquaintance with the Buddha's teachings, not free from defilements.

In the ensuing discussion regarding Sāriputta's passing away, the Buddha mentions a division of aspects of the path to liberation that revolves around five "aggregates", thereby employing terminology similar to the basic analysis of individual experience into bodily form, feeling, perception, formations, and consciousness as five aggregates of clinging, discussed in Chapter 2. Whereas clinging to these five aggregates prevents one from reaching awakening, the five aggregates of liberation mentioned in the present context are rather what leads to awakening and reflects its successful attainment. The first three correspond to the three trainings mentioned in Chapter 8; the remaining two are related to the completion of such training. The whole set of five reads as follows:

- virtue,
- concentration,
- wisdom,
- liberation,
- knowledge and vision of liberation.

The *Saṃyukta-āgama* discourse translated above also mentions another aspect of the teaching that Sāriputta has not taken away at the time of his death, although this is not found in the *Saṃyutta-nikāya* parallel. This aspect of the teaching is the thirty-seven qualities and practices that are on the side of awakening, *bodhipakkhiyā dhammā*, in the sense of being qualities that are conducive to awakening:[19]

- the four establishments of mindfulness,
- the four right efforts,
- the four bases for supernormal power,
- the five faculties,
- the five powers,
- the seven factors of awakening,
- the noble eightfold path.

In this way the *Saṃyukta-āgama* version reinforces the point made in both discourses with respect to the five aggregates

19 For a detailed study see Gethin 1992.

of liberation, namely that Sāriputta's passing away has not resulted in any loss or damage to those aspects of the path and to those qualities and practices that lead one to meditative mastery of the mind and eventually to awakening.

In addition to contrasting the attitudes of the fully awakened Cunda and the trainee Ānanda with respect to the passing away of Sāriputta, the discourse also offers a tool for relating to grief, illustrating self-reliance with the evocative image of an island. The way to become self-reliant and reliant on the Dharma is to be found in the cultivation of the four *satipaṭṭhāna*s. This is the way to become like an island to oneself and at the same time to rely on the Dharma, namely through the practice of mindfulness. Mindfulness enables one to understand as it really is what happens within and around oneself, and also to understand how this relates to the teachings, the Dharma.

In the case of experiencing grief because of the death of a loved one, a central aspect of the teachings to be recollected with mindfulness would be impermanence. Reminding oneself that "life ends in death" or that "what arises ... is of a nature to be destroyed", the sense of a personal loss, even perhaps of some sort of injustice done to oneself, fades away and the very same death can turn from an occasion for grief to an occasion for insight.

Becoming an island by relying on the Dharma in this way one can in turn also become a true support for others who are affected by the loss of those who are dear to them. It is precisely mindfulness that facilitates opening one's heart to the grief of others without going so far as to suffer together with them, simply by holding their sorrow in the open space of one's mind without judgements or reactivity. The simple tool of mindfulness thereby offers a middle-path approach that avoids the two extreme reactions when confronted with grief: searching for some (quite possibly sensual) type of distraction or else immersing oneself in sorrow and pain. Instead one becomes an island to oneself and to others by just remaining aware.

The Buddha's empowering advice to become an island to oneself in this way brings me back to the topic of mindfulness and the four *satipaṭṭhāna*s, which already came to the fore in several discourses as appropriate when facing disease or pain. Be it in relation to disease of the body or dis-ease of the mind through grief and sorrow, the potential of mindfulness is a recurrent theme in the instructions offered in the early discourses.

XV

DYING AND THE DIVINE ABODES

XV.1 INTRODUCTION

With this chapter my exploration shifts from how to deal with grief experienced at the death of others to the qualities required at the actual moment of passing away. In the discourse taken up below, Sāriputta is still alive and engages in compassionate teaching activities, the beneficiary of which is a sick brahmin householder by the name of Dhānañjāni.[1] The episode in question is found in a discourse in the *Madhyama-āgama* and its *Majjhima-nikāya* parallel,[2] the earlier parts of which report that Sāriputta had come to know that Dhānañjāni was engaging in unethical behaviour. This had motivated Sāriputta to come for a visit and give a teaching that resulted in Dhānañjāni changing his behaviour.

The part of the discourse translated below takes place on a later occasion, when Dhānañjāni has fallen ill and is on his deathbed. On being informed of his condition, Sāriputta again comes to visit and deliver a teaching. In this teaching he leads the dying Dhānañjāni through a mental tour of the following realms of existence:[3]

---

1 Dhānañjāni seems to appear only in the present discourse; see Malalasekera 1937/1995: 1159.

2 MN 97 at MN II 184,25 (translated Ñāṇamoli 1995/2005: 791).

3 In MN 97 at MN II 193,25 the first three are realms, the remainder are beings. In MĀ 27 only the first is clearly a realm; in the case of the remainder it remains open to interpretation whether the Chinese character used signifies the *deva*s or their respective realms.

- hell,
- animals,
- ghosts,
- humans,
- heavenly Four Great Kings,
- *deva*s of the Thirty-three,
- Yāmā *deva*s,
- Tusitā *deva*s,
- *deva*s who delight in creating,
- *deva*s who wield power over others' creations,
- Brahmā *deva*s.

As with the existence of *deva*s discussed in Chapter 7, there can be little doubt that for the ancient Indian audience, as well as for the Buddha and his disciples, these various realms and their celestial inhabitants were considered a reality. Acknowledging this as an aspect of the ancient Indian worldview does not mean that one needs to believe in these realms or in these celestial beings in order to benefit from a discourse in which they are described. In early Buddhist thought the external world outside and the internal world of one's own mind are seen as intrinsically interrelated, so much so that a tour through early Buddhist cosmology is at the same time a tour through various types of mental states.[4] This makes it certainly meaningful to approach the description of various realms in the present discourse as illustrations of mental states, as long as this is done without clinging to such an approach as the only correct and valid reading of such descriptions found in ancient texts.

By way of simplification, the first group of three, comprising hell, animals, and ghosts, can be seen as representative of modes of thinking and acting that are below good standards of human ethics and conduct. The group from the heavenly Four Great Kings up to *deva*s who wield power over others' creations is part of what Buddhist cosmology considers the sense-sphere heavens, in which sense pleasures far superior to those available to human beings can be experienced. The last in the list, the Brahmā *deva*s, belong to the heavens of the

---

4 On the close relationship between cosmology and meditation in Buddhist thought see, e.g., Gethin 1997.

form realm, in which sensuality has been at least temporarily left behind, corresponding to the experience of meditative absorption.

XV.2 TRANSLATION[5]

[A monastic said]: "Venerable Sāriputta, the brahmin Dhānañjāni is now sick, quite seriously ill, because of which he might pass away."[6]

Having heard this being said, the venerable Sāriputta took his robe and bowl, left the Southern Mountains and approached Rājagaha. He stayed in the Bamboo Grove, the Squirrels' Feeding Ground.

Then, at daybreak when the night was over, the venerable Sāriputta put on his robe, took his bowl, and approached the house of the brahmin Dhānañjāni. The brahmin Dhānañjāni saw from afar that the venerable Sāriputta was coming. Having seen it, he in turn wanted to get up from his bed.[7] Seeing that the brahmin Dhānañjāni wanted to get up from his bed, the venerable Sāriputta in turn stopped him, saying: "Brahmin Dhānañjāni, do not get up from the bed. There is another bed; I will seat myself separately."

Then the venerable Sāriputta sat on that bed. Being seated, he said: "Dhānañjāni, how is your ailment now? Are you eating and drinking much or little? Is the affliction decreasing and not increasing?"[8]

Dhānañjāni replied: "My ailment is becoming serious. I am not eating or drinking. The affliction is still increasing and I do not experience a decrease. Venerable Sāriputta, it is just as if a

5 The translated part is taken from MĀ 27 at T I 457c22 to 458b14; for a translation of the entire discourse see Bingenheimer et al. 2013: 176–88 and for a comparative study of MN 97 and MĀ 27 Anālayo 2011a: 566–72.

6 Whereas in MĀ 27 an unnamed monastic, on being asked by Sāriputta about Dhānañjāni, provides this information, in MN 97 at MN II 191,34 Dhānañjāni himself sends a messenger to inform the Buddha and Sāriputta about his sick condition and to invite Sāriputta to come for a visit.

7 MN 97 does not report that Dhānañjāni tried to get up.

8 MN 97 reports no enquiry about eating and drinking, nor any indication given in this respect by Dhānañjāni.

strong man were to cleave one's head with a sharp knife, only giving rise to extreme pain. Now my headache is also just like that. Venerable Sāriputta, it is just as if a strong man were to keep tightening a rope around one's head, only giving rise to extreme pain. Now my headache is also just like that.

"Venerable Sāriputta, it is just as if a cow butcher or his son were to cut up the belly of a cow with a sharp knife, only giving rise to extreme pain. Now my stomach ache is also just like that. Venerable Sāriputta, it is just as if two strong men were to take hold of a weak man and roast him over a fire, only giving rise to extreme pain. Now my bodily pains are also just like that, my whole body is giving rise to pain, which is still increasing and not decreasing."[9]

The venerable Sāriputta said: "I will now question you, Dhānañjāni, answer according to your understanding. Brahmin Dhānañjāni, what do you think, what is better, being in hell or being an animal?" Dhānañjāni replied: "Being an animal is better."

[The venerable Sāriputta] asked again: "Dhānañjāni, what is better, being an animal or being a ghost?" Dhānañjāni replied: "Being a ghost is better."

[The venerable Sāriputta] asked again: "Dhānañjāni, what is better, being a ghost compared to being a human?" Dhānañjāni replied: "Being a human is better."

[The venerable Sāriputta] asked again: "Dhānañjāni, what is better, being a human or being [one of] the Four Heavenly Kings?" Dhānañjāni replied: "Being [one of] the Four Heavenly Kings is better."

[The venerable Sāriputta] asked again: "Dhānañjāni, what is better, being [one of] the Four Heavenly Kings or being [one of] the devas of the Thirty-three?" Dhānañjāni replied: "Being [one of] the devas of the Thirty-three is better."

[The venerable Sāriputta] asked again: "Dhānañjāni, what is better, being [one of] the devas of the Thirty-three or being [one of] the Yāmā devas?" Dhānañjāni replied: "Being [one of] the Yāmā devas is better."

---

9 In MN 97 at MN II 193,1 the corresponding first three similes illustrate the violent winds that are affecting Dhānañjāni; the fourth illustrates his fever.

[The venerable Sāriputta] asked again: "Dhānañjāni, what is better, being [one of] the Yāmā devas or being [one of] the Tusitā devas?" Dhānañjāni replied: "Being [one of] the Tusitā devas is better."

[The venerable Sāriputta] asked again: "Dhānañjāni, what is better, being [one of] the Tusitā devas or being [one of] the devas who delight in creating?" Dhānañjāni replied: "Being [one of] the devas who delight in creating is better."

[The venerable Sāriputta] asked again: "Dhānañjāni, what is better, being [one of] the devas who delight in creating or being [one of] the devas [who wield power over] others' creations?" Dhānañjāni replied: "Being [one of] the devas [who wield power over] others' creations is better."

[The venerable Sāriputta] asked again: "Dhānañjāni, what is better, being [one of] the devas [who wield power over] others' creations or being [one of] the Brahmā devas?" Dhānañjāni replied: "Being [one of] the Brahmā devas is supreme, being [one of] the Brahmā devas is supreme."

The venerable Sāriputta said:[10] "Dhānañjāni, the Blessed One who knows and sees, the Tathāgata, free from attachment, fully awakened, has taught four divine abodes. By cultivating these, cultivating them much, one, that is a clansman or a clanswoman, who has removed sensual desires, given up thoughts of sensuality, with the breaking up of the body at death will be born among Brahmā devas.[11] What are the four?

"Dhānañjāni, a learned noble disciple dwells pervading one direction with a mind imbued with mettā, and in the same way the second, third, and fourth directions, the four intermediate directions, above and below, completely and everywhere. Being without mental shackles, resentment, ill will, or contention, with

---

10 MN 97 at MN II 194,26 reports Sāriputta reflecting that, as brahmins aspire to the world of Brahmā, he will teach the brahmin Dhānañjāni the path to companionship with Brahmā.

11 MN 97 does not mention explicitly that these four divine abodes have been taught by the Buddha. Instead of a clansman or clanswoman, or the subsequently mentioned noble disciple, in MN 97 the description of the practice of the divine abodes has a monastic as its subject. Since the instructions are aimed at a lay person, this is a good example of an instance where the usage of the term *bhikkhu* cannot be meant to restrict the instructions to fully ordained male monastics only; see also p. 66 note 1.

a mind imbued with mettā that is supremely vast and great, boundless and well developed, [the noble disciple] dwells pervading the entire world.

"A learned noble disciple dwells pervading one direction with a mind imbued with compassion, *and in the same way the second, third, and fourth directions, the four intermediate directions, above and below, completely and everywhere. Being without mental shackles, resentment, ill will, or contention, with a mind imbued with compassion that is supremely vast and great, boundless and well developed, the noble disciple dwells pervading the entire world.*

"A learned noble disciple dwells pervading one direction with a mind imbued with sympathetic joy, *and in the same way the second, third, and fourth directions, the four intermediate directions, above and below, completely and everywhere. Being without mental shackles, resentment, ill will, or contention, with a mind imbued with sympathetic joy that is supremely vast and great, boundless and well developed, the noble disciple dwells pervading the entire world.*

"A learned noble disciple dwells pervading one direction with a mind imbued with equanimity, and in the same way the second, third, and fourth directions, the four intermediate directions, above and below, completely and everywhere. Being without mental shackles, resentment, ill will, or contention, with a mind imbued with equanimity that is supremely vast and great, boundless and well developed, [the noble disciple] dwells pervading the entire world.

"Dhānañjāni, these are reckoned to be the four divine abodes taught by the Blessed One who knows and sees, the Tathāgata, free from attachment, fully awakened. By cultivating these, cultivating them much, one, that is a clansman or clanswoman, who has removed sensual desires, given up thoughts of sensuality, with the breaking up of the body at death will be born among Brahmā devas."[12]

Then the venerable Sāriputta, having taught Dhānañjāni the teaching on [rebirth among] the Brahmā devas, rose from his seat and left. The venerable Sāriputta went out from Rājagaha

---

12 In his reply to the instruction received, in MN 97 at MN II 195,16 Dhānañjāni asks Sāriputta to pay respect on his behalf at the Buddha's feet.

and, before he had reached the Bamboo Grove, the Squirrels' Feeding Ground, during that interval, the brahmin Dhānañjāni, by cultivating the four divine abodes, removing sensual desires, and giving up thoughts of sensuality, with the breaking up of the body at death was born among Brahmā devas.

XV.3 DISCUSSION

The *Majjhima-nikāya* and *Madhyama-āgama* discourses continue with the Buddha telling Sāriputta that Dhānañjāni could have been led even further. Evidently Sāriputta had not been aware of this and had therefore adjusted his instruction to what the brahmin Dhānañjāni had clearly revealed, namely that the Brahmā world was of supreme attraction for him.[13] This reflects a basic attitude of respecting the patient's wishes and inclinations by trying to accommodate them to the best of one's ability.

The Buddha's comment then can be read as making the point that one should beware of underestimating a dying patient's spiritual potential. Sāriputta had known Dhānañjāni for a long time and perhaps for this reason had not been fully aware of the degree to which the brahmin's mental disposition had changed with the onset of death, so much so that he could have been led to attain a level of awakening. Although Sāriputta did not take maximum advantage of this opportunity, it needs to be kept in mind that without his intervention the brahmin Dhānañjāni would probably not even have been able to reach such a lofty rebirth.

The actual means to his rebirth is the cultivation of the four divine abodes, *brahmavihāra*. These are *mettā*, compassion, sympathetic joy, and equanimity, which I surveyed briefly in Chapter 4. Elsewhere I have discussed in more detail the practice of radiating these four divine abodes.[14] Of particular significance for the present context is the divine or celestial condition of the mind reached through dwelling in these four *brahmavihāra*s. Independent of whether one believes in the

13 Martini 2011: 144 comments that Sāriputta "had given an instruction limited in scope on account of the Brahmins' firm devotion to the (attainment of) the Brahmā-world".

14 Anālayo 2015b: 54–7 and 159f.

existence of celestial realms, as described in early Buddhist cosmology, what in the end counts is learning to cultivate the mind in such a way that heaven on earth manifests within. Such heaven on earth comes into existence based on going beyond and leaving behind sensuality, which is substantially different from the type of attitudes fostered by the divine abodes. Having left sensuality behind, one here and now ascends to heaven simply by dwelling in these four sublime mental attitudes in a boundless manner, without imposing any limit.

As the case of Dhānañjāni shows, such cultivation is in principle possible even when one is seriously sick and in considerable pain. Facing the pain of death in this way can be a powerful approach to cultivating non-attachment. It results in a degree of freedom of the mind that leads one at least temporarily beyond attachment to sensuality and results in a truly divine mode of passing away. Total freedom from attachment, however, requires the cultivation of insight. The impact of insight at the time of one's own death will be a continuing topic in the next chapters.

XVI

DEATHBED INSTRUCTIONS

XVI.1 INTRODUCTION

The discourse in this chapter again features Sāriputta's compassionate teaching activities. Besides Sāriputta, the present episode shares two protagonists with Chapter 9, namely the sick householder Anāthapiṇḍika and Ānanda, who is visiting out of concern for the sick householder, a similarity that exemplifies the close relationship between disease and death. Whereas in the episode in Chapter 9 Anāthapiṇḍika recovers from his disease, in the present instance Anāthapiṇḍika is on his deathbed. As is appropriate in such a situation, Sāriputta gives him a penetrative teaching on insight.

The *Anāthapiṇḍikovāda-sutta* agrees with its parallels in the *Saṃyukta-āgama* and the *Ekottarika-āgama* that, at the end of the insight teaching received from Sāriputta, Anāthapiṇḍika is in tears because he had not received such profound instructions earlier. Elsewhere I have examined this statement in detail, based on a translation of the *Saṃyukta-āgama* version of the present discourse.[1] Although the statement on its own could give the impression that teachings on insight were withheld from the laity, closer inspection of other relevant passages rather shows that the present passage is best understood against

1 Anālayo 2010b.

the background of Anāthapiṇḍika's personality in the way this emerges from other discourses.

As mentioned in Chapter 9, Anāthapiṇḍika had become a stream-enterer during his first meeting with the Buddha and thus was on safe ground from the viewpoint of early Buddhist soteriology. Other discourses give the impression that he had little interest in teachings on insight and the practice of meditation. He apparently found his satisfaction in acting as a donor, reflected also in the name Anāthapiṇḍika, "Feeder of the Destitute", which he had acquired even before becoming a Buddhist.

A discourse in the *Aṅguttara-nikāya* and its parallels in the *Saṃyukta-āgama* and in Tibetan translation report the Buddha telling Anāthapiṇḍika that, in addition to supporting monastics, he should also develop the bliss of meditation.[2] This conveys the impression that to engage in meditation was not his natural inclination. In another discourse in the *Aṅguttara-nikāya* and its parallels the Buddha recommends to Anāthapiṇḍika the cultivation of insight as being more fruitful than providing the Buddha and his monastics with food and lodging.[3] This shows the Buddha trying to make Anāthapiṇḍika realize that he should not rest content with mere giving, but should also develop insight.

Such passages give the impression that the case of Anāthapiṇḍika does not reflect any partiality in the dispensation of liberating teachings. In fact the discourse given to Mānadiṇṇa, translated in Chapter 8, makes it quite evident that lay disciples must have received teachings on insight, otherwise he could hardly have become a non-returner. The same is even more evident in the case of the lay disciple Citta, to be taken up in Chapter 22, who had even become an outstanding teacher

---

2 AN 5.176 at AN III 207,1 (translated Bodhi 2012: 789) and its parallels SĀ 482 at T II 123a6 and D 4094 *nyu* 73b3 or Q 5595 *thu* 118a8.

3 In AN 9.20 at AN IV 396,1 (translated Bodhi 2012: 1277) the recommendation is to cultivate awareness of impermanence, which two parallels, MĀ 155 at T I 678a4 and T 73 at T I 879c16, combine with awareness of the other two characteristics. Another parallel, D 4094 *ju* 172a1 or Q 5595 *tu* 198a3, combines impermanence with dispassion, cessation, and disappearance. Two more parallels, T 72 at T I 878c26 and EĀ 27.3 at T II 645a6, recommend the absence of delighting in the whole world. Yet another parallel, T 74 at T I 882a10, mentions signlessness. All of these topics are of course closely related to liberating insight.

of the Dharma himself. The present instance does imply, however, that insight was not forced on those who showed themselves unreceptive to it. On the present occasion of being on his deathbed, Anāthapiṇḍika has apparently become more receptive to such teachings than he was earlier.

Below I translate the first part of the *Ekottarika-āgama* account of what precedes Anāthapiṇḍika's passing away, which has a parallel in the *Anāthapiṇḍikovāda-sutta* of the *Majjhima-nikāya*, as well as in the *Saṃyukta-āgama*.[4]

XVI.2 TRANSLATION[5]

Thus have I heard. At one time the Buddha was staying at Sāvatthī in Jeta's Grove, Anāthapiṇḍika's Park. At that time the householder Anāthapiṇḍika's body had become seriously sick.

Then, with his purified divine eye that is free from contaminations, Sāriputta saw that the householder Anāthapiṇḍika's body had become seriously sick.[6] He looked for Ānanda and told him: "Come with me to enquire about the householder Anāthapiṇḍika's [condition]." Then Ānanda replied: "You know that this is the right time."

Then, when the time had come, [Sāriputta] and Ānanda put on their robes,[7] took their bowls, and entered Sāvatthī to beg for food, gradually approaching the house of the householder Anāthapiṇḍika. They in turn sat down. Then, being seated, Sāriputta said to the householder Anāthapiṇḍika:

"Is your disease now increasing or decreasing? Do you experience gradually becoming free from the pain of the disease, without it increasing in severity?"

---

4 MN 143 at MN III 258,1 (translated Ñāṇamoli 1995/2005: 1109) and SĀ 1032 at T II 269c8 (translated Anālayo 2010b); for a comparative study see also Anālayo 2011a: 821–5.

5 The translated part is taken from EĀ 51.8 at T II 819b11 to 819c13.

6 In MN 143 at MN III 258,2 Anāthapiṇḍika sends a messenger to inform Sāriputta of his condition and invite him for a visit; according to SĀ 1032 at T II 269c9 Sāriputta had heard of Anāthapiṇḍika's condition. None of the parallel versions brings in the divine eye.

7 The translation is based on adopting a variant that adds a reference to "putting on robes", which is usually part of the standard description of getting ready to beg for food.

The householder Anāthapiṇḍika replied: "My affliction is now extreme and there is little to rely on. I experience an increase, I do not experience a decrease."[8]

Sāriputta replied: "Now householder, you should recollect the Buddha, that is, the Tathāgata, who is an arahant, fully awakened, endowed with knowledge and conduct, well-gone, knower of the worlds, an unsurpassable person, a charioteer of the path of Dharma,[9] a teacher of devas and men, called a Buddha, a Blessed One.[10]

"You should also recall and recollect the Dharma, the Tathāgata's Dharma which is extremely profound, to be respected and to be praised, beyond comparison, and cultivated by noble ones.

"You should also recollect the Community, the Community of the Tathāgata, where seniors and juniors are harmonious and do not quarrel,[11] the noble Community that is accomplished in all qualities, being accomplished in virtue, accomplished in concentration, accomplished in wisdom, accomplished in liberation, accomplished in ⟨knowledge⟩ and vision of liberation,[12] namely the Community of the four pairs and the eight persons. This is called the noble Community of the Tathāgata that is to be respected and to be praised, it is a supreme field of merit in the world.

"Householder, if you cultivate recollection of the Buddha, recollection of the Dharma, and recollection of the ⟨noble⟩

---

8 In MN 143 at MN III 259,9 and SĀ 1032 at T II 269c14 Anāthapiṇḍika illustrates his sick condition with the standard set of similes (both discourses abbreviate).

9 The expression "an unsurpassable person, a charioteer of the path of Dharma" is a translation error regularly occurring in Chinese texts of what in the original would have been the expression "unsurpassable leader of persons to be tamed"; see Minh Chau 1964/1991: 326 and Nattier 2003: 227.

10 MN 143 and SĀ 1032 do not report any instruction on recollection of the Buddha, the Dharma, and the Community.

11 The reference to the absence of quarrel is specific to the present version of recollection of the Community and usually not found in descriptions in the early discourses of the qualities of the noble Community.

12 The translation is based on adopting a variant that adds "liberation" and on emending a reference to "wisdom" to read "knowledge".

Community,[13] your merit will be beyond calculation, [enabling] the gaining of the deathless taste of the sphere of cessation.[14]

"If a clansman or clanswoman has recollected these three, which are worthy of respect, the Buddha, the Dharma, and the noble Community, it is certainly impossible that they could fall into the three evil destinies.[15] If a clansman or clanswoman cultivates recollection of these three, which are worthy of respect, they will certainly afterwards ascend to a good realm among devas or men.

"Householder do not cling to forms and do not cling to consciousness in dependence on forms,[16] do not cling to sounds and do not cling to consciousness in dependence on sounds, do not cling to odours and do not cling to consciousness in dependence on odours, do not cling to tastes and do not cling to consciousness in dependence on tastes, do not cling to tangibles and do not cling to consciousness in dependence on tangibles, do not cling to mental [objects] and do not cling to consciousness in dependence on mental [objects].[17]

"Do not cling to this world or the next world, and do not cling to consciousness in dependence on this world or the next world.[18] Do not cling to craving and do not cling to consciousness in dependence on craving. The reason is that in dependence on craving there is clinging, in dependence on clinging there is becoming, in dependence on becoming there is birth, and in dependence on birth there is death,[19] worry, grief, pain, and vexation beyond calculation."[20]

---

13 The expression "noble" is an emendation of what in the original text reads "monastic". This does not fit the context, since the monastic Community is the object of taking refuge, not the object of recollection; see in more detail Anālayo 2015b: 84f.

14 The translation is based on adopting a variant that adds "taste".

15 Since Anāthapiṇḍika was a stream-enterer, he was anyway beyond rebirth in the three "evil destinies".

16 Regarding the translation "do not cling" see p. 86 note 13.

17 The need to avoid clinging to any of the six senses is the topic with which Sāriputta begins his instructions in MN 143 at MN III 259,12 and SĀ 1032 at T II 269c16; in MN 143 this leads on to a detailed analysis of experience through the six sense-doors.

18 MN 143 at MN III 261,4 also mentions the need to avoid clinging to this world and the next world, which is not taken up in SĀ 1032.

19 The translation is based on adopting a variant that adds "in dependence on birth there is".

20 This last part does not have a parallel in MN 143 or SĀ 1032.

XVI.3 DISCUSSION

The instructions in the *Ekottarika-āgama* discourse next bring in the five aggregates and then apply the law of dependent arising to each of the six sense-doors, an exposition without a counterpart in the other versions. The other versions also have no counterpart to the beginning of the instructions delivered by Sāriputta in the *Ekottarika-āgama* discourse regarding recollection of the Buddha, the Dharma, and the Community.

The description of this recollection in the *Ekottarika-āgama* version offers further details regarding the objects of the first three limbs of stream-entry mentioned in Chapter 9, the three jewels. The first of these is the Buddha, described with a standard series of epithets that throw into relief the qualities of one who is fully awakened and acts as a compassionate teacher. In the case of the Dharma, its profound and respect-inspiring qualities come together with it being what noble ones cultivate. These make up the noble Community, qualified as accomplished in the five qualities of virtue, concentration, wisdom, liberation, and the knowledge and vision of being liberated (corresponding to the five aggregates of liberation mentioned in Chapter 14).

Of further interest is the mention of "the four pairs and the eight persons" in the description of the noble Community, a reference found similarly in such descriptions in other early discourses.[21] The eight persons that make up the four pairs are those on the path to one of the four levels of awakening and those who have reached one of these four levels.

The *Dakkhiṇāvibhaṅga-sutta* and its parallels list those who are on the way to the realization of one of the levels of awakening among different recipients of gifts.[22] In line with later notions of the path as consisting of a single mind-moment on the brink of awakening, the Pāli commentary on this passage reasons that someone may attain the path just as he or she is about to receive

21 See, e.g., AN 5.179 at AN III 212,26 (translated Bodhi 2012: 793) and its parallel MĀ 128 at T I 616c26.

22 MN 142 at MN III 254,28 (translated Ñāṇamoli 1995/2005: 1103) and its parallels MĀ 180 at T I 722b14, T 84 at T I 903c27, D 4094 *ju* 255b2 or Q 5595 *tu* 291a2, a Tocharian fragment, Ji et al. 1998: 182, and an Uighur fragment, Geng and Klimkeit 1988: 202.

offerings.[23] This seems contrived and it can safely be assumed that the *Dakkhiṇāvibhaṅga-sutta* and its parallels would not have allotted a special place to those on the way to the realization of a particular level of awakening, alongside those who have already reached it, if this were to designate only those whose breakthrough to liberation happens to take place precisely at the moment they are receiving a gift.[24]

From the viewpoint of the early discourses, the notion of being on the path to a particular level of awakening does not refer to a momentary event that occurs just before the actual attainment, but rather has a prolonged period of practice in view that will eventually culminate in realizing the corresponding level of awakening. This in turn implies that the noble Community comprises not only those who have realized stream-entry or are right on the brink of such attainment, but also those who seriously practise for such attainment. These, too, are part of one of the three jewels and worthy of recollection. This makes it easier to implement this form of recollection. One need not overly concern oneself with who has indeed reached at least the first of the four levels of awakening; instead one can simply recollect those who seriously practise the path to awakening.

Turning to the actual insight instruction found similarly in the three versions, the teaching given by Sāriputta focuses on the need to avoid clinging to any aspect of experience by way of the six sense-doors. This is precisely what the time of approaching death requires above all: letting go of any clinging. This perhaps most salient point to emerge from the present discourse will be a recurring topic in subsequent chapters of my exploration. In the present case, the three versions confirm that this instruction was given at a time when death was close, as the householder Anāthapiṇḍika passed away soon after having received Sāriputta's penetrative instructions.

Besides throwing into relief the importance of non-attachment at the time of passing away, a more specific point made by the present discourse, if read keeping in mind the information offered in other discourses about Anāthapiṇḍika, is that someone might be capable of opening up to deeper insight

23 Ps V 72,15.
24 See also Gethin 1992: 131f and Bodhi 2012: 68–70.

only at the time of death. In conjunction with the discourse studied in the last chapter, this suggests the need for those who are in the presence of someone close to death to be mindful of the patient's mental attitude, keeping an eye out for signs of a mental opening up. It is precisely when death draws near that patients might finally muster the courage to face what they have so far tried to avoid at all costs.

XVII

NON-ATTACHMENT AND TERMINAL DISEASE

XVII.1 INTRODUCTION

This chapter features another lay disciple who on the verge of death receives instructions. This time the Buddha himself, on hearing about the condition of the sick lay disciple, out of compassion comes to visit and give instructions. The present discourse, found in the *Saṃyukta-āgama* and in the *Saṃyutta-nikāya*, has two lay protagonists.[1] These are the sick householder Dīghāvu and his father, the householder Jotika.

The instructions delivered by the Buddha to Dīghāvu combine the four limbs of stream-entry with instructions on insight, in particular on six types of perception. Besides the insight instructions given by the Buddha on this occasion, the present discourse also addresses the issue of family relationships at the time of approaching death. Here the householder Jotika embodies the proper attitude when facing the fact that his son is terminally ill and about to pass away.

1 SN 55.3 at SN V 344,8 (translated Bodhi 2000: 1790). The two lay protagonists Dīghāvu and Jotika seem to feature only on this occasion, so that no further information appears to be available; see Malalasekera 1937/1995: 1085 and 970 (no. 2), who distinguishes the Jotika of the present discourse from the treasurer of Rājagaha by the name Jotika.

XVII.2 TRANSLATION[2]

Thus have I heard. At one time the Buddha was staying at Rājagaha in the Bamboo Grove, the Squirrels' Feeding Ground. Then the body of the young man Dīghāvu, the son of the householder Jotika, had fallen seriously sick.

Then the Blessed One, hearing that the body of the young man Dīghāvu had fallen seriously sick,[3] put on his robe in the morning and took his bowl to enter the town of Rājagaha to beg for food. He gradually approached the house of the young man Dīghāvu. When the young man Dīghāvu saw from afar the Blessed One, he wanted to get up, supporting himself on the bed.[4]

Having seen it, the Buddha said to him: "Householder, do not get up, your affliction will increase." The Buddha sat down and said to the young man Dīghāvu: "How is it, Dīghāvu, is the disease bearable? Is the affliction of the body increasing or is it decreasing?"

The young man Dīghāvu said to the Buddha: "I have not recovered from the illness and my body is not at ease; the pains keep increasing and there is no relief. It is just as if many strong men were to take hold of a weak man, put a rope around his head and with both hands pull it tight, so that he is in extreme pain. My pain now exceeds that.

"It is just as if a cow butcher with a sharp knife were to cut open a living cow's belly to take its internal organs. How could that cow endure the pains in its belly? My belly is now more painful than that cow's.

"It is just as if two strong men were to grab one weak person and hang him over a fire, roasting both his feet. The heat of both my feet now exceeds that.[5] The pain of the disease is still increasing and not decreasing."

[The Buddha said]: "Young man [Dīghāvu], you should therefore train yourself like this: 'I have unshakeable faith in the Buddha, *unshakeable faith* in the Dharma, unshakeable faith

2 The translated discourse is SĀ 1034 at T II 270a18 to 270b14.

3 In SN 55.3 at SN V 344,14 Dīghāvu sends his father Jotika to inform the Buddha of his situation.

4 SĀ 1034 here gives the same indication as SĀ 1031 (translated above p. 75) that the remainder of the introductory narration should be supplemented from the discourse by Khemaka.

5 In SN 55.3 Dīghāvu does not employ any similes to illustrate his sick condition.

in the Community, and I am accomplished in noble virtue.'[6] You should train yourself like this."[7]

The young man [Dīghāvu] said to the Buddha: "Blessed One, I am now in possession of all of the four types of unshakeable faith, as declared by the Blessed One. I constantly have unshakeable faith in the Buddha, *unshakeable faith* in the Dharma, unshakeable faith in the Community, and I am accomplished in noble virtue."

The Buddha said to the young man [Dīghāvu]: "Relying on the four types of unshakeable faith, you should further cultivate six perceptions that partake of knowledge. What are the six? That is, the perception of impermanence in all formations, the perception of *dukkha* in what is impermanent, the perception of not-self in what is *dukkha*, the perception of contemplating the nutriments,[8] the perception of not delighting in the whole world, and the perception of death."[9]

The young man [Dīghāvu] said to the Buddha: "[Blessed One], I am now in possession of all of the six perceptions that partake of knowledge, cultivated by relying on the four types of unshakeable faith, as declared by the Blessed One. Yet I have this thought: 'After my death, I do not know: how will it be for my father, the householder Jotika?'"

Then the householder Jotika said to the young man Dīghāvu: "For the time being stop thinking of looking after me.[10] Now just listen to the Blessed One teaching the Dharma, pay attention to it, and keep it in mind, so that you can gain for a long time benefit, peace, happiness, and welfare."[11]

Then the young man Dīghāvu said: "I shall practise the perception of impermanence in all formations, the perception of

6 SN 55.3 additionally offers a description of the qualities of each of the three jewels and qualifies noble virtue as conducive to concentration.

7 I take it that this injunction is meant to encourage recollection of these four limbs of stream-entry; that is, the passage would not imply that the Buddha was unaware of Dīghāvu's possession of these qualities.

8 This reference most likely refers to the four nutriments of food, contact, intention, and consciousness. These are described, e.g., in SN 12.63 at SN II 98,1 (translated Bodhi 2000: 597) and its parallel SĀ 373 at T II 102b18, together with a set of stark similes illustrating their nature.

9 The last three perceptions differ in SN 55.3 at SN V 345,25, which instead lists the perceptions of abandoning, dispassion, and cessation.

10 The translation "looking after" is based on a variant reading.

11 SN 55.3 does not mention the gaining of benefit, etc., although the same is clearly implicit.

> *dukkha* in what is impermanent, the perception of not-self in what is *dukkha*, the perception of contemplating the nutriments, the perception of not delighting in the whole world, and the perception of death, constantly keeping them in front of me."
>
> The Buddha said to the young man [Dīghāvu]: "You have now yourself declared the fruit of once-return."[12]
>
> The young man Dīghāvu said to the Buddha: "Blessed One, may the Blessed One stay here and take food in our house."[13] Then the Blessed One accepted the invitation by [remaining] silent.
>
> Various types of clean and delicious food and drink were promptly prepared and respectfully offered [on behalf of] the young man Dīghāvu. The meal being over, the Blessed One further taught the Dharma in various ways to the young man [Dīghāvu]. Having instructed, taught, illuminated, and delighted [the young man Dīghāvu], he rose from his seat and left.

XVII.3 DISCUSSION

Whereas the *Saṃyukta-āgama* discourse stops at this point, the *Saṃyutta-nikāya* parallel reports what happened after the Buddha had left. It proceeds as follows:[14]

> Then the lay disciple Dīghāvu passed away not long after the Blessed One had left. Then many monastics approached the Blessed One. Having approached and paid respect to the Blessed One, they sat to one side.
>
> Sitting to one side those monastics said to the Blessed One: "Venerable sir, the lay disciple called Dīghāvu, whom the Blessed One instructed with a brief instruction, has passed away. What is his destination? What is his future lot?"
>
> [The Buddha said]: "Monastics, the lay disciple Dīghāvu was

---

12 It is not clear how the mere statement of being determined to practise the six perceptions could function as a declaration of the attainment of the second level of awakening. In SN 55.3 the Buddha only declares his level of attainment after he has passed away, by which time he had become a non-returner.

13 SN 55.3 does not report any invitation for food etc.

14 The translated part is taken from SN 55.3 at SN V 346,6 to 346,19.

wise, he practised in accordance with the Dharma and did not trouble me on account of the Dharma.[15] Monastics, through the destruction of the five lower fetters the lay disciple Dīghāvu is of spontaneous birth and will attain final Nirvāṇa there, without returning from that world."

In this way in the Pāli version the insight instructions given by the Buddha result in the sick Dīghāvu being able to let go of his worries about his father and reaching non-return. Besides the differing conclusions, another difference between the two versions concerns the six perceptions that the Buddha taught to Dīghāvu. The *Saṃyutta-nikāya* differs on the last three, which in its presentation are:

- perception of abandoning,
- perception of dispassion,
- perception of cessation.

The same perceptions, in the same sequence, are part of the meditative programme delineated in the *Girimānanda-sutta*, introduced in Chapter 12 and to be discussed further in the conclusion.

The first three perceptions, common to the two versions of the present discourse, correspond to the three characteristics, a fundamental insight teaching in early Buddhist thought. The three perceptions are:

- perception of impermanence in all formations,
- perception of *dukkha* in what is impermanent,
- perception of not-self in what is *dukkha*.

These three perceptions reflect a basic pattern in the cultivation of liberating insight.[16] The foundation to be laid is clear and continuous awareness of the fact that all formations, *saṅkhāra*, without exception, are of a changing nature. Next

---

15 In the Siamese edition of SN 55.3 the Buddha instead qualifies Dīghāvu as a speaker of truth; the same edition also does not have the term "me" in the reference to troubling on account of the Dharma, which is also not found in the PTS edition, but occurs only in the Burmese and Ceylonese editions.

16 For a more detailed discussion of this pattern see Anālayo 2012c: 43–8.

comes the insight that what is impermanent cannot yield lasting satisfaction; therefore it must be unsatisfactory, *dukkha*. What is unsatisfactory and bound to change is in turn not fit to be regarded as one's self, which by definition would have to be permanent in order to deserve being reckoned one's "self" (according to conceptions of a self in the ancient Indian setting). This insight leads to the perception of not-self, *anattā*. It is precisely the freedom of attachment that comes from realizing *dukkha* which fuels progress in deepening the realization of not-self.

In practical terms, cultivating these three perceptions starts with attending to all aspects of one's present experience as a process, as something that changes. Once perception of impermanence is well established in this way, one keeps attending to the same changing process of experience with an attitude of dissatisfaction and disenchantment. Still aware of the same impermanent process, one then cultivates the willingness to let go of patterns of identification with and appropriation of any aspect of what is experienced.

Based on this basic pattern for the cultivation of insight, instead of proceeding with abandoning, dispassion, and cessation, the *Saṃyukta-āgama* version translated above lists the following three perceptions:

- perception of contemplating the nutriments,
- perception of not delighting in the whole world,
- perception of death.

The first of these three, the perception of contemplating the nutriments, most likely refers to the four nutriments:

- food,
- contact,
- intention,
- consciousness.

The teaching on the nutriments reveals the way these four nourish the continuity of existence and serve as its essential conditions.[17] Food provides nourishment for the body;

17 On the four nutriments see in more detail Nyanaponika 1967/1981.

contact nourishes feeling. Just as the stimulation of physical hunger results in the search for food, so mental hunger for stimulation results in the search for contact. Intention is a central nourishment from the viewpoint of the early Buddhist doctrine of karma, representing the conditioning influence of intentional deeds on what and who one is and will become through the mediating force of one's plans and aspirations. Finally the desire for experience as such is how consciousness comes to nourish the continuity of existence.

Contemplation of these four nutriments and the way they nourish and thereby condition the continuity of one's own existence can result in a powerful "perception that partakes of knowledge", in the sense of revealing the degree to which one's very being depends on the input provided by these nutriments.

The other two perceptions in the *Saṃyukta-āgama* version are the perception of not delighting in the whole world and the perception of death. The first of these already came up in Chapter 12 as part of the instructions to Girimānanda and will be discussed further in the conclusion. In the present context it forms a natural continuation from contemplation of the four nutriments, which is precisely meant to undermine one's delight in existence. Next comes recognition of one's own mortality through the perception of death, a topic to which I return in more detail in Chapter 24.

As mentioned in the introduction to this chapter, a specific contribution made by the present discourse is to touch on the subject of family relationships at the time of approaching death. Jotika selflessly tries to ensure that his son Dīghāvu makes best use of this precious opportunity to progress in insight and non-attachment in the Buddha's presence. In fact the qualities and meditative perceptions mentioned by the Buddha are familiar terrain for Dīghāvu. Yet it seems as if worry about his father had prevented him from giving wholehearted attention to them. Jotika's attitude in this situation is exemplary of the way one should handle the impending death of someone whom one holds dear. The chief aim should be to encourage the dying person to let go of concerns and worries, instead of living out one's own attachments. In this way, in line with the central import of the instructions given by the Buddha to Dīghāvu,

Jotika himself practises and at the same time encourages his own son in the one thing that matters most when facing death: non-attachment.

XVIII

ADVICE ON PALLIATIVE CARE

XVIII.1 INTRODUCTION

This chapter continues with the topic of non-attachment at the time of impending death, in particular towards those who are close and dear. The discourse in question presents instructions on palliative care given by the Buddha at the request of a Sakyan lay disciple.

The discourse takes place on an occasion when the Buddha is visiting his home country. The Buddha's presence affords his Sakyan lay disciples the opportunity to associate regularly with him and his monastic disciples. Aware of the fact that he will be leaving them again to resume his wandering lifestyle, the Sakyan lay disciples come to the Buddha in order to have one particular question clarified. This question is an expression of their compassionate concern, as they want to make sure they know how to care properly for the sick and dying. Receiving instructions on this topic from the Buddha will help to ensure that, once the Buddha and his monastic disciples have set out travelling again, the Sakyan lay disciples will have a basic guideline to follow in order to attend to the best of their ability to anyone who falls seriously sick and is about to pass away.

The *Saṃyukta-āgama* discourse translated below has a parallel in the *Saṃyutta-nikāya*.[1] The protagonist in the *Saṃyutta-*

---

1 SN 55.54 at SN V 408,6 (translated Bodhi 2000: 1834).

nikāya version is a single Sakyan lay disciple by the name of Mahānāma, whereas the *Saṃyukta-āgama* discourse instead features a group of Sakyan lay disciples whose leader is called Nandiya.[2]

XVIII.2 TRANSLATION[3]

Thus have I heard. At one time the Buddha was dwelling at Kapilavatthu in Nigrodha's Park. Then a group of many Sakyans had come together in the communal hall for discussion. Their discussion went in such a way that some Sakyans then said to the Sakyan Nandiya:[4]

"There are times when we get to approach the Buddha and respectfully make offerings; there are times when we do not get to do this. There are times when we get to associate with and make offerings to the monastics with whom we are acquainted; there are times when we do not get to do this.[5] Furthermore we do not know: how should a wise lay disciple instruct another wise male lay disciple or a wise female lay disciple who is sick and subject to pain, how to instruct them and teach them the Dharma?[6] We should now together approach the Blessed One and ask him about this matter. As the Blessed One instructs us, so we will respectfully receive it."

Then Nandiya together with the Sakyans approached the Buddha. They paid respect at his feet and withdrew to stand to one side. [Nandiya] said to the Buddha: "Blessed One, we Sakyans came together in the communal hall for discussion. Our discussion went in such a way that some Sakyans said to me:

2 On Mahānāma and Nandiya see Malalasekera 1938/1998: 514f (no. 3) and 27 (no. 2).

3 The translated discourse is SĀ 1122 at T II 297c29 to 298b13.

4 Instead of recording a meeting of the Sakyans, SN 55.54 at SN V 408,8 reports that the male monastics were making new robes for the Buddha in the expectation that he would soon set out travelling again, which then motivated the lay disciple Mahānāma to approach the Buddha.

5 SN 55.54 does not draw attention to the irregularity of access to the Buddha and his monastic disciples, although the same is implicit in its indication that the Buddha would soon go travelling again.

6 SN 55.54 at SN V 408,22 explicitly mentions only a male lay disciple being sick, although it can safely be taken for granted that the instruction similarly applies to the case of a female lay disciple who is sick.

"'Nandiya, sometimes we meet the Tathāgata and respectfully make offerings; sometimes we do not meet him. Sometimes we approach and meet the monastics with whom we are acquainted, associate with and make offerings to them; sometimes we do not get to do this. *Furthermore we do not know how a wise lay disciple should instruct another wise male lay disciple or a wise female lay disciple who is sick and subject to pain, how to instruct them and teach them the Dharma. We should now together approach the Blessed One and ask him about this matter.* As the Buddha instructs us, so we will respectfully receive it.'

"Now we ask this question from the Blessed One: How should a wise lay disciple instruct another wise male lay disciple or a wise female lay disciple who is sick and subject to pain, how to instruct them and teach them the Dharma?"

The Buddha said to Nandiya: "Suppose a wise lay disciple were to approach another wise male lay disciple or a wise female lay disciple who is sick and subject to pain. [The wise lay disciple] should guide them in relation to the three occasions for consolation, saying: 'Friend, you should be accomplished in unshakeable confidence in the Buddha, *unshakeable confidence* in the Dharma, and unshakeable confidence in the Community.'[7]

"Having guided them in relation to the three occasions for consolation, one should further ask: 'Are you emotionally attached to your mother and father?' If they are emotionally attached to their mother and father, they should be taught to let go and should be told: 'If by being emotionally attached to your mother and father you could stay alive, such emotional attachment would be acceptable. Since you will not stay alive because of being emotionally attached, what use is it to be emotionally attached?'[8]

---

7 SN 55.54 at SN V 408,29 also mentions noble virtue as a fourth consolation, *assāsa*. Its presentation also has a more affirmative character, in the sense of assuring the sick that they have these types of consolation, whereas SĀ 1122 conveys more the sense that the sick should be encouraged in recollecting their being accomplished in these types of consolation.

8 The instruction in SN 55.54 at SN V 409,6 is that one will anyway die, whether one is attached to one's parents or not, hence one should give up one's attachment.

"If they say that they are no [longer] emotionally attached to their mother and father, one should praise them and rejoice in it.[9] Then one should ask them further: 'Do you have thoughts of attachment to your ⟨partner⟩ and children,[10] your servants, your wealth and possessions?[11] If they say that they have thoughts of attachment to them, they should be taught to let go *and should be told: 'If by having thoughts of attachment to your ⟨partner⟩ and children, your servants, your wealth and possessions you could stay alive, such thoughts of attachment would be acceptable. Since you will not stay alive because of having thoughts of attachment, what use is it to have thoughts of attachment?'*

"If they say that they no [longer] have thoughts of attachment to *their ⟨partner⟩ and children, their servants, their wealth and possessions*, one should praise them and rejoice in it. Then one should ask them further: 'Do you have thoughts of attachment to the five types of human sensual pleasure?' If they say that they have thoughts of attachment to *the five types of human sensual pleasure*, they should be told: 'The five types of human sensual pleasure are foul, impure, and corrupting, a stinky place, inferior to the five types of sublime celestial sense pleasure.' They should be taught to let go of the five types of human sensual pleasure and be taught to aspire to the five types of celestial sense pleasure.[12]

"If they in turn say that their mind has already become far removed from their earlier thoughts of attachment to the five types of human sensual pleasure [and that they aspire for] the

---

9 Here and below SN 55.54 does not mention that one should praise the sick for letting go of their attachment and rejoice in it.

10 The text speaks of one's "wife", which only fits the case of male lay disciples who are sick. Since the discourse earlier explicitly mentioned that the instruction should be applicable also to female lay disciples, I have employed the expression "partner" in order for it to become gender-neutral.

11 SN 55.54 at SN V 409,12 only mentions wife and children.

12 Instead of the celestial sense pleasures in general, SN 55.54 at SN V 409,25 takes up the same topic in more detail with additional steps that proceed through the various realms of the sense-sphere heavens recognized in early Buddhist cosmology, namely the heavenly Four Great Kings, the *deva*s of the Thirty-three, the Yāma *deva*s, the Tusitā *deva*s, the *deva*s who delight in creating, and the *deva*s who wield power over others' creations.

five types of sublime celestial sense pleasure, one should praise them and rejoice in it. Then one should tell them further: 'The sublime celestial sense pleasures are impermanent, *dukkha*, and empty, they are of a nature to change.[13] The [pleasures] of the *deva*s of [the realm] of form are superior to the five celestial sense pleasures.'

"If they in turn say that they have let go of thoughts of attachment to celestial sense pleasures and have [instead] thoughts of attachment to the superior pleasures of the form realm, one should praise them and rejoice in it. Then one should instruct them further: 'The pleasures of the form realm are also impermanent and of a nature to change. The cessation of formations, Nirvāṇa, is the joy of renunciation. You should relinquish thoughts of attachment to the form realm and delight in the peace of Nirvāṇa, delight in what is the highest, what is supreme.' [If] noble disciples have already been able to relinquish thoughts of attachment to the form realm and delight in Nirvāṇa, one should praise them and rejoice in it.[14]

"Nandiya, in this way a noble disciple has been instructed and guided step by step to attain the absence of clinging and Nirvāṇa,[15] which is just as if a monastic has been liberated for a hundred years [by attaining] Nirvāṇa."[16]

When the Buddha had spoken this discourse, hearing what the Buddha had said the Sakyans and Nandiya rejoiced in it and were delighted. They paid homage and left.

---

13 SN 55.54 at SN V 410,16 introduces a comparable insight reflection only in relation to the Brahmā world (which is the counterpart to the form realm in SĀ 1122).

14 SN 55.54 at SN V 410,18 contrasts the impermanence of the Brahmā world to the cessation of personality.

15 The part translated as "absence of clinging" would more literally be "not giving rise to", which patently fails to make sense in the present context. This confirms, as already mentioned above, p. 86 note 13, that the underlying Indic original would have referred to the absence of clinging, a reference that was then misunderstood by the Chinese translator due to the similarity between the two terms *uppāda*, "arising", and *upādāna*, "clinging".

16 The implications of this reference in SĀ 1122 become clearer on consulting the counterpart in SN 55.54 at SN V 410,21, which proclaims that there is no difference between the liberation reached by a lay disciple at this juncture and that of a monastic whose mind has been liberated for a hundred years.

XVIII.3 DISCUSSION

When one is on the verge of death, there can be no excuse for continuing with attachment and clinging. Or, according to the reasoning proposed in the *Saṃyutta-nikāya* parallel, whether one is attached or not, one will die anyway. Therefore one should let go of one's attachments. This reflects the proper attitude that emerged also from the discourse in the previous chapter on the householder Dīghāvu and his father Jotika, as well as from the instructions to the dying Anāthapiṇḍika in Chapter 16.

The present discourse continues with the theme of celestial sense pleasures, already broached in Chapter 15. These pleasures are treated in more detail in the *Saṃyutta-nikāya* version by proceeding through the different realms also mentioned in the instruction given by Sāriputta to the brahmin Dhānañjāni in Chapter 15, up to the pleasures of the form realm or Brahmā world.

Instructions of the type given also in the present discourse involve a gradual refinement of the basic drive for happiness. In the context of the gradual path of training for a monastic, such gradual refinement proceeds from the happiness of blamelessness due to virtuous conduct to the happiness of contentment and sense-restraint. Based on these one then experiences the happiness of deepening concentration experiences until eventually the happiness of liberation is reached.[17] In the present instance the same basic principle is applied to the case of a sick lay disciple, in the form of a guided meditation that through a step-by-step diminishing of attachments leads onwards to ever more refined types of happiness.

In a modern-day situation such a guided meditation would need to be adjusted to those who are unfamiliar with these celestial realms, so as to find a way of leading the mind of the patient gradually from what is gross to what is refined, and eventually all the way to total freedom from attachments, in whatever way best suits the character, inclinations, and beliefs of the patient. The basic pattern on which to model such adjustment would be to proceed gradually from whatever attachment manifests for the patient at that time to increasing

17 For a more detailed discussion see Anālayo 2007b.

degrees of non-attachment, facilitating whatever degree of letting go at that time is possible for the patient.

The gradual procedure of a refinement of the basic drive for happiness becomes particularly evident in the injunction found in the *Saṃyukta-āgama* version translated above, according to which each time the patients have let go of what is gross and settled on something more refined one "should praise them and rejoice in it". In this way the patients receive continuous support in the quest to implement this gradual refinement of happiness, until eventually they become able to let go completely and arrive at a very high level of freedom from attachments, precisely by following this gradual approach.

Besides providing this basic directive for Buddhist palliative care, the present discourse also highlights the potential of the time of approaching death in leading to a degree of liberation that earlier would not have been possible in this way. As the final part of both discourses explicitly proclaims, the time of death can be an occasion for a lay disciple to progress to the same level of liberation as that gained by an accomplished monastic through gradual cultivation a long time ago. Such remarkable progress takes place simply by allowing the implications of impending death to transform and liberate the mind.

The transformative impact that death can have on one's mind, a transformation that ideally has been cultivated well before the moment comes when one is about to expire, has been expressed by Reynolds in the following manner:

> Death continues to function as a limit that calls into question the value of all of the satisfactions and pleasures that can be realized within this-worldly existence ... for those who truly understand ... the painful implications of death's continuing recurrence in the ongoing process of life, death, rebirth, and redeath, the only appropriate response is quite obviously the response of the Buddha himself and of the Buddhist saints who follow in his footsteps. In the case of such Noble Beings the impermanent, death-infected, suffering-filled character of phenomenal reality is recognized; as a result, desire is snuffed out and thus Nibbana (release from the power of death) is attained.[18]

18 Reynolds 1992: 160f.

Those who are released in this way from the power of death will of course still pass away, but the way they do so becomes a manifestation of their inner freedom, of their unshakeable mental health even at the time when the body is sick and about to fall apart. A tool of central importance to gain such release from the power of death is mindfulness, as can be seen in the discourse taken up in the next chapter. In this way, besides being the appropriate mode for facing physical pain or the mental pain of grief, and in addition to furnishing the required quality of receptivity when attending to the terminally ill, mindfulness can come to one's aid even at the last moments of life.

XIX

MINDFUL DYING

XIX.1 INTRODUCTION

In the discourse translated in this chapter the Buddha acts again in his compassionate role: this time he visits the monastic sick ward on his own initiative to give instructions and guidance. Somewhat similarly to the discourse to the Sakyans taken up in the last chapter, here, too, the Buddha offers general instructions appropriate for those who are on the verge of death.

A central theme in the last chapter was enabling lay disciples to assist other lay disciples, with a natural focus on consolation and the need to give up the types of attachment usually associated with living a lay life. In the present context the Buddha instead guides monastics in how to face their own death. In early Buddhist thought the decision to go forth as a monastic is representative of the inspiration to make the cultivation of meditation and liberating insight the main concern of one's life. It is for practitioners of a similar orientation that the present discourse will be of particular interest.

The focus of this chapter's instruction is on the experience of feeling. This is a natural choice for a teaching given to those who are sick and in pain. The instruction highlights how the three types of feeling relate to the underlying tendencies. Just as in Chapter 3, out of the entire list of seven such underlying tendencies, those three are singled out that are of direct relevance to the experience of the three types of feeling:

- the underlying tendency to sensual desire (↔ pleasant feeling),
- the underlying tendency to aversion (↔ painful feeling),
- the underlying tendency to ignorance (↔ neutral feeling).

In line with the simile of the two arrows offered in the discourse translated in Chapter 3, the task to experience feeling without reactivity is a central aspect in the teaching given in the discourse translated below from the *Saṃyukta-āgama*, which has a parallel in the *Saṃyutta-nikāya*.[1]

XIX.2 TRANSLATION[2]

Thus have I heard. At one time the Buddha was staying at Sāvatthī in Jeta's Grove, Anāthapiṇḍika's Park.[3] At that time a group of many monastics had come to be together in the sick ward; many monastics were sick at that time.[4]

Then, in the afternoon, the Blessed One rose from his meditation and approached the sick ward. He sat in front of the great group on a prepared seat. Being seated, he said to the monastics:

"You should await the time [of your death] with right mindfulness and clear comprehension, in accordance with my instructions.

"Monastics, what is right mindfulness? That is, monastics, one establishes mindfulness by contemplating the body as a body internally, with energetic effort, right mindfulness, and clear comprehension, overcoming desire and discontent in the world. One establishes mindfulness by contemplating the body as a body externally, *with energetic effort, right mindfulness, and clear comprehension, overcoming desire and discontent in the world*. One establishes mindfulness by contemplating the body as a body

1 SN 36.7 at SN IV 210,21 (translated Bodhi 2000: 1266).
2 The translated discourse is SĀ 1028 at T II 268b27 to 269a11.
3 According to SN 36.7 at SN IV 210,21, the Buddha was rather staying in the Great Wood at Vesālī.
4 SN 36.7 does not report that many monastics were sick.

internally-and-externally, *with energetic effort, right mindfulness, and clear comprehension, overcoming desire and discontent in the world.*[5]

"One establishes mindfulness by contemplating feelings as feelings internally, *with energetic effort, right mindfulness, and clear comprehension, overcoming desire and discontent in the world. One establishes mindfulness by contemplating feelings as* feelings externally, *with energetic effort, right mindfulness, and clear comprehension, overcoming desire and discontent in the world. One establishes mindfulness by contemplating feelings as* feelings internally-and-externally, *with energetic effort, right mindfulness, and clear comprehension, overcoming desire and discontent in the world.*

"One establishes mindfulness by contemplating the mind as mind internally, *with energetic effort, right mindfulness, and clear comprehension, overcoming desire and discontent in the world. One establishes mindfulness by contemplating the mind as* mind externally, *with energetic effort, right mindfulness, and clear comprehension, overcoming desire and discontent in the world. One establishes mindfulness by contemplating the mind as* mind internally-and-externally, *with energetic effort, right mindfulness, and clear comprehension, overcoming desire and discontent in the world.*

"One establishes mindfulness by contemplating dharmas as dharmas internally, *with energetic effort, right mindfulness, and clear comprehension, overcoming desire and discontent in the world. One establishes mindfulness by contemplating dharmas as* dharmas externally, *with energetic effort, right mindfulness, and clear comprehension, overcoming desire and discontent in the world.* One establishes mindfulness by contemplating dharmas as dharmas internally-and-externally, with energetic effort, right mindfulness, and clear comprehension, overcoming desire and discontent in the world. Monastics, this is called right mindfulness.

"Monastics, what is clear comprehension? That is, monastics, when coming and going one is established in clear comprehension, when looking and observing, when bending,

---

5 SN 36.7 does not explicitly mention the distinction between internal, external, and internal-and-external *satipaṭṭhāna* practice.

stretching, lowering or raising [any limb], when carrying one's robes and bowl, when walking, standing, sitting, lying down, when [falling] asleep or waking up, even up to fifty or sixty times,[6] and in accordance with when one speaks or is silent, one practises clear comprehension.[7] Monastics, this is called clear comprehension.

"Monastics, to one who is established in this way in right mindfulness and clear comprehension, pleasant feelings can arise in dependence on conditions, not independent of conditions. What are the conditions on which they depend? That is, they depend on the body. One reflects: 'This body of mine is impermanent, it is conditioned; and the mind arisen in dependence on it [is also impermanent and conditioned]. Pleasant feelings are also impermanent and conditioned; and the mind arisen in dependence on them [is also impermanent and conditioned].'[8]

"One contemplates the body and pleasant feelings as impermanent, contemplates their arising and passing away, contemplates being free from desire, contemplates cessation, and contemplates letting go of them. Having contemplated body and pleasant feeling as impermanent, *having contemplated their arising and passing away, having contemplated being free from desire, having contemplated cessation, and having contemplated* letting go, whatever underlying tendency one has to passionate desire in relation to the body and pleasant feelings will no longer affect one.

"To one who is in this way with right mindfulness and clear comprehension, painful feelings arise in dependence on conditions, not independent of conditions. What are the conditions on which they depend? They depend in this way on the body. One reflects: 'This body of mine is impermanent, it is conditioned; and the mind arisen in dependence on it

6 This reference is somewhat obscure and probably the result of a textual error. Attempting to make sense of it, perhaps it could be interpreted as referring to clear comprehension while falling asleep and waking up repeatedly during the night, even if this should happen fifty or sixty times.

7 SN 36.7 at SN IV 211,11 additionally mentions eating, drinking, consuming food, and tasting, as well as defecating and urinating, as occasions for clear comprehension.

8 SN 36.7 does not refer to the mind arisen in dependence on the body or on feelings.

[is also impermanent and conditioned]. Painful feelings are also impermanent and conditioned; and the mind arisen in dependence on them [is also impermanent and conditioned].'

"One contemplates the body and painful feelings as impermanent, *contemplates their arising and passing away, contemplates being free from desire, contemplates cessation, and contemplates letting go. Having contemplated body and painful feeling as impermanent, having contemplated their arising and passing away, having contemplated being free from desire, having contemplated cessation, and having contemplated* letting go, the underlying tendency herein to irritation and anger in relation to the [body] and to painful feelings will no longer affect one.

"To one who is in this way with right mindfulness and clear comprehension, neutral feelings arise in dependence on conditions, not independent of conditions. What are the conditions on which they depend? That is, they depend on the body. One reflects: 'This body of mine is impermanent, it is conditioned; and the mind arisen in dependence on it [is also impermanent and conditioned]. Neutral feelings are also impermanent and conditioned; and the mind arisen in dependence on them [is also impermanent and conditioned].'

"One contemplates the body and neutral feelings as impermanent, *contemplates their arising and passing away, contemplates being free from desire, contemplates cessation, and contemplates letting go. Having contemplated body and neutral feeling as impermanent, having contemplated their arising and passing away, having contemplated being free from desire, having contemplated cessation, and having contemplated* letting go, whatever underlying tendency one has to delusion in relation to the body and neutral feelings will no longer affect one.[9]

"The learned noble disciple who contemplates like this becomes disenchanted with bodily form, *becomes disenchanted with* feeling, *becomes disenchanted with* perception, *becomes disenchanted with* formations, and becomes disenchanted with consciousness. Being disenchanted [the noble disciple] becomes dispassionate. Being dispassionate [the noble disciple] becomes liberated. Being

9 The translation is based on a variant reading that avoids a repetition of the reference to the underlying tendency; see also Yìnshùn 1983c: 40 note 18.

liberated [the noble disciple] knows and sees: 'Birth for me has been eradicated, the holy life has been established, what had to be done has been done, I myself know that there will be no receiving of further existence.'"[10]

Then the Blessed One spoke this poem:[11]

"When one experiences pleasant feelings
And is unable to understand pleasant feelings,
Then one is affected by the underlying tendency to
  passionate desire
Without seeing an escape from it.
"When one experiences painful feelings
And is unable to understand painful feelings,
Then one is affected by the underlying tendency to aversion
Without seeing a way to escape from it.
"In the case of neutral feelings,
As the Fully Awakened One has taught,
On being also unable to understand them
One will in the end not cross over to the other shore.
"If a monastic is energetic
And has right comprehension that does not waver,
Then in relation to all that is felt
[Such a] one is able to understand it with complete wisdom.
"Being able to understand all that is felt,
Here and now the influxes are eradicated.
Being based on wisdom, when passing away
One [attains] Nirvāṇa and is beyond being reckoned."

When the Buddha had spoken this discourse, hearing what the Buddha had said the monastics were delighted and received it respectfully.

---

10 SN 36.7 at SN IV 213,1 instead describes insight and non-attachment in relation to each of the three feelings, as well as in relation to feelings terminating with the body and with life. SN 36.7 then illustrates the situation of total freedom from attachment towards feelings and their becoming cool after death with the example of an oil lamp that is extinguished due to its wick and oil being exhausted.

11 SN 36.7 does not report any stanzas spoken by the Buddha on this occasion.

XIX.3 DISCUSSION

The above description of how to experience feeling without giving rise to reactivity puts the spotlight on mindfulness, which in both versions involves cultivating the four *satipaṭṭhānas*. The *Saṃyutta-nikāya* version does not explicitly differentiate between the internal and external dimensions of such *satipaṭṭhāna* practice, although the same can safely be assumed to be implicit, given that these dimensions are part of the classical exposition of *satipaṭṭhāna* in the *Satipaṭṭhāna-sutta* and its parallels.[12] In addition to right mindfulness in the form of the four *satipaṭṭhānas*, the discourse translated above and its *Saṃyutta-nikāya* parallel mention clear comprehension, which is one of the exercises included under contemplation of the body in the *Satipaṭṭhāna-sutta* and its *Madhyama-āgama* parallel.[13]

Equipped with a foundation in these meditative practices, one directs attention to the arising of feeling, a crucial link in dependent arising, *paṭicca samuppāda*. This central doctrine in early Buddhist thought describes the conditioned genesis of *dukkha* through a series of causal relations, often but not invariably taking the form of twelve links:

- ignorance,
- formations,
- consciousness,
- name-and-form,
- six senses,
- contact,
- feeling,
- craving,
- clinging,
- becoming,
- birth,
- old age and death.

The crucial link in this conditional sequence, where mindfulness can make a world of difference, is between

12 See Anālayo 2013b: 15f.
13 MN 10 at MN I 7,5 (translated Ñāṇamoli 1995/2005: 147) and its parallel MĀ 98 at T I 582b20; see also Anālayo 2013b: 50–2.

feeling and craving. Whereas the six senses, contact, and the conditioned arising of feeling in dependence on these are a basic given in the experience of human beings, feeling does not necessarily have to give rise to craving. It is precisely at this juncture that, through mindful awareness of the nature of feeling, the tendency to react with craving can be gradually diminished and eventually eradicated.

Directing the spotlight of awareness on the changing nature of feelings, based on being established in mindfulness and clear comprehension, directly counteracts the underlying tendencies. These are the proclivities in the mind to react with desire to pleasant feelings, with aversion to painful feelings, and with delusion to neutral feelings. In this way mindfulness training can bring about a substantial change in one's mental conditioning. All it takes is to be as continuously as possible aware of feelings as impermanent phenomena.

The basic realization of the impermanence of feelings, a naturally prominent feature in the experience of sickness and imminent death, leads on to dispassion and liberation. In this way, contemplating the experience of pain at the time of being ill and close to death can culminate in the realization of full awakening. In terms of the poem offered in the *Saṃyukta-āgama* discourse translated above, by fully understanding the true nature of all that is felt, one can cross over to the other shore and transcend being reckoned in any way.

XX

THE LIBERATING POTENTIAL OF DEATH

XX.1 INTRODUCTION

In this chapter the Buddha features once again in his role of compassionate visitor to a seriously sick patient in order to offer the gift of his instructions. The discourse translated below from the *Saṃyukta-āgama*, just like its parallel in the *Aṅguttara-nikāya*,[1] does not record the actual instructions given by the Buddha. The emphasis in both discourses is instead on the potential in principle of giving instructions at the time of terminal disease, and thereby on how the moment of death can be turned into a moment of liberation.

XX.2 TRANSLATION[2]

Thus have I heard. At one time the Buddha was staying at Sāvatthī in Jeta's Grove, Anāthapiṇḍika's Park. At that time the venerable Phagguna was staying in the Eastern Park, the Hall of Migāra's Mother.[3] He was seriously sick.

The venerable Ānanda approached the Buddha, paid respect at his feet, and withdrew to stand to one side. He said to the

1 AN 6.56 at AN III 379,5 (translated Bodhi 2012: 936).
2 The translated discourse is SĀ 1023 at T II 266c9 to 267b4.
3 AN 6.56 does not provide specifications about where either the Buddha or Phagguna was staying.

Buddha: "Blessed One, the venerable Phagguna, who is staying in the Eastern Park, the Hall of Migāra's Mother, is seriously sick. Of monastics who are sick like this, many have passed away.[4] It would be good if the Blessed One could please approach the venerable Phagguna in the Eastern Park, the Hall of Migāra's Mother, out of compassion."

Then the Blessed One consented by [remaining] silent. When the afternoon had arrived, he rose from his meditation and approached the venerable Phagguna in the Eastern Park, the Hall of Migāra's Mother.[5] He sat on a prepared seat and taught the venerable Phagguna the Dharma in various ways, instructing, teaching, illuminating, and delighting him. Having instructed, taught, illuminated, and delighted [Phagguna], he rose from his seat and left.

Soon after the Blessed One had left, the venerable Phagguna passed away. Just at the time of his passing away his faculties were joyful, his countenance was clear, and the colour of his skin was bright.[6]

Then the venerable Ānanda, having taken care of the venerable Phagguna's bodily remains, approached the Buddha, paid respect at the Buddha's feet, and withdrew to stand to one side. He said to the Buddha:

"Blessed One, the venerable Phagguna passed away soon after the Blessed One had come [back]. Right at the time of passing away his faculties were joyful, and the colour of his skin was clear, bright, and lustrous. How is it, Blessed One, where has he been reborn? What birth has he taken? What is his afterlife?"[7]

---

4 An indication that many monastics in this condition had passed away is not given in AN 6.56.

5 AN 6.56 at AN III 379,15 reports that Phagguna tried to get up, whereupon the Buddha told him to remain as he was. AN 6.56 also records Phagguna describing his sick condition with the similes of cleaving the head with a sword, of tightening a strap around the head, of cutting up the belly of a cow, and of a weak man being roasted over a pit of hot coals by two strong men.

6 AN 6.56 at AN III 380,25 only mentions the condition of his faculties.

7 In AN 6.56 at AN III 381,4 Ānanda only describes the condition of Phagguna's faculties, without enquiring about his rebirth. In reply, the Buddha explains that Phagguna had eradicated the five lower fetters, a statement similar to what is found in SĀ 1023 towards the end of the discourse. AN 6.56 continues by introducing the ensuing exposition with the announcement that there are six benefits of listening to the Dharma and of reflecting on its meaning at the proper time.

The Buddha said to Ānanda: "Suppose earlier, when not yet sick, a monastic had not abandoned the five lower fetters. At the time of experiencing the arising of a disease, the body is afflicted, tending to become weak, and the mind is distressed.[8] One is able to hear the great teacher's instruction, who in various ways instructs and teaches the Dharma.[9] Having heard the Dharma, one eradicates the five lower fetters. Ānanda, this is the benefit of the great teacher instructing and teaching the Dharma.[10]

"Again, Ānanda, suppose earlier, when not yet sick, a monastic had not abandoned the five lower fetters. Later a disease arises, the body comes to be afflicted, tending to become weak. One does not receive the great teacher's instruction, instructing and teaching the Dharma. Yet, one encounters instruction from other learned and senior practitioners of the holy life, who instruct and teach the Dharma. Having got to hear the Dharma, one eradicates the five lower fetters. Ānanda, this is called the benefit of being instructed and taught, of hearing the Dharma.

"Again, Ānanda, suppose earlier, when not yet sick, a monastic had not abandoned the five lower fetters. *Later a disease arises, the body comes to be afflicted, tending to become weak.* One does not hear the great teacher's instruction, instructing and teaching the Dharma, and one also does not hear instructions from other learned and senior practitioners of the holy life, who instruct and teach the Dharma. Yet, being alone and in a quiet [place], one gives attention to the Dharma one has earlier received, evaluating it and contemplating it, and one gains the eradication of the five lower fetters. Ānanda, this is called the benefit to be gained by giving attention to and contemplating the Dharma one has earlier heard.

"Again, Ānanda, suppose earlier, when not yet sick, a monastic had abandoned the five lower fetters, but had not attained the supreme liberation through the destruction of craving, being

---

8 Here and below, AN 6.56 at AN III 381,14 simply speaks of the time of death.

9 Here and below, AN 6.56 at AN III 381,16 additionally mentions qualities of the Dharma, which is good in the beginning, middle, and end, etc., and reveals the pure holy life.

10 The translation "teaching" is based on adopting a variant reading, which is the same as the formulation used in the original earlier.

well liberated in the mind from the influxes by not clinging.[11] Later one gets a disease, the body comes to be afflicted, tending to become weak. One is able to hear the great teacher's instruction, who instructs and teaches the Dharma, and one gains the supreme liberation through the destruction of craving, dispassion, and the liberation from the influxes by not clinging. Ānanda, this is called the benefit of the great teacher teaching the Dharma.

"Again, Ānanda, suppose earlier, when not yet sick, a monastic had abandoned the five lower fetters, but had not attained the supreme liberation through the destruction of craving, dispassion, and the liberation from the influxes by not clinging. [Later] one experiences the arising of a bodily disease, encountering a serious ailment. One does not get the great teacher's instruction, instructing and teaching the Dharma. Yet, one gets instructions from other learned and senior practitioners of the holy life, who instruct and teach the Dharma, and one gains the supreme liberation through the destruction of craving, dispassion, and the liberation from the influxes by not clinging. Ānanda, this is called the benefit of being instructed and taught, of hearing the Dharma.

"Again, Ānanda, suppose earlier, when not yet sick, a monastic had abandoned the five lower fetters, but had not attained the supreme liberation through the destruction of craving, dispassion, and the liberation from the influxes by not clinging. [Later] a bodily disease arises, a serious ailment arises. One does not get the great teacher's instruction, instructing and teaching the Dharma, and one does not get instructions from other learned and senior [practitioners of the holy life], who instruct and teach the Dharma. Yet, being alone and in a quiet place, one gives attention to the Dharma one has earlier heard, evaluating it and contemplating it, and one gains the supreme liberation through the destruction of craving, dispassion, and the liberation from the influxes by not clinging. Ānanda, this is called the benefit to be gained from giving attention to the Dharma one has earlier heard.

11 Regarding the translation "not clinging" see p. 86 note 13. AN 6.56 at AN III 382,11 refers to full awakening with the expression "unsurpassed destruction of the acquisitions".

"How could it be that the monastic Phagguna did not acquire joyful faculties, a clear appearance, and bright and lustrous bodily skin colour? Earlier, when not yet being sick, the monastic Phagguna had not abandoned the five lower fetters. On personally hearing instructions from the great teacher, who instructed and taught him the Dharma, he eradicated the five lower fetters."

The Blessed One declared that the venerable Phagguna had experienced non-return.[12] When the Buddha had spoken this discourse, hearing what the Buddha had said the venerable Ānanda rejoiced in it and was delighted. He paid homage and left.

XX.3 DISCUSSION

A minor detail in the discourse translated above, also mentioned in the Pāli parallel, is that the Buddha visits the sick Phagguna only after having engaged in his meditation practice. This is particularly noteworthy in the *Saṃyukta-āgama* version, where the Buddha has been informed of Phagguna's ailment and the text explicitly indicates that many who have been in the same condition have passed away. In fact in both versions Phagguna does pass away soon after the Buddha's visit.

The fact that the Buddha nevertheless is not portrayed as immediately rushing over to see Phagguna can be taken to convey that the compassionate concern to assist those who are sick or even on the verge of death should not result in neglecting one's own practice. In the present discourse, even a fully awakened one does not immediately go out to meet the patient, but instead takes the time to engage in his formal sitting meditation. This is clearly not because of a lack of concern for the sick, but needs to be read alongside the depiction of the Buddha being willing even to wash a sick monastic himself, mentioned above in Chapter 4. These two episodes simply reflect aspects of the same compassionate attitude.[13]

---

12 Such a statement by the reciters has no counterpart in AN 6.56. The preceding passage, in which the Buddha declares Phagguna's attainment, has a counterpart at an earlier juncture in AN 6.56; see above note 7.

13 On the Buddha's practice of seclusion as an expression of his compassion see Anālayo 2015b: 16f.

The example set by the Buddha in the present case makes it even more essential for those who have not yet reached awakening to maintain a regular meditation practice, in order to be able to approach others with the inner peace and strength that come from their own practice. Without in this way properly taking care of oneself, it will not be possible to take care of others to the best of one's own abilities.

Another aspect of the discourse translated above is the liberating potential of the Dharma at the time of death. The importance of the time of death is also taken up in the *Mahākammavibhaṅga-sutta* and its *Madhyama-āgama* parallel. The two discourses examine the complexity of karma, showing that even if someone had earlier performed bad deeds with the potential of leading to a lower rebirth, it is still possible that at the time of death, through becoming established in a wholesome mental condition, such lower rebirth can be avoided. This does not mean, of course, that the karmic retribution for the bad deeds has been rendered completely inoperative, but only that it will not come to fruition on this occasion. The relevant passage from the *Madhyama-āgama* proceeds as follows:[14]

> Suppose someone did not refrain from killing, from stealing, from sexual misconduct, and from falsehood ... yet at the time of death [this person] gives rise to a wholesome state of mind, a state of mind endowed with teachings that are connected with right view. Because of this and for this reason, with the breaking up of the body at death [this person] is reborn in a good realm of existence, in heaven.

This extract needs to be read in conjunction with a description of the predicament of one who has not maintained moral conduct and has to face approaching death. Such a condition is described in the *Madhyama-āgama* parallel to the *Bālapaṇḍita-sutta* in the following way:[15]

---

14 MĀ 171 at T I 708b13f and 708b21 to 708b22, counterpart to MN 136 at MN III 214,17 (translated Ñāṇamoli 1995/2005: 1064).

15 The translated passage is taken from MĀ 199 at T I 759b25 to 759c6. In the parallel MN 129 at MN III 164,24 (translated Ñāṇamoli 1995/2005: 1017) the fool experiences such regret even just when lying down to rest, without being sick. Another parallel, T 86 at T I 907a26, begins by describing how the fool takes a rest, but then continues by noting that

A fool engages in evil bodily conduct, engages *in evil verbal conduct*, and engages in evil mental conduct. Suppose [the fool] then becomes sick and experiences pain. Whether [the fool] is sitting or lying on a bed, sitting or lying on a bench, sitting or lying on the ground, in the body extreme pains and severe pains arise such as to make one wish to cut off one's life. Whatever evil bodily conduct, *evil* verbal *conduct*, and evil mental conduct [the fool] has done, at that time that hangs over [the fool].

It is just as if, in the late afternoon, when the sun descends behind a tall mountain, its shadow hangs over the ground. In the same way whatever evil bodily conduct, *evil* verbal *conduct*, and evil mental conduct [the fool] has done, at that time that hangs over [the fool].

[The fool] thinks: "This is my evil bodily conduct, *evil* verbal *conduct*, and evil mental conduct, which are hanging over me. Formerly I have not done what is meritorious; I have done much evil.

"If there is a place for those who have done evil, who have been fierce and brutal, who have been unprincipled in their affairs, who have not done what is meritorious and not done what is wholesome, who have not made for themselves a lifelong refuge from fear, on which to rely, I will be going to that bad place."

From this arises regret. Regret having arisen, [the fool] will die unworthy, will end life in an unwholesome way.

The manifestation of regret and guilt in relation to something unwholesome done previously is indeed an easily observable feature among the terminally ill.[16] It would therefore be best if, while still being alive, one avoids as much as possible the creation of the conditions for the frightful shadow of evil conduct to arise, thereby establishing oneself in a condition of fearlessness through having maintained virtuous conduct, as described above in Chapter 9.

---

the fool is sick. A quotation of a version of the present passage in the *Śrāvakabhūmi* also indicates that the one who has committed misconduct is sick; see Śrāvakabhūmi Study Group 1998: 124,11 and its Chinese parallel in T 1579 at T XXX 408c26. This makes it probable that MN 129 has lost a reference to being sick, which fits the context better than merely taking a rest.

16 See, e.g., Saunders and Baines 1983/1989: 52.

In case one has not been successful in this respect, however, if at the moment of passing away one can at least give rise to a wholesome state of mind that is connected with right view, this can become like a ray of sunshine that temporarily dispels the shadow of remorse for wrongs done in the past. Here right view in particular points to developing an understanding in line with the four noble truths, such as taking responsibility for the ignorant craving that motivated one's past unwholesome conduct and using this honest acknowledgement as the basis for cultivating the type of insight and freedom from attachment that leads beyond such craving.

At the crucial moment of being about to die, the perspective afforded by the Dharma in this way can provide the catalyst for transformation and have a decisive impact, either in terms of one's prospective rebirth or else in terms of making a deeper breakthrough that earlier, while one was still healthy, had not been possible. Even if one does not find the rebirth perspective in the passages above relevant, the last moment before death can undoubtedly be a powerful time to transform and improve one's mental dispositions.

Ideally such a breakthrough relies on the support of those who can provide guidance in non-attachment and insight. All being well, companions in the practice of the Dharma will be present to assist and encourage, even perhaps read out Dharma passages that one has earlier selected for this purpose. However, one can hardly take for granted that at the time of one's death such support will be available. It must be for this reason that the discourse translated above takes up the alternative that "one gives attention to the Dharma one has earlier heard, evaluating it and contemplating it." This offers an alternative in case circumstances are such that, at the time of passing away, one finds oneself without the support of fellow Dharma practitioners or teachers.

This in turn points to the need to equip oneself with sufficient knowledge of the Dharma, so that one is indeed able to contemplate it at such a time. Sufficient in the sense that, in case one has to face death on one's own, one is ready to do so. In this way the present discourse suggests the importance of learning and internalizing the Dharma, in particular the chief teachings on insight and non-attachment.

Whatever passages one may find particularly useful in this respect, it would be helpful to make sure one is well acquainted with them. In the ancient context this meant memorization. Although nowadays texts are much more readily accessible, one cannot be sure that such access will be available at the time of death. A sudden accident could happen and one might find oneself not only without the guidance of companions in the practice of the Dharma, but also without access to one's personal library, be this digital or in print. This makes it advisable to develop some degree of close acquaintance with at least a short selection of teachings, even just a few verses or pithy instructions, so that one is able to reflect on their import on one's own. A guide to proper selection could be to imagine as vividly as possible one's own passing away, in order to try out what passages or reflections would be most useful at such a time. Cultivating such self-reliance will provide a solid foundation for making best use of the liberating potential of the time of one's own death.

XXI

THE POWER OF INSIGHT AT THE TIME OF DYING

XXI.1 INTRODUCTION

The discourse in this chapter once again documents the Buddha's compassion. This time he goes to visit a newly ordained monastic who has not yet had the time to form close relationships with monastic companions or lay supporters. His condition in a way parallels the situation of a hospitalized patient who does not receive frequent visits from relatives or friends, and who is therefore all the more in need of kindness from the nurses and doctors attending on him or her.

The discourse translated below is the first of two consecutive discourses in the *Saṃyukta-āgama* in which the Buddha goes to visit an unknown and recently ordained monastic. Each of these *Saṃyukta-āgama* discourses has a counterpart in the *Saṃyutta-nikāya*.[1]

XXI.2 TRANSLATION[2]

Thus have I heard. At one time the Buddha was staying at Sāvatthī in Jeta's Grove, Anāthapiṇḍika's Park. At that time there was a certain monastic, young and new to the training, who had

1 The parallel to SĀ 1025 (translated here) is SN 35.74 at SN IV 46,1 (translated Bodhi 2000: 1157); the parallel to SĀ 1026 is SN 35.75.

2 The translated discourse is SĀ 1025 at T II 267c7 to 268a19.

recently gone forth in this teaching and discipline and who had few friends. He had come for a visit alone and was without an attendant. He was staying in a monastic dwelling for visitors by the side of the village and he was seriously sick.

Then a group of many monastics approached the Buddha, paid respect with their heads at his feet, and withdrew to sit to one side.[3] They said to the Buddha: "Blessed One, there is a monastic, young and new to the training *who has recently gone forth in this teaching and discipline and has few friends. He has come for a visit alone and is without an attendant.* He is staying in a monastic dwelling for visitors by the side of the village. He is seriously sick. Of monastics who have been sick like this, many have died and not survived. It would be good if the Blessed One were to approach that dwelling place, out of compassion."

Then the Blessed One consented by [remaining] silent. In the afternoon of the same day, after rising from his meditation, he approached that dwelling place. On seeing the Blessed One from afar, that sick monastic wanted to get up, supporting himself on the bed.

The Buddha said to the monastic: "Stay on your bed and do not get up. How is it, monastic, are your afflictions bearable?"[4]

The monastic replied: "I am not recovering from the illness and my body is not at ease; the pains keep increasing and there is no relief. It is just as if many strong men were to take hold of a weak man, put a rope around his head and with both hands pull it tight, so that he is in extreme pain. My pain now exceeds that.

"It is just as if a cow butcher with a sharp knife were to cut open a living cow's belly to take its internal organs. How could that cow endure the pains in its belly? My belly is now more painful than that cow's.

"It is just as if two strong men were to grab one weak person and hang him over a fire, roasting both his feet. The heat of both my feet

3 In SN 35.74 at SN IV 46,2 a single monastic informs the Buddha of the sick condition of a newly ordained monastic without acquaintances. SN 35.74 does not mention that the Buddha sat in meditation before approaching the sick monastic.

4 SĀ 1025 abbreviates and indicates that this should be supplemented by the description in the discourse by Khemaka, SĀ 103 (see above p. 91). SN 35.74 does not have any similes illustrating the sick monastic's condition.

now exceeds that. The pain of my disease is still increasing and not decreasing."

The Buddha said to the sick monastic: "I will now question you, answer me according to your understanding. Do you have nothing to regret?" The sick monastic said to the Buddha: "Blessed One, I truly have something to regret."

The Buddha said to the sick monastic: "Do you gain being without violation of the precepts?" The sick monastic said to the Buddha: "Blessed One, I truly have not violated the precepts."

The Buddha said to the sick monastic: "If you have not violated the precepts, what is it that you regret?" The sick monastic said to the Buddha: "Blessed One, I am young and have recently gone forth, I have not attained any superior knowledge and vision of a state beyond [the ability of ordinary] men. I have this thought: 'I know the time of passing away has come. Where will I be reborn?' Therefore regret has arisen."[5]

The Buddha said to the [sick] monastic: "I will now question you, answer me according to your understanding. How is it, monastic, does eye-consciousness exist because of the existence of the eye?"[6] The [sick] monastic said to the Buddha: "It is like this, Blessed One."

[The Buddha] asked further: "What do you think, monastic, does eye-contact exist because of the existence of eye-

---

5 Instead of being concerned about so far not having reached any knowledge and vision "of a state beyond [the ability of ordinary] men", *uttarimanussadhamma* (on which see Anālayo 2008a), in SN 35.74 at SN IV 47,5 the monastic states that he knows the Buddha's teaching not to be merely for the sake of purification of morality, but rather for the sake of dispassion. In the other Pāli version, SN 35.75 at SN IV 48,4, which otherwise proceeds similarly to SN 35.74, the monastic protagonist knows the teaching to be for the sake of final Nirvāṇa without clinging. In both versions this motivates the Buddha to give an exposition on the nature of the sense-spheres, evidently with the aim to guide each monastic towards dispassion or final Nirvāṇa without clinging.

6 The teaching given in SN 35.74 at SN IV 47,15 (as well as in SN 35.75) begins with the impermanent nature of each sense-sphere, then points out that what is impermanent is *dukkha*, and what is *dukkha* should not be regarded as "this is mine, this I am, this is my self." Whereas the two Pāli versions have the same teaching, SĀ 1026 at T II 268a22 reports a different teaching given by the Buddha, compared to the present exposition in SĀ 1025. Instead of taking up the six sense-spheres, the teaching in SĀ 1026 concerns the not-self nature of the body with consciousness and any external signs.

consciousness, and conditioned by eye-contact do painful, or pleasurable, or neutral feelings arise within?" The [sick] monastic said to the Buddha: "It is like this, Blessed One."

The Buddha asked further: "How is it, monastic, does ear-consciousness exist because of the existence of the ear?*" The sick monastic said to the Buddha: "It is like this, Blessed One."*

The Buddha asked further: "What do you think, monastic, does ear-contact exist because of the existence of ear-consciousness, and conditioned by ear-contact do painful, or pleasurable, or neutral feelings arise within?" The sick monastic said to the Buddha: "It is like this, Blessed One."

The Buddha asked further: "How is it, monastic, does nose-consciousness exist because of the existence of the nose?*" The sick monastic said to the Buddha: "It is like this, Blessed One."*

The Buddha asked further: "What do you think, monastic, does nose-contact exist because of the existence of nose-consciousness, and conditioned by nose-contact do painful, or pleasurable, or neutral feelings arise within?" The sick monastic said to the Buddha: "It is like this, Blessed One."

The Buddha asked further: "How is it, monastic, does tongue-consciousness exist because of the existence of the tongue?*" The sick monastic said to the Buddha: "It is like this, Blessed One."*

The Buddha asked further: "What do you think, monastic, does tongue-contact exist because of the existence of tongue-consciousness, and conditioned by tongue-contact do painful, or pleasurable, or neutral feelings arise within?" The sick monastic said to the Buddha: "It is like this, Blessed One."

The Buddha asked further: "How is it, monastic, does body-consciousness exist because of the existence of the body?*" The sick monastic said to the Buddha: "It is like this, Blessed One."*

The Buddha asked further: "What do you think, monastic, does body-contact exist because of the existence of body-consciousness, and conditioned by body-contact do painful, or pleasurable, or neutral feelings arise within?" The sick monastic said to the Buddha: "It is like this, Blessed One."

The Buddha asked further: "How is it, monastic, does mind-consciousness exist because of the existence of the mind?*" The sick monastic said to the Buddha: "It is like this, Blessed One."*

The Buddha asked further: "What do you think, monastic, does mind-contact exist because of the existence of mind-consciousness, and conditioned by mind-contact do painful, or pleasurable, or neutral feelings arise within?" The sick monastic said to the Buddha: "It is like this, Blessed One."

[The Buddha asked further]: "How is it, monastic, if there is no eye, is there no eye-consciousness?" The [sick] monastic said to the Buddha: "It is like this, Blessed One."

[The Buddha] asked further: "Monastic, if there is no eye-consciousness, is there no eye-contact? If there is no eye-contact, do painful, or pleasurable, or neutral feelings not arise within, conditioned by eye-contact?[7] The [sick] monastic said to the Buddha: "It is like this, Blessed One."

The Buddha asked further: "How is it, monastic, if there is no ear, *is there no ear-consciousness?" The sick monastic said to the Buddha: "It is like this, Blessed One."*

The Buddha asked further: "Monastic, if there is no ear-consciousness, is there no ear-contact? If there is no ear-contact, do painful, or pleasurable, or neutral feelings not arise within, conditioned by ear-contact?" The sick monastic said to the Buddha: "It is like this, Blessed One."

The Buddha asked further: "How is it, monastic, if there is no nose, *is there no nose-consciousness?" The sick monastic said to the Buddha: "It is like this, Blessed One."*

The Buddha asked further: "Monastic, if there is no nose-consciousness, is there no nose-contact? If there is no nose-contact, do painful, or pleasurable, or neutral feelings not arise within, conditioned by nose-contact?" The sick monastic said to the Buddha: "It is like this, Blessed One."

The Buddha asked further: "How is it, monastic, if there is no tongue, *is there no tongue-consciousness?" The sick monastic said to the Buddha: "It is like this, Blessed One."*

The Buddha asked further: "Monastic, if there is no tongue-consciousness, is there no tongue-contact? If there is no tongue-contact, do painful, or pleasurable, or neutral feelings not arise within,

---

7 The translation "eye-contact" follows a correction in the CBETA edition. Instead of "eye", the original has another Chinese character of similar appearance that rather means "limit", clearly the result of a copyist's error.

conditioned by tongue-contact?" The sick monastic said to the Buddha: "It is like this, Blessed One."

The Buddha asked further: "How is it, monastic, if there is no body, *is there no body-consciousness?" The sick monastic said to the Buddha: "It is like this, Blessed One."*

The Buddha asked further: "Monastic, if there is no body-consciousness, is there no body-contact? If there is no body-contact, do painful, or pleasurable, or neutral feelings not arise within, conditioned by body-contact?" The sick monastic said to the Buddha: "It is like this, Blessed One."

The Buddha asked further: "How is it, monastic, if there is no mind, *is there no mind-consciousness?" The sick monastic said to the Buddha: "It is like this, Blessed One."*

The Buddha asked further: "Monastic, if there is no mind-consciousness, is there no mind-contact? If there is no mind-contact, do painful, or pleasurable, or neutral feelings not arise within, conditioned by mind-contact?" The sick monastic said to the Buddha: "It is like this, Blessed One."

[The Buddha said]: "Monastic, therefore you should give proper attention to this teaching in this way, to attain a good passing away and a good afterlife."

At that time, having in various ways taught the Dharma to the sick monastic, having instructed, taught, illuminated, and delighted him, the Blessed One rose from his seat and left.

Then the sick monastic passed away soon after the Blessed One had left. At the time of passing away his faculties were joyful, his countenance was clear, and the colour of his skin was bright.

Then a group of many monastics approached the Buddha, paid respect with their heads at his feet, and withdrew to sit to one side. They said to the Buddha: "Blessed One, regarding that young monastic who was seriously sick, the venerable one has by now already passed away. Just at the time of passing away his faculties were joyful, his countenance was clear, and the colour of his skin was bright. How is it, Blessed One, where has the monastic been reborn in this way? What birth has he taken? What is his afterlife?"

The Buddha said to the monastics: "That monastic's passing away has been truly valuable. Having heard me teach the

Dharma, he clearly understood. Being fearless in the Dharma, he attained final Nirvāṇa. You should now reverentially take care of his bodily remains."[8]

At that time the Buddha made the supreme declaration regarding that monastic. When the Buddha had spoken this discourse, hearing what the Buddha had said the monastics were delighted and received it respectfully.

XXI.3 DISCUSSION

The present discourse again shows the liberating potential of the time of death. The discourse translated in the preceding chapter highlighted that one who has not eradicated the five lower fetters can eradicate them at the time of death, or else that one who has already eradicated them can progress to full awakening. In the present instance the entire progress, from being unawakened to becoming fully liberated, takes place at the time of death. This serves as a complement to the indication given in Chapter 18 that a lay disciple can equal the liberation of a fully awakened monastic through complete freedom from attachment at the time of death. All these discourses point to the powerful potential of insight at the time of passing away.

The mode of non-attachment proposed in the present discourse and its Pāli parallel is based on the six sense-spheres, which are employed in the two versions in different ways for the cultivation of insight. The six sense-spheres are:

- eye and forms,
- ear and sounds,
- nose and odours,
- tongue and tastes,
- body and tangibles,
- mind and mind-objects.

---

8 SN 35.74 at SN IV 47,27 simply reports that during the exposition given by the Buddha the monastic attained stream-entry. In the case of SN 35.75 at SN IV 48,12, the monastic reaches full awakening. Neither of the two reports that the respective monastic passed away soon after the Buddha's instruction; therefore, neither has a counterpart to the ensuing episode in SĀ 1025, according to which the other monastics enquired about him.

The basic point behind this analysis is to disclose the composite and therefore conditioned nature of experience. Such disclosure begins by analytically setting apart the different avenues of experience according to the respective senses. Notably the mind and its objects are considered on a par with the five physical senses, instead of being in some way seen as superior to them. By taking up each sense as a distinct sphere of experience in turn, the conditionality of experience can be discerned more easily.

Following the *Saṃyutta-nikāya* version, one should then attend to the impermanent nature of each sense-sphere. Based on this, one then realizes that what is impermanent is *dukkha*, and what is *dukkha* is not fit to be regarded as "this is mine, this I am, this is my self." This follows the pattern of building up insight in relation to the three characteristics discussed above in Chapter 17.

In the *Saṃyukta-āgama* discourse translated above the emphasis is more on the conditioned nature of feelings that arise due to the experience of contact through any of these six senses. This conditionality has its contrast in the absence of feeling due to the absence of the conditions for its arising. The significance of the exposition on absence in the *Saṃyukta-āgama* version could easily be underestimated as being a simple complement to the previous part on the existence of the senses etc. A deeper significance emerges once this is viewed as offering a pointer to Nirvāṇa, wherein the senses and their objects are indeed absent, and any type of feeling as well. Understood in this way, the teaching given in the discourse translated above proceeds from exposing the conditionality of felt experience to pointing the mind towards the unconditioned, both being part of an instruction that clearly functions as a guided meditation.

From a practical viewpoint one might even combine the two approaches described in the *Saṃyukta-āgama* and *Saṃyutta-nikāya* versions respectively. This could be done by first of all clearly recognizing that any feeling experienced is the conditioned product of a particular sense and its corresponding type of consciousness. What is conditioned must be impermanent, and being impermanent it is incapable of yielding lasting satisfaction and therefore not adequate for identifying with or being appropriated as "mine". Based on such insight, one then inclines the mind towards the unconditioned. Cultivating such profound inclination at the time of death, after having fragmented experience into its component units and aroused penetrative insight into the true nature of these components, can safely be expected to have an immensely liberating potential.

XXII

THE LAST WORDS OF AN ACCOMPLISHED LAY DISCIPLE

XXII.1 INTRODUCTION

After several chapters on death as an occasion for developing insight, this chapter and the next turn to the case of those already highly accomplished in insight, whose death becomes an occasion for them to teach others. Similarly to the case of Khemaka, discussed in Chapter 11, in the discourse in the present chapter the patient is the one who delivers teachings. This feat is performed by the householder Citta, who in the early discourses features as a highly accomplished lay practitioner.[1]

A discourse in the *Saṃyutta-nikāya* and its *Ekottarika-āgama* parallel present Citta as an exemplary householder. The two versions agree in reporting the Buddha's recommendation that a mother instruct her son, should he decide to live the lay life, to take the householder Citta as his example.[2] The Buddha explains that Citta is one of two householders who serve as a standard for male lay disciples.

---

1 For biographical sketches of Citta see Malalasekera 1937/1995: 865f (no. 1) as well as Nyanaponika and Hecker 1997: 365–72. Pāsādika 1972: 23 points out that Citta, in his role as a wise and exemplary lay disciple, can be considered a precursor to Vimalakīrti.

2 SN 17.23 at SN II 235,18 (translated Bodhi 2000: 688) and EĀ 9.1 at T II 562a23.

According to the listing of eminent disciples in the *Aṅguttara-nikāya*, Citta was foremost among male lay disciples in teaching the Dharma. The *Ekottarika-āgama* counterpart considers him foremost in wisdom among male lay disciples.[3]

Citta's meditative abilities come to the fore in a discourse that also shows him wittily defeating the leader of the Jains in a debate type of situation, an occasion during which Citta affirms his ability to attain absorption.[4] Another discourse presents him as having been an adept not only in concentration but also in insight, as he had attained non-return.[5]

Several discourses record him exercising his teaching skills even towards monastics. One of these discourses reports a group of monastics discussing and expressing different opinions on the working mechanism of the fetters. Citta joins them and clarifies the situation with the help of a simile about two oxen yoked together.[6] Neither of the oxen is the fetter of the other, but the yoke between the two is what binds them together. Similarly, neither the senses nor their objects are in themselves fetters. Instead the fetter is to be found in the desire that arises in dependence on them.

It is telling that in this discourse monastics, representing withdrawal from the world, receive such a clarification from an accomplished lay practitioner. While living in the world and thereby in a situation less conducive to intensive practice, Citta has clearly been successful in handling the experience of sense-objects in his household life in such a way as to diminish his fetters and desires. He is living proof that the problem lies in the yoke between the two oxen, not just in the oxen themselves.

---

3 AN 1.14 at AN I 26,5 (translated Bodhi 2012: 112) and its parallel EĀ 6.1 at T II 559c10.

4 In SN 41.8 at SN IV 298,29 (translated Bodhi 2000: 1327) he describes his ability to attain all four absorptions, whereas in the parallel SĀ 574 at T II 152c15 he only mentions the first two absorptions (which appears to be due to the topic of debate with the leader of the Jains and need not imply that at the time of this encounter he had only reached the ability to attain the first two absorptions).

5 SN 41.9 at SN IV 301,22 (translated Bodhi 2000: 1329) and its parallel SĀ 573 at T II 152b11.

6 SN 41.1 at SN IV 282,32 (translated Bodhi 2000: 1315) and its parallel SĀ 572 at T II 152a15.

On another occasion Citta is on record for explaining in detail to a monastic the meaning of a short saying by the Buddha,[7] and on yet another occasion he clarifies to another monastic the distinctions between different types of liberation of the mind.[8] Besides throwing into relief Citta's profound wisdom, these instances serve to confirm a point made earlier, in that the early discourses do not consider insight to be the sole domain of monastics. Not only do lay disciples receive profound teachings and reach high levels of awakening, but they are also shown as capable of teaching the Dharma to their monastic brethren and clarifying issues for them, as is clearly the case for Citta.

In the discourse translated below from the *Saṃyukta-āgama*, which has a parallel in the *Saṃyutta-nikāya*,[9] Citta is on his deathbed. As yet another instance of his exemplary role, he dies teaching the Dharma and displaying the freedom from attachment of one who has reached a high level in the cultivation of liberating insight.

XXII.2 TRANSLATION[10]

Thus have I heard. At one time the Buddha was staying in Ambāṭaka in the Mango Grove, together with a company of many senior monastics.[11]

At that time the householder Citta was sick and in pain. He was surrounded by his relatives. A group of many devas had approached the householder. They said to the householder Citta:[12] "Householder, you should make an aspiration to become a universal monarch, [and you will gain the results in accordance with your aspiration]."[13]

7 SN 41.5 at SN IV 292,1 (translated Bodhi 2000: 1321) and its parallel SĀ 566 at T II 149b14.
8 SN 41.7 at SN IV 296,9 (translated Bodhi 2000: 1325) and its parallel SĀ 567 at T II 149c20.
9 SN 41.10 at SN IV 302,19 (translated Bodhi 2000: 1330).
10 The translated part is taken from SĀ 575 at T II 153a3 to 153b12.
11 SN 41.10 does not report the Buddha's whereabouts.
12 SN 41.10 at SN IV 302,21 specifies what kind of *deva*s had come, namely those dwelling in parks, groves, trees, herbs, and forests.
13 The supplemented part seems to be required here, as it is part of what Citta later quotes as having been said by the *deva*s when reporting the conversation to his relatives.

The householder Citta said to the devas: "If one becomes a universal monarch, that is also impermanent, dukkha, empty, and not-self."

Then the householder's relatives said to the householder [Citta]: "You should collect your mindfulness, you should collect your mindfulness."

The householder Citta said to his relatives: "Why are you instructing me: 'Collect your mindfulness, collect your mindfulness?'"

The relatives said: "You said: 'That is impermanent, dukkha, empty, and not-self.' For this reason we instructed you: 'Collect your mindfulness, collect your mindfulness.'"

The householder [Citta] said to his relatives: "Devas have approached me and said to me: 'You should make an aspiration to become a universal monarch, and you will gain the results in accordance with your aspiration.' I replied: 'Such a universal monarch is also impermanent, dukkha, empty, and not-self.'"

The relatives said to the householder Citta: "What is it about a universal monarch that those devas have instructed you to aspire for?"

The householder [Citta] replied: "The universal monarch rules according to the right Dharma. Because of seeing this benefit, the devas have come and instructed me to aspire for it."[14]

The relatives said: "What is your mental attitude now, how will it be for you?"[15]

The householder said: "Relatives, my only intention now is not to encounter again birth in a womb, not to increase the dust of the cemeteries, and not to receive [again] blood and breath. I do not see in me the five lower fetters, as taught by the Blessed One. I do not see in myself a single of these fetters that has not been removed, such a fetter which, on not being removed, would lead to being reborn in this world."[16]

Then the householder Citta rose up from his bed, sat down

---

14 SN 41.10 at SN IV 303,18 adds that those *deva*s knew that Citta was a virtuous person of good conduct and thus had the qualities to enable him to realize this aspiration.

15 Instead of enquiring about his aspiration, in SN 41.10 at SN IV 303,28 the relatives ask Citta to give them an exhortation.

16 This paragraph is without a counterpart in SN 41.10, which does not have an explicit reference to his attainment of non-return.

cross-legged, [set up] right mindfulness in front, and spoke this poem:[17]

"Cloth and food that have been stored up
Extensively and with much trouble,
Offering them to a highly advanced field of merit
Breeds the five types of strength.
"What by means of an aspiration can be desired
By ordinary people who dwell at home,
All such benefits I have attained.
Already I have escaped from many troubles.
"What in the world is heard and spoken about,
I am far removed from these many troublesome affairs.
Joy arises on understanding that there will be little trouble
In pursuing full awakening.
"Make offerings to those who uphold morality,
To those who well cultivate the holy life,
To arahants, whose influxes are eradicated,
Who are the disciples of the Sage.
"To encounter excellent ones like these
Is the supreme and best of occasions.
Constantly engage in offerings to these persons
And in the end you will obtain great fruit.
"Engaging in many offerings,
Offerings made to this excellent field of merit,
On passing away from this world
You will be born spontaneously in heaven.
"Being fully endowed with the five [celestial] sense pleasures,
Your mind will be immeasurably delighted.
Because of not being stingy
One gains this sublime fruit.
In whatever place you receive rebirth,
You will always be happy."[18]

---

17 SN 41.10 does not report that he sat up. In SN 41.10 at SN IV 304,1 Citta begins his teaching by encouraging his relatives in unshakeable confidence in the Buddha, the Dharma, and the Community.

18 This long poem has as its counterpart a single sentence in SN 41.10 at SN IV 304,14, in which Citta recommends that his relatives engage in giving.

Having spoken this poem, the householder Citta passed away and was reborn among the Avihā and Ātappa devas.[19]

XXII.3 DISCUSSION

The recommendation given to Citta by the *deva*s concerns the universal monarch, *cakkavattin*. The universal monarch, who makes the Dharma his foremost concern and governs the whole world in a righteous manner, without relying on force or coercion, is a recurring motif in early Buddhist discourse.[20] In the present context this motif serves to highlight the superiority of liberating insight even over the option of establishing a peaceful society governed by Dharma in the whole world. This comes out with additional poignancy as the speaker is a lay person and not a monastic who has, at least ideally, left the world behind. Yet the same lay speaker is also one who is endowed with profound insight and high meditative accomplishment. For such a one the idea of becoming a *cakkavattin* is therefore just something else that is also impermanent, *dukkha*, empty, and not-self.

A point to be taken from all this could be that, however glorious one may imagine one's own future and beneficial activities for the sake of others to be, nothing whatsoever should take total priority over progressing to liberation. Citta can in several ways serve as a powerful icon of successful lay practice. But at the same time he also exemplifies the importance of really breaking through one's inner bondages and fetters, and not using one's responsibilities and living circumstances as an excuse for settling for a half-hearted compromise with one's own defilements.

The *deva*s in the discourse translated above were evidently unaware of Citta's high level of accomplishment, which made it impossible for him to be reborn as a human, be it as a universal

19 SN 41.10 at SN IV 304,20 only reports that Citta passed away, without noting where he was reborn. SĀ 575 continues by reporting how, reborn as a *deva* in the Pure Abodes, Citta visits the Mango Grove, where he reveals his identity to a monastic who at night had gone outside his hut to practise walking meditation.

20 For a more detailed study of the *cakkavattin* motif see Anālayo 2011c, 2012f, and 2014e.

monarch or otherwise.[21] Citta's relatives in turn were unaware of the presence of the *deva*s, wherefore they thought that he was confused when they heard him talk, leading them to try to bring him back to his senses. This was not required and the remainder of the discourse shows Citta clarifying the situation for them, just as he had clarified it for the *deva*s, before he breathes his last.

The reference to his rebirth among the Avihā and Ātappa *deva*s denotes two realms of what are called the "Pure Abodes" (*suddhāvāsa*) in early Buddhist cosmology. These are sublime celestial realms in which only non-returners are reborn. The place of his rebirth concords with Citta's own assertion that he had eradicated the five lower fetters.

Before reaching such lofty rebirth, Citta teaches others right up to his very last moment, showing that, even though he is beyond the option of becoming a benevolent ruler, he is at the same time full of compassion towards those who are in his presence. That the teaching he delivers happens to be on generosity needs to be considered alongside the wisdom he displays elsewhere. His choice of this particular topic is best read as reflecting his awareness of the inclinations and proclivities of his audience. Instead of delivering one of the profound teachings that the discourses surveyed at the outset of this chapter show him as being capable of giving, he encourages those who are right now present with him in what he knows will be most beneficial for them and probably also most easily understood and put into practice by his audience. This is a matter of such concern for him that, in the *Saṃyukta-āgama* version translated above, he even sits up to give this last teaching. His passing away in both versions is an inspiring example of how one should teach others, namely by compassionately adjusting to the audience's level of receptivity.

---

21 Nyanaponika and Hecker 1997: 372 comment that "in recommending Citta to be a world monarch the devas must have been unaware of his attainment, which made it impossible for him to return to the human realm."

XXIII

THE BUDDHA'S MEDITATIVE PASSING AWAY

XXIII.1 INTRODUCTION

The present chapter shows the continuity of the Buddha's compassionate teaching activities even when on the verge of his own death. The translated passages present him consoling the grieving Ānanda and then instructing his assembled disciples. The first of these two episodes shares with the discourse in Chapter 14 the motif of Ānanda's grief and the Buddha's providing of solace, with the difference that in the present instance it is the Buddha's own impending passing away which causes Ānanda's distress. The Buddha's advice to Ānanda provides a helpful example of how to work with grief. To balance out excessive focus on the impending loss of his beloved teacher, Ānanda is made to recollect the manifold benefits he gained through his long-time close association with the Buddha. Similarly, the impending loss of a beloved one can be put into perspective by cultivating one's appreciation, even gratitude, for all the positive experiences shared with that person in the past.

The teaching activity of the Buddha in the second episode complements the example of Citta in the last chapter, where the patient on his deathbed still delivers teachings to those around him. Just as Citta passes away after giving a teaching to his assembled relatives, so the Buddha passes away after giving a last teaching to his assembled disciples.

The two passages translated below are from the *Dīrgha-āgama* parallel to the *Mahāparinibbāna-sutta* of the *Dīgha-nikāya*, which, together with a Sanskrit fragment parallel and discourse versions found in the *Ekottarika-āgama* and as individual translations into Chinese, records the final events in the life of the Buddha.[1] After the first of the two passages taken up, the *Mahāparinibbāna-sutta* and its parallels record some other intervening episodes before reporting the Buddha's last teaching to his disciples and his passing away by putting his meditative mastery into practice one last time. In what follows I translate only these two episodes – Ānanda's grief and then the Buddha's final words and last meditation.

XXIII.2 TRANSLATION (1)[2]

At that time Ānanda was standing behind the Buddha, holding onto the bed and weeping in grief, unable to control himself. He said sobbingly: "So soon does the Tathāgata [attain] extinction! So quickly does the Blessed One [attain] extinction! So rapidly does the great Dharma sink into obscurity! The excellent one among living beings is withering away! The eye of the world is ceasing! Why do [I say] that? Receiving the Buddha's kindness I attained the level of a trainer. I have not yet accomplished my task, yet the Buddha is [now attaining] extinction."

At that time the Blessed One, who knew it, asked on purpose: "Where is the monastic Ānanda now?"[3] Then the monastics said to the Tathāgata: "The monastic Ānanda is now standing behind the Buddha, holding onto the bed and weeping in grief, unable to

1 The first episode recording Ānanda's sorrow can be found in DN 16 at DN II 143,20 (translated Walshe 1987: 265), Waldschmidt 1951: 294, T 5 at T I 169b10, T 6 at T I 184c21, T 7 at T I 200b4, and EĀ 42.3 at T II 751a21.

2 The translated parts are taken from DĀ 2 at T I 25b26 to 25c11 and 26b19 to 26c8; complete translations of DĀ 2 are available in German, French, and English; see Weller 1939 and 1940, Jin 2013, and Ichimura 2015: 63–171. For a comparative study of the *Mahāparinirvāṇa* narrative see Waldschmidt 1944 and 1948; for a study of the moment of the Buddha's actual passing away and a critical examination of some suggestions made by other scholars in relation to this episode see Anālayo 2014a.

3 DN 16 at DN II 143,24 does not note that the Buddha knew what was happening; in fact here Ānanda has gone away to cry.

control himself. He says sobbingly: 'So soon does the Tathāgata [attain] extinction! So quickly does the Blessed One [attain] extinction! So rapidly does the great Dharma sink into obscurity! The excellent one among living beings is withering away! The eye of the world is ceasing! Why do [I say] that? Receiving the Buddha's kindness I attained the level of a trainer. I have not yet accomplished my task, yet the Buddha is [attaining] extinction.'"[4]

The Buddha said to Ānanda: "Stop, stop, do not grieve and cry. Ever since you have been attending on me, you have engaged in undivided and boundless bodily deeds of mettā, you have engaged in *undivided and boundless* verbal deeds of mettā, and you have engaged in undivided and boundless mental deeds of mettā. Ānanda, you have respectfully supported me. This is of enormous great merit. Of all those who respectfully support devas, Māras, Brahmās, recluses, and brahmins, none is equal to you.[5] Be energetic and you will soon accomplish awakening."[6]

XXIII.3 TRANSLATION (2)

[The Buddha said]: "Therefore, monastics, do not be negligent. Through not being negligent, I reached right awakening myself. An immeasurable multitude of goodness as well can be attained by not being negligent. All the ten thousand things remain being impermanent." These were the Tathāgata's last words.[7]

Then the Blessed One entered the first absorption.[8] He rose from the first absorption and entered the second absorption. He rose from the second absorption and entered the third absorption. He rose from the third absorption and entered the fourth absorption.

4 The description of his grief in DN 16 at DN II 143,21 is shorter and mainly concerned with his status as a trainer.

5 Such a comparison is not found in DN 16, where the Buddha additionally highlights that whatever has come into being will inevitably have to pass away.

6 At this juncture the text continues with other events that precede the Buddha's actual passing away.

7 In DN 16 at DN II 156,1 the Buddha simply says: "Formations are impermanent, strive on with diligence."

8 The translation is based on a variant that dispenses with an additional reference to "concentration".

He rose from the fourth absorption and entered concentration on the sphere of [infinite] space. He rose from concentration on the sphere of [infinite] space and entered concentration on the sphere of [infinite] consciousness. He rose from concentration on the sphere of [infinite] consciousness and entered concentration on nothingness. He rose from concentration on nothingness and entered concentration on neither-perception-nor-non-perception. He rose from concentration on neither-perception-nor-non-perception and entered concentration on the cessation of perception [and feeling].[9]

Then Ānanda asked Anuruddha: "Has the Blessed One attained Nirvāṇa?"

Anuruddha said: "Not yet, Ānanda. The Blessed One is now in the concentration on the cessation of perception [and feeling]. Formerly I heard from the Buddha that he will attain Nirvāṇa on rising from the fourth absorption."

Then the Blessed One rose from concentration on the cessation of perception [and feeling] and entered concentration on neither-perception-nor-non-perception. He rose from concentration on neither-perception-nor-non-perception and entered concentration on nothingness. He rose from concentration on nothingness and entered concentration on the sphere of [infinite] consciousness. He rose from concentration on the sphere of [infinite] consciousness and entered concentration on the sphere of [infinite] space.

He rose from concentration on the sphere of [infinite] space and entered the fourth absorption. He rose from the fourth absorption and entered the third absorption. He rose from the third absorption and entered the second absorption. He rose from the second absorption and entered the first absorption.

He rose from the first absorption and entered the second absorption. He rose from the second absorption and entered the third absorption. He rose from the third absorption and entered the fourth absorption. Rising from the fourth absorption, the Buddha [attained] final Nirvāṇa.

---

9 The attainment of cessation is not mentioned in the PTS edition of another record of the Buddha's last meditation in SN 6.15 at SN I 158,11. This appears to be due to a loss of text; see also Bodhi 2000: 442 note 421 and Anālayo 2014a: 8f.

XXIII.4 DISCUSSION

The final instruction given by the Buddha in the discourse translated above draws attention to the impermanence of all things. The *Dīgha-nikāya* parallel similarly throws into relief impermanence, as does the Sanskrit fragment parallel.[10] In this way the Buddha seems to use his own death to give a teaching to his disciples, firmly establishing them in perception of impermanence as the central conclusion to be drawn on witnessing his passing away. The same conclusion is of course similarly to be drawn on witnessing the passing away of anyone else. In fact perception of impermanence can be seen as a converging point of the various perspectives on the cultivation of insight in relation to disease and death, surveyed in the previous chapters. Comparable to a key that unlocks the treasury of liberating wisdom, insight into impermanence indeed deserves the place of honour of having been the theme of the Buddha's last instruction.

After providing this highlight on impermanence as the crucial insight to be kept in mind, in the above account the Buddha for a last time demonstrates the superiority of a meditatively matured mind even at the time of death, thereby documenting the benefits of diligent practice, also mentioned in his last instructions. The Buddha's last meditation consists in a progression through the entire range of different levels of concentrative attainments recognized in early Buddhist thought.[11] These begin with the four absorptions, which are as follows, listed together with a brief indication of their chief affective tone:

- first absorption: joy and happiness born of seclusion,
- second absorption: joy and happiness born of concentration,
- third absorption: happiness,
- fourth absorption: equanimity.

The first of these four absorptions is characterized by the presence of a subtle degree of application of the mind and

10 DN 16 at DN II 156,1 and Waldschmidt 1951: 394.
11 For a practice-oriented survey of the absorptions and immaterial attainments see Catherine 2008.

its sustaining, *vitakka* and *vicāra*, as well as by the experience of joy and happiness born of seclusion from sensuality and involvement with the external world.[12] With the second absorption, application of the mind and its sustaining are left behind and the resultant experience is one of joy and happiness born of concentration in the full sense of the term.[13] With the third absorption, joy subsides and only happiness is left. Mindfulness, which is present throughout the gradual deepening of one's absorption practice, becomes prominent enough at this juncture to merit explicit mention as a characteristic feature of this experience. With the fourth absorption, even happiness fades away, and the resultant experience of a deeply stable mind firmly established in equanimity is at the same time an experience of superbly pure mindfulness.

Once this level of meditative mastery of the mind has been gained, the four immaterial attainments can be cultivated. These are based on the level of concentration attained with the fourth absorption. Their successive attainment takes place through refining the object of concentration:[14]

- the sphere of infinite space,
- the sphere of infinite consciousness,
- the sphere of nothingness,
- the sphere of neither-perception-nor-non-perception.

With the first of these, the object used previously for the cultivation of the four absorptions is left behind and replaced by the notion of infinite space. Next the experience of infinite space is attended to from the viewpoint of the mind that experiences such infinite space, resulting in the experience of infinite consciousness, which becomes the object of one's concentrative absorption. Attending to the insubstantiality of consciousness gives way to the experience of nothingness as the object of absorption attainment. The gradual refinement of perception that has led up to this point continues to an even deeper experience, wherein perception itself no longer fully

12 For a more detailed study of the first absorption see Anālayo 2014d.
13 For a more detailed study of the second absorption see Anālayo 2016.
14 On these objects as part of a gradual meditation on emptiness see Anālayo 2015b.

functions. The resultant attainment is therefore one where one is neither fully perceptive nor completely devoid of perception.

On the eve of his passing away the Buddha reportedly went through all of these eight levels of concentrative experience and continued with a final step that forms the culmination point of this series of meditative attainments, namely the cessation of perception and feeling. As already discussed in Chapters 6 and 7, the sick Anuruddha and the Buddha himself did not avail themselves of their ability to enter cessation when being in pain, instead choosing to dwell in the four *satipaṭṭhānas*. In the present setting the Buddha similarly chooses not to pass away in the cessation of perception and feeling. In fact it is precisely Anuruddha in the present episode who points this out to Ānanda, who had the impression that the Buddha had already passed away.

Instead of passing away in the cessation attainment, the Buddha traces the meditative trajectory leading up to the cessation of perception and feeling all the way back down to the first absorption. The ability to attain all these levels of concentrative experience in ascending and descending order is characteristic of the highest level of meditative mastery. From the first absorption the Buddha again begins the upward progression until he reaches the fourth absorption. It is after being in the fourth absorption that he passes away. He thereby passes away from an experience that is characterized not only by a profound depth of concentration, but also by a completely purified degree of mindfulness in combination with equanimity.

In this way the Buddha's last meditation can be seen to offer two indications. One is his meditative mastery as a result of his earlier diligent practice, whereby on the verge of death the Buddha is shown to be so self-possessed that he is able to accomplish a meditative tour through the entire range of possible concentrative attainments, in both ascending and descending order. The other indication is that, with all these different experiences available, he chooses to pass away from a mental condition in which mindfulness has become particularly purified. This is in line with a recurrent theme throughout other chapters in this book, which keep on showing the potential and importance of mindfulness when facing disease and death. This is the one quality to be cultivated most of all when experiencing pain or grief, when caring for others, or when passing away oneself, from the very first steps taken on the path all the way to its consummation: mindfulness.

In this way the Buddha's last instruction and final meditation throw into relief the importance of insight into impermanence and of mindfulness, both to be practised with diligence. How to go about cultivating mindfulness in a truly diligent manner in relation to the most threatening aspect of impermanence, one's own mortality, is the theme of the next chapter.

XXIV

RECOLLECTION OF DEATH

XXIV.1 INTRODUCTION

The discourses translated in the preceding chapters have in various and complementary ways highlighted the need to face impermanence, in particular death, as well as the potential of mindfulness in this respect. The set of discourses on the theme of death began in Chapter 13 with the topic of the inevitability of death, based on the episode of King Pasenadi's grief at the death of his grandmother.

The inevitability of death is also central to the present chapter, which presents instructions on how to direct mindfulness to one's own mortality as an actual meditation practice. These instructions can be found in a discourse in the *Ekottarika-āgama*, translated below, which has parallels in two discourses in the *Aṅguttara-nikāya*.[1] The parallel versions agree that the Buddha examined how his monastic disciples were practising recollection of death and found them to lack diligence in developing this practice to its fullest potential. He then gave instructions on how to become truly diligent in relation to the challenging task of fully facing one's own mortality.

---

1 AN 6.19 at AN III 303,23 and AN 8.73 at AN IV 316,22 (translated Bodhi 2012: 876 and 1219).

XXIV.2 TRANSLATION[2]

Thus have I heard. At one time the Buddha was staying at Sāvatthī in Jeta's Grove, Anāthapiṇḍika's Park.[3] At that time the Blessed One said to the monastics: "You should cultivate the perception of death and give attention to the perception of death."[4]

Then one monastic among those seated there said to the Blessed One: "I constantly cultivate giving attention to the perception of death." The Blessed One said: "How do you give attention to cultivating the perception of death?"

The monastic said to the Buddha: "At the time of giving attention to the perception of death, I have the aspiration to remain [alive] for seven days and give attention to the seven awakening factors. In the Tathāgata's teachings that would be of much benefit and I will not regret passing away after that. Blessed One, it is like this that I give attention to the perception of death."

The Blessed One said: "Stop, stop, monastic, this is not [truly] an undertaking of the practice of the perception of death. This is called being of a negligent nature."

Again one monastic said to the Blessed One: "I am capable of cultivating the perception of death." The Blessed One said: "How do you cultivate attending to the perception of death?"

The monastic said to the Buddha: "Now I have this reflection: 'I have the aspiration to remain [alive] for six days and, having given attention to the right teachings of the Tathāgata, then might reach the end of life. This will thus be for my good fortune.' In this way I attend to the perception of death."

The Blessed One said: "Stop, stop, monastic, you are also of a negligent nature. This is not [truly] attending to the perception of death."

---

2 EĀ 40.8 at T II 741c27 to 742b2 (partially translated Anālayo 2013b: 104). On the practice of recollection of death in general see Boisvert 1996 and Karunaratne 2002.

3 AN 6.19 at AN III 303,23 and AN 8.73 at AN IV 316,22 instead have the Brick Hall at Nādika as their venue.

4 In AN 6.19 at AN III 304,4 and AN 8.73 at AN IV 317,4 the Buddha highlights the benefits of recollection of death in leading to the deathless. As Bodhi 2012: 1753 note 1283 comments, "it is interesting to note that mindfulness of death culminates in the deathless."

Again a monastic said to the Buddha: "I aspire to remain [alive] for five days." Someone said: "*I aspire to remain alive* for four days." Someone said: "*I aspire to remain alive* for three days." Someone said: "*I aspire to remain alive* for two days." Someone said: "*I aspire to remain alive* for one day."

At that time the Blessed One said to the monastics: "Stop, stop, monastics, this is also being of a negligent nature. This is not [truly] attending to the perception of death."

At that time there was again one monastic who said to the Blessed One: "I am able to cultivate the perception of death effectively."[5] The monastic said to the Buddha: "When the time has come, I put on my robes, take the alms bowl, and enter Sāvatthī to beg for alms.[6] Having begged for alms I turn back to leave Sāvatthī and return to my place. I enter my meditation hut to give attention to the seven factors of awakening. Then I might reach the end of life. It is thus that I attend to the perception of death."

The Blessed One said: "Stop, stop, monastic, this is also not [truly] giving attention to cultivating the perception of death. Monastics, you all spoke of negligent ways of practice. This is not [truly] of the nature of cultivating the perception of death."

At that time the Blessed One further spoke to the monastics: "Those who are able to be like the monastic Vakkalī,[7] they are indeed reckoned to be giving attention to the perception of death. That monastic is well able to give attention to the perception of death, being disenchanted with this foul and unclean body.

"If a monastic gives attention to the perception of death, collecting his mindfulness in front,[8] with a mind that is unshaken, being mindful of the exhalation and the inhalation for the time it takes for them to go out and return, and during that period he gives attention to the seven awakening factors, that would

5 The translation "effectively" is based on a variant.

6 The addition of the expression "to beg for alms" is based on a variant.

7 AN 6.19 and AN 8.73 do not mention Vakkalī. According to the listings of outstanding disciples in AN 1.14 at AN I 24,15 (translated Bodhi 2012: 110) and EĀ 4.5 at T II 557c20, Vakkalī was foremost among those liberated by faith; for a comparative study of the canonical records of his suicide see Anālayo 2011d.

8 The translation "mindfulness" is based on a variant.

indeed be of much benefit [to him] in the Tathāgata's teaching.[9]

"This is because all formations are entirely empty, they all become appeased, they rise and cease, they are all [like] a magical illusion that is without any true essence.[10]

"Therefore, monastics, you should give attention to the perception of death in the interval between an out-breath and an in-breath, so that you will be liberated from birth, old age, disease, death, grief, worry, pain, and vexation.[11] In this way, monastics, should you train yourselves."[12]

At that time the monastics, hearing what the Buddha had said, were delighted and received it respectfully.

XXIV.3 DISCUSSION

The two parallels in the *Aṅguttara-nikāya* begin with a monastic who imagines staying alive for a single day and night in order to give attention to the Buddha's teaching.[13] The shorter of the two discourses then continues with living for a single day, for the time of a single meal, the time of swallowing several mouthfuls, the time of a single mouthful, and the time of breathing in and out. The longer of the two discourses adds to these the time of half a day and the time of half a meal. In both *Aṅguttara-nikāya* versions the Buddha commends those who expect to live for the time it takes to swallow a single mouthful or the time of breathing in and out.

The central message conveyed in these two discourses as well as in the *Ekottarika-āgama* version translated above is that recollection of death needs to be applied directly to the present moment. This need arises from the certainty of death,

---

9 AN 6.19 and AN 8.73 do not mention the awakening factors.

10 AN 6.19 and AN 8.73 do not make such a statement.

11 AN 6.19 at AN III 306,15 and AN 8.73 at AN IV 319,32 conclude by highlighting that training in the recollection of death can lead to the destruction of the influxes.

12 The translation is based on a variant.

13 AN 6.19 at AN III 304,9 and AN 8.73 at AN IV 317,9. A discourse quotation in T 1509 at T XXV 228a25, translated in Lamotte 1970: 1424, begins with the idea of living for seven years and then proceeds to seven months, seven days, six days, five days, four days, three days, two days, one day, the time of a meal, and the time of breathing in and out. The Buddha commends the last case.

combined with the uncertainty of when death will come. Those who envisage their own death taking place at some time in the future, even if this is only a single day, are considered to be negligent in their practice. Instead of such "negligence", acknowledging one's own mortality needs to be coupled with diligence, with the awareness that death can happen right now, in the sense that death is *right now* approaching *me*. As Bowker explains,

> mindfulness of Death is a concentration ... on the fact that death (*maraṇa*) is approaching *me*. It is not a meditation on death in general, but on its application to me.[14]

This application to oneself and the emphasis on relating it to the present moment differ substantially from common ways of thought. Wayman notes that

> mankind does not ordinarily think this way. Therefore ... there is implied a kind of conversion of the mind, a "death" from previous ways of thinking by way of contemplating death.[15]

In this way, from a Buddhist viewpoint the existential question that death poses to human beings can be solved in life, in fact it can *only* be solved in life. Furthermore, it not only *can* be solved; it *must* be solved.[16] As Klima points out, this requires

> an intimate confrontation with the painful and disappointing tendency of the body to fall apart and die. It is the practitioners' belief that only by coming to terms with this truth can one ever escape from being emotionally subject to it.[17]

Facing one's own death when still alive offers the best preparation for being able to live well the actual moment of death. The potential of such practice is that it enables one to live without the deadening effects of the fear of death. Only once death has become a natural part of life will it be possible to go beyond the influence of existential fear and thereby come fully alive to life as it unfolds in the present moment. The pervasiveness

---

14 Bowker 1991: 187.
15 Wayman 1982: 289.
16 Schmidt-Leukel 1984: 166.
17 Klima 2002: 173 and 198.

of the existential fear of death has been formulated by Becker as follows:

> The idea of death, the fear of it, haunts the human animal like nothing else; it is a mainspring of human activity – activity designed largely to avoid the fatality of death, to overcome it by denying in some way that it is the final destiny of man.[18]

The repercussions of the fear of death on various aspects of human behaviour have been studied in detail in modern psychology, leading to the development of the Terror Management Theory, which studies how human beings manage the existential terror of their own mortality.[19] The basic problem could be summarized in this way:

> The fear of death is rooted in an instinct for self-preservation that humans share with other species. Although we share this instinct with other species, only we are aware that death is inevitable – that is, that our self-preservation instinct will inevitably be thwarted. This combination of an instinctive drive for self-preservation with an awareness of the inevitability of death creates the potential for paralyzing terror.[20]

Research undertaken on this paralysing terror has led to a better understanding of what appears to be an ingrained reaction to being made aware of one's own mortality, namely by attempting to turn attention away from it.

> When thoughts of death are in current focal attention, the individual responds ... by either distracting oneself from the issue or pushing the problem of death into the distant future by denying one's vulnerability.[21]

The terror of death, as long as it is unresolved, leads to the construction of defence mechanisms. One of these consists in pushing death into the distant future, precisely the problem that according to the *Ekottarika-āgama* discourse and its parallels met with the Buddha's criticism. Another defence mechanism

18 Becker 1973: xvii.
19 Greenberg et al. 1986; see also Burke et al. 2010.
20 Harmon-Jones et al. 1997: 24.
21 Pyszczynski et al. 2004: 445.

comes into play as soon as awareness of one's own mortality is no longer at the forefront of one's attention.

> Death thoughts are often too threatening to be kept in focal attention for an extended time ... once death thoughts have receded from focal attention, people rely on a dual-component, cultural anxiety buffer, consisting of a cultural worldview and self-esteem, to manage the implicit knowledge of their inevitable death. People create and maintain a system of beliefs and practices (a cultural worldview) that provides order and meaning in life, standards of value to attain, and protection against death in the form of symbolic immortality.[22]

In this way, fear of death extends its various arms like a polyp, building up and fortifying one's sense of identity. This provides the background for the relationship drawn in the early Buddhist texts between recollection of death and awakening, the realization of the deathless. Fear of death is intimately connected with one's holding on to a sense of personality, *sakkāya*. One who has fully realized the truth of not-self thereby goes beyond the fear of death.

The medicine required to bring about this cure is surprisingly simple: attending to the possibility that one's own death could happen right here and now. All it requires is bringing one's own mortality into present-moment awareness. Such practice can have a considerable transformative effect not only for oneself, but also in relation to others. As Kübler-Ross points out,

> if all of us would make an all-out effort to contemplate our own death, to deal with our anxieties surrounding the concept of death, and to help others familiarize themselves with these thoughts, perhaps there could be less destructiveness around us.[23]

One can undertake this type of practice of bringing one's own mortality into present-moment awareness, in accordance with the above instructions, through mindfulness of the breath. In the conclusion that follows I will explore detailed instructions for mindfulness of breathing that involve sixteen distinct

---

22 Niemic et al. 2010: 345.
23 Kübler-Ross 1969/1982: 12.

steps of practice. In the case of recollection of death, the task is simpler. Mindfulness of each breath just needs to be yoked firmly to awareness of the fact that this breath could be the last breath one will take.

The actual practice I like to recommend for this involves relating the perception of one's own mortality especially to the inhalations. In this way with every breath coming in one is aware that this could be one's last inhalation, and with every exhalation one trains oneself to let go and relax.

Practising in this way enables one to adjust the intensity of one's recollection of death so as to maintain mental balance and to proceed in accordance with one's personal abilities and the requirements of the present situation. At times the thought of one's death can become quite challenging, even leading to fear and agitation. If this should happen, one emphasizes being aware of the exhalations and of letting go. This helps to calm the mind. At other times it can happen that practice has become somewhat sluggish or automatic; the fact of one's own mortality is not really making an impact on the mind. In such a situation one puts more emphasis on the inhalations, on the fact that this could be the last breath taken in.

There can be no doubt that one will breathe one's last breath sooner or later, and with equal certainty this moment is coming closer and closer with every breath one takes. Therefore the present breath, even if not the last, is certainly one breath closer to death.

Every breath, closer to death.
Every breath, closer to death.
Every breath, closer to death.

CONCLUSION AND MEDITATION INSTRUCTIONS

INTRODUCTION

In what follows I first briefly summarize some of the key points that emerge from the preceding twenty-four chapters on how to face disease and death. Then I describe one practical approach to the meditative instructions given to the sick Girimānanda in the discourse translated in Chapter 12.

The base line and foundational reference point for the early Buddhist perspective on disease and death is the teaching on the four noble truths. The honest acknowledgement to oneself that one's own craving and clinging are contributory causes to the experience of *dukkha* is the indispensable diagnostic groundwork for administering the medicine of early Buddhist wisdom to the case of being afflicted by disease and death. Integral to this teaching is the eightfold path aimed at realizing a state of total mental health through full awakening. Although early Buddhist mental training has much to offer for healing and palliative care, its final aim reaches far beyond.

Based on this foundational reference point, a central distinction between the bodily and mental components of the experience of pain comes into play. By avoiding the arrow of mental pain, the mind can be kept healthy even when the body is sick. Keeping the mind healthy requires meditational training, especially in mindfulness, the first of the awakening factors and the primary quality cultivated through the practice of the four *satipaṭṭhāna*s. As the discourses surveyed in this study show, the potential of mindfulness in facing pain and leading to healing was not lost on the early Buddhists. This is the case to such an extent that even those able to dwell in states of deep concentration, which could be used to suppress feelings completely, rather opt to face pain with mindfulness.

Besides mindfulness, another key aspect in the early Buddhist attitude towards disease and death is the recurrent emphasis on non-attachment, particularly in relation to the five aggregates of clinging and the six sense-spheres. Here the foundation for deepening non-attachment is insight into their impermanence, their resultant inability to provide lasting satisfaction, and the conclusion that they are empty. The cultivation of insightful freedom from attachment rests on a foundation in virtuous conduct, which in itself provides a source of fearlessness when one is sick and close to death.

When guiding others through their last moments, a gradual refinement of the innate drive to happiness can be employed to enable the dying to pass away with as much inner peace and absence of gross forms of clinging as possible. A helpful practice for the time of death is dwelling in the divine abodes, *brahmavihāra*s, which offer access to the experience of "heaven on earth" within one's own mind.

Not only in the case of disease, but also when facing death, the power of mindfulness proves its worth, enabling one to remain balanced with the experience of feelings and withstand their tendency to trigger unwholesome reactions in the mind. Approached in this way, the time of dying can become a potent occasion for the arising of liberating insight. Besides proving its worth as an aid to facing one's own death, mindfulness can also play a transformative role in relation to the experience of grief. In order to recollect one's own mortality, mindfulness of breathing can be used to make oneself fully take on board the fact that one might live only until the next breath.

The central perspectives that emerge from the passages surveyed so far can be brought together within the meditative frame of the instructions to Girimānanda, which involve insight into the impermanent nature of the five aggregates of clinging, the empty nature of the six sense-spheres, the nature of the body to become sick, the need to purify the mind, the vision of total mental health as the final goal, and detailed instructions on mindfulness of breathing. Implementing the meditation programme that brought about Girimānanda's recovery from illness offers an approach to integrating chief aspects of the early Buddhist attitude to disease and death into one's personal meditation practice.

THE MEDITATION INSTRUCTIONS TO GIRIMĀNANDA

In what follows I present one possible way in which the instructions given in the *Girimānanda-sutta* and its Tibetan parallel, translated in Chapter 12, can be put into practice. Needless to say, my intention is only to provide an inspiration for practice, without any implicit claim that what I present is the only correct way to go about it. Practitioners should feel free to adjust to their personal requirements and inclinations what I present here merely as an example.

Just to recapitulate, the Buddha tells Ānanda to present the following ten perceptions to the sick Girimānanda:

- the "perception of impermanence" in the five aggregates,
- the "perception of not-self" in the six senses and their objects,
- the "perception of lack of beauty" in the anatomical constitution of the body,
- the "perception of danger" in the body's tendency to become sick,
- the "perception of abandoning" unwholesome thoughts,
- the "perception of dispassion" as a conduit to Nirvāṇa,
- the "perception of cessation" as a conduit to Nirvāṇa,
- the "perception of not delighting in the whole world" as a conduit to Nirvāṇa,
- the "perception of impermanence in all formations" as a conduit to Nirvāṇa,
- "mindfulness of breathing" in sixteen steps.

As discussed in Chapter 12, the first four perceptions in the *Girimānanda-sutta* correspond to the four distortions: mistaken projections of permanence, a self, attractiveness, and pleasure on a reality that is the opposite of these. The correspondences are as follows:

perceptions:	distortions:
1) impermanence	a) permanence in what is impermanent
2) not-self	c) self in what is not-self
3) lack of beauty	d) attractiveness in what is unattractive
4) danger	b) pleasure in what is *dukkha*

The perceptions of dispassion (6), of cessation (7), of not delighting in the whole world (8), and of impermanence in all formations (9) form another set of four. The single perceptions (5 and 10) involve a subdivision into fours. The perception of abandoning (5) concerns the removal of sensual thoughts (5a), of ill will (5b), of harmfulness (5c), and of any other evil and unwholesome quality (5d); the sixteen steps of mindfulness of breathing (10) come in four tetrads that correspond to the four *satipaṭṭhāna*s. The fourfold rhythm underlying the entire set of ten perceptions is as follows:

- impermanence (1), not-self (2), lack of beauty (3), danger (4);
- abandoning sensual desire (5a), ill will (5b), harmfulness (5c), unwholesomeness (5d);
- dispassion (6), cessation (7), not delighting in the whole world (8), impermanence in all formations (9);
- mindfulness of breathing: first tetrad (10a), second tetrad (10b), third tetrad (10c), and fourth tetrad (10d).

The four *satipaṭṭhāna*s are of additional relevance to appreciating the instructions to Girimānanda. As I briefly mentioned in Chapter 6, a comparative study of the instructions on *satipaṭṭhāna* in the *Satipaṭṭhāna-sutta* and its Chinese *Āgama* parallels suggests the following main themes for the four *satipaṭṭhāna*s: contemplating the true nature of the body in terms of its lack of attractiveness, as well as its empty and mortal nature (A), contemplating the nature of feelings (B), contemplating the nature of the mind (C), and contemplating *dharma*s in such a way as to cultivate the mental conditions conducive to awakening (D).

In the instructions to Girimānanda corresponding themes have already been broached before the onset of mindfulness of breathing. In fact the perception concerned with the body's lack of beauty (3) corresponds to one of the contemplations of the body found in all versions of the *Satipaṭṭhāna-sutta*.[1]

The perception of danger or impediments (4) begins in the *Girimānanda-sutta* and its Tibetan parallel with the summary statement that the body is productive of much pain. This is one of the three types of feeling, the topic of the second *satipaṭṭhāna*. The perception of abandoning (5) is clearly concerned with the mind, being based on the same basic distinction between what is wholesome and what is unwholesome that also informs the first states of mind listed in the *Satipaṭṭhāna-sutta* and its parallels for contemplation of the mind. The next perceptions (6 to 9) in the *Girimānanda-sutta* incline the mind towards the final goal and are thereby a thematic counterpart to the building up of the awakening factors that is central to the fourth *satipaṭṭhāna* in the *Satipaṭṭhāna-sutta* and its parallels.

The resulting correspondences between the third to ninth perceptions in the *Girimānanda-sutta* and the four *satipaṭṭhāna*s are as follows:

perceptions:	*satipaṭṭhāna*:
3) lack of beauty	A) body
4) danger	B) feelings
5) abandoning	C) mind
6) to 9) dispassion etc.	D) *dharma*s

From this viewpoint, then, mindfulness of breathing in the *Girimānanda-sutta* works through meditative terrain already covered with the seven preceding perceptions, and these in turn take off based on the foundation in insight laid by the first two perceptions. Mindfulness of breathing thereby in a way summarizes and rounds off what has been taken up earlier and at the same time combines these different themes into a single

1 Regarding counterparts to the first two perceptions in AN 10.60, contemplation of the five aggregates is absent from the Chinese *Āgama* parallels to MN 10. Contemplation of the six sense-spheres, besides not being found in all versions, concerns the arising of a fetter, not contemplation of not-self; see Anālayo 2013b: 169–74.

unified whole, based on awareness of the changing process of breathing.

The narrative setting of the *Girimānanda-sutta* also has some bearing on putting into practice the instructions to Girimānanda. On the reasonable assumption that Ānanda's recitation functioned as a guided meditation, Girimānanda would have meditatively progressed through these ten meditations concurrently with Ānanda's recitation. This enables one to gauge the time it might take to complete the entire programme of ten meditations.

Assuming a measured type of recitation, it would not take more than twenty or thirty minutes to recite the entire discourse. Even allowing for short intervals after each of the ten perceptions to let the instructions sink into the mind, it seems reasonable to assume that it took no more than an hour, and quite possibly even less, to conclude the entire recitation. The *Girimānanda-sutta* and its Tibetan parallel make it clear that, in whatever way Girimānanda followed the recitation, it was certainly successful, as it led to his recovery. Based on this it seems reasonable to assume that progressing through all ten perceptions within a single meditation session of forty-five to sixty minutes would be in line with what the text seems to indicate.

Needless to say, familiarizing oneself with each of these practices will indubitably take considerably more time. It may be recommendable to take up each on its own for a while, and only later combine them all into a single meditative progression. Little additional information about Girimānanda is known, so it is not clear how familiar he would already have been with some or most of these practices. Perhaps what was new to him was only the way they are woven together into a continuous succession of meditative experiences.

Be that as it may, once one has achieved familiarity with these ten perceptions, it should be possible to complete the entire meditation programme within a single sitting. The advantage of having such a variety of meditative themes within a relatively limited time period is that the mind is kept engaged, making it less probable that it will succumb to distraction. Even if that were to happen, a distraction will more easily and swiftly be noticed. In this way one can enliven practice and avoid it turning into a monotonous duty performed somewhat automatically.

Based on building up the meditative continuity that this type of approach facilitates, one might then continue for the remainder of one's meditation period with a less structured form of practice, such as just being aware of the changing flow of experience in the present moment.[2] Based on these preliminary observations, we are now ready to turn to the actual practice.

THE PERCEPTION OF IMPERMANENCE (1)

According to the relevant instructions, translated in Chapter 12, one should contemplate as follows:

> Bodily form is impermanent, feeling is impermanent, perception is impermanent, formations are impermanent, consciousness is impermanent. One should contemplate these five aggregates of clinging as impermanent.

This first perception involves the five aggregates that one tends to cling to:

- bodily form,
- feeling,
- perception,
- formations,
- consciousness.

As already discussed in Chapter 2, the physical body tends to be clung to as the location "where I am", feeling provides an opportunity to cling to "how I am", perceptions can become the object of clinging to "what I am", formations provide the foundation of clinging to "why I am" acting in a certain way, and consciousness furnishes the basis for clinging to experience as "whereby I am". To counter such clinging, the required medicine is to direct mindfulness to the impermanent nature of each of these five individually and also to all five in combination.

I suggest to begin actual practice by becoming aware of the body in the sitting posture. Such whole-body awareness can serve as a helpful foundation for continuity of mindfulness

2 This would be in line with what in Anālayo 2003: 267 I suggest as a summary of key elements of *satipaṭṭhāna* meditation: "keep calmly knowing change."

throughout the entire meditative programme described in the instructions to Girimānanda.

The knowing of the body in the sitting posture should then be accompanied by the understanding that this body is impermanent. It keeps changing at the cellular level at every moment, and eventually it will pass away, fall apart, and disintegrate in its entirety.

The way to know that the whole body is now in the sitting posture involves a form of proprioceptive awareness, the ability to sense the position of the body and come to know it clearly without even needing to open one's eyes. This way of feeling the body is a manifestation of the aggregate of feeling. Awareness of this aspect of the meditative experience of the body in the sitting posture opens the vista to the second of the five aggregates. What is further required at this point is the understanding that feelings also change; they are impermanent.

The knowing of the body in the sitting posture requires the ability of the mind to recognize that this is the "body" and that it is in the "sitting posture". This is the domain of the third aggregate of perception. Recognizing this part of the same meditative experience of the body in the sitting posture needs to be accompanied by the understanding that perception, too, is of a changing nature.

The decision to attend to the body in the sitting posture, just as at times the tendency of the mind to get lost in some fantasy or thought, is an expression of the aggregate of formations. These also keep changing; the very fact of getting distracted is clear proof that formations must also be impermanent.

The knowing of all these facets of the experience of the body in the sitting posture is performed by consciousness, the last of the five aggregates. The fact that such knowing can involve different objects implies in turn that consciousness must also be of a changing nature. If it were unchanging, it would forever know only one single thing.[3]

3 In the words of Gunaratana 2014: 109, "the mind does not remain static when it becomes aware of the changes in conditioned things ... in other words, our awareness of impermanence is also impermanent. That is why the mind, while watching ... impermanence ..., drifts away from this awareness." For an application of the present perception of impermanence to mindfulness of breathing see Gunaratana 2014: 17f.

In this way the five-aggregate scheme can be employed to distinguish these five facets of the basic situation of sitting in the meditation posture, followed by being aware of them as processes, as changing, without anything permanent to be found anywhere. After going through the aggregates one by one, one can then rest in awareness of all aggregates in combination as a mere flux. Practice is proceeding properly if one is clearly aware of the process character of all aspects of what one might cling to as "I".

THE PERCEPTION OF NOT-SELF (2)

Having dwelled for as long as one finds suitable in the perception of impermanence, one moves on to perception of not-self, in the sense of the empty nature of all aspects of sense experience. The instructions for this perception are to contemplate as follows:

> The eye is not-self and forms are not-self, the ear is not-self and sounds are not-self, the nose is not-self and odours are not-self, the tongue is not-self and tastes are not-self, the body is not-self and tangibles are not-self, the mind is not-self and mind-objects are not-self. These six internal and six external sense-spheres are not-self.

To get started it would be helpful to open the eyes just a little and allow the gaze to rest on some spot in front, without looking at anything in particular.

Next one turns awareness to the eyes, more specifically to the faculty of vision in the eyes, with the understanding that the physical basis for the ability to see is not-self. It is not-self in the sense of being empty of anything permanent in it, empty of anything that one could truly and forever own or possess. Attention next shifts from the eyes to what is seen. Whatever objects come within the range of vision, they certainly are also not-self, that is, they are empty of anything permanent in them, empty of anything that one could truly and forever own or possess.

From the eyes, which one might now or a little later close again, one proceeds to becoming aware of the ears, of the faculty of hearing, and turns attention to what is heard. Ideally one has retired to a secluded spot, as explicitly recommended in the instructions, according to which one should go to sit in a forest under a tree or in an empty hut. Yet even in such places something will make itself heard, sooner or later. This is all the more the case when one is not able to practise in a secluded spot. By turning "disturbances" into part of the practice, the present meditation can have a remarkable effect. Whatever the sound one is hearing may be, it is also not-self. No need to take it up, appropriate it, make it "my" disturbance, and then become annoyed with it.

The same procedure applies to the nose and whatever odours one might smell, even if this is rather indistinct. Similarly one directs awareness to the tongue together with tastes, which during the meditation sitting will often just be the basic taste of one's own saliva.

The body and tangibles provide easily noticeable objects for the application of the not-self strategy. Part of the body must be touching the ground, in addition to which there is the touch sensation of one's clothing and any meditation gear. At times pain can manifest because of sitting for a long time without changing posture. Whatever it is, body and tangibles are not-self.

Finally comes the mind, which sooner or later tends to become distracted. Even when totally distracted by some thought or fantasy, all that is required is a moment of smiling recognition with the understanding that this, too, is not-self, and one is back in the present moment.

From having cultivated the perception of not-self in relation to each of these six sense-spheres individually, practice can proceed to being aware of the whole set of six senses and their objects as sharing the characteristic of being empty. A sign of proper practice is the recognition of the empty nature of all aspects of experience, internal and external, without exception.

THE PERCEPTION OF THE LACK OF BEAUTY (3)

The perception of the lack of beauty corresponds to the instructions on contemplating the anatomical parts of the body in the *Satipaṭṭhāna-sutta*. Additional information provided by this discourse and its *Madhyama-āgama* parallel comes from a simile, which illustrates the appropriate attitude when undertaking this exercise with the example of looking at a container with various grains inside.[4] The implication appears to be that, just as when seeing various grains one would not feel sexually attracted, in the same way one should cultivate an attitude towards the body that is free of sensual attachment. In order to emerge from obsession with the sexual attractiveness of one's own body, and its correlate in the sexual attractiveness of the bodies of others, it can at times be a skilful means to emphasize the less appealing and even disgusting aspects of the body. However, this should be done with circumspection and with a clear overall aim to arrive at the balance of freedom from attachment, instead of resulting in a loss of balance through excessive revulsion.

The basic instruction in the Tibetan version introduces various anatomical parts of the body with the injunction that one "should reflect distinctly on this body from the top of the head down to the soles of the feet, covered by skin, full of many impurities". The Pāli version similarly enjoins that one should "examine this same body up from the soles of the feet and down from the top of the hair, enclosed by skin and full of many impurities".

For the sake of facilitating the cultivation of the present perception, I like to suggest a simplification. This is based on a passage in the *Sampasādanīya-sutta* and its parallels, which describe a progression of practice from contemplating the different anatomical parts to contemplating just the bones, leaving aside skin and flesh.[5] This implies that the anatomical parts listed in the *Sampasādanīya-sutta*, which correspond to the listing in the *Satipaṭṭhāna-sutta*, can be subsumed under three headers:

- skin,
- flesh,
- bones.

---

4 MN 10 at MN I 57,20 (translated Ñāṇamoli 1995/2005: 147) and its parallel MĀ 98 at T I 583b9; see also Anālayo 2013b: 67f.

5 DN 28 at DN III 105,12 (the translation by Walshe 1987: 420 does not do full justice to the original) and its parallels DĀ 18 at T I 77b17 and T 18 at T I 256a12; see also Anālayo 2013b: 72f.

Once familiarity with these three parts has been achieved, those who wish to do so could expand this mode of contemplation so as to cover all of the individual anatomical parts listed in the discourse for this perception.

To implement the simplified version and make this as much as possible a matter of direct experience, I suggest employing a body scan. Actual practice can have as its starting point awareness of the whole body in the sitting posture, followed by a body scan that attends in particular to the skin. Beginning with the skin on the head, such a scan proceeds by sensing the skin in the neck area, the shoulders, etc., all the way down to the feet. At first it might be preferable to take arms and legs singly, but eventually these can be done concurrently.

Having completed one body scan attending to the skin from head to feet, for the sake of continuity the next scan attending to the fleshy parts of the body, including the organs, could start from the feet and gradually move up to the head. This in turn can lead to a third scan attending to the bones from head to feet.

During the actual scan, the task is to simply be aware of the location of the skin, flesh, or bones. At times it naturally happens that one will have a direct sense or feel of these parts of the body. Such a distinct feel is not necessary, however, since the purpose of the exercise is not to cultivate bodily sensitivity up to the point that one is able to feel one's skin or flesh and bones distinctly throughout the entire body. General awareness of the respective parts of the body is quite sufficient for the exercise to fulfil its purpose. This purpose is to combine a grounding of mindfulness in the body with a clear awareness that the body is made up of skin, flesh, and bones. Such awareness then should be accompanied by the understanding that, however useful skin, flesh, and bones are to keep this body alive, they are not in themselves sexually attractive.

Having done the three body scans in this way, meditation can proceed to being aware of the whole body in the sitting posture, made up of skin, flesh, and bones, as something that is not in itself sexually alluring. A sign of practice correctly carried out is a growing sense of freedom from attachment to sensuality along with the realization that the entire concern with sexual attractiveness is the product of mental projections onto what is fundamentally of the same nature as various grains in a container.

THE PERCEPTION OF DANGER (4)

The instruction for this perception in the Tibetan version introduces a long list of diseases with the statement that "this body has much pain and many impediments. In this body many diseases arise." The Pāli version is similar, with the minor difference that it speaks of "danger" instead of "impediment".

Similarly to the preceding perception, in the present case I also like to recommend a simplification, based on the above summary statement that introduces the listing of various diseases in the *Girimānanda-sutta* and its Tibetan parallel. This summary statement highlights that the physical body is subject to much pain and many diseases. My suggestion is to implement this basic understanding without going into each of the various individual diseases listed in the discourse. Once familiarity with this simplified approach has been gained, it is of course open to those who are so inclined to move on to a mode of contemplation that takes up each of the sicknesses and afflictions explicitly mentioned in the instructions for this perception.

The simplified approach can be combined with yet another body scan. Given that the previous perception of the body's lack of beauty involved three body scans, the last of which ended with the feet, for the purpose of continuity one could start from the feet and gradually move up to the head. During this body scan one is aware of each part of the body with the clear understanding that this particular part can become sick and turn into a source of pain. With the scan completed, one rests in whole-body awareness combined with a clear recognition of the vulnerability of the body, of its "danger" in becoming an "impediment" through falling prey to disease and pain.

Executing this type of practice does not necessarily require going into various details about what particular type of illness may affect the bodily area which one is at present attending to, or exactly in what way this illness could result in pain and affect the rest of the body. At times this happens naturally and can strengthen the impact of this perception, but the main purpose of the exercise is served as long as one is clearly aware that each and every part of the body could potentially become sick, whether it be due to external influences or internal causes.

The diseases to which the body can fall prey include lethal ones. The listing in the discourse translated in Chapter 12 refers to cancer, for example, and several of the other diseases mentioned in it could become so severe as to bring about death. Directing awareness to this inherent "danger" of the body opens the door to making recollection of death an integral part of the present exercise. In terms of actual practice, when resting in whole-body awareness, after having completed the body scan, one can allow the mortality of the body to stand out as a particularly prominent aspect of the body's vulnerability in general, in particular being aware that one cannot be totally sure one will still be alive even just in the next moment. Such awareness could then be related to the breath in the manner described in Chapter 24. In this way, after a body scan with attention to the various possible diseases that can afflict the body, one rests in awareness of the whole body as well as of the breath, with each inhalation knowing that this could be one's last breath and with each exhalation cultivating an attitude of letting go.

Much like the previous perception, the present meditative practice should also be carried out with an eye on balance. When awareness of the vulnerability of the body becomes too challenging, one can attend to the fact that at present one does not have most of the various illnesses that the body could in principle give rise to. Awareness of the potential of the body to become sick can therefore, whenever needed, be complemented by keeping in view the fact that it has not succumbed to all of these possible illnesses. In this way one can ensure that inner balance is maintained.

Proper cultivation of this perception has a remarkable potential to transform one's attitude towards the body. Clear appreciation of one's own body's vulnerability makes it much less probable that one will engage in risky types of activities merely for the sake of personal entertainment. In particular in the case of falling sick, the present perception shows its full worth. A major difficulty with becoming sick can be the unwitting assumption that one is sort of entitled to health, that being without illness is the base-line condition of one's body. Regular cultivation of the present perception will make it unmistakeably clear that such assumptions are projections of the mind that do not accord with reality. It is not at all surprising that one should become sick. Properly considered, it is surprising that one does not become ill more often and more seriously.

The realization that it is perfectly natural to become sick and experience pain can considerably reduce the stressful mental repercussions of falling ill. In addition, familiarity with this perception offers a tool to switch perspective, in the sense that, having become afflicted with one particular disease, one is free to attend as well to one's not being afflicted at present with quite a range of other diseases. Alongside becoming aware of pain in one particular part of the body, one can broaden attention to include also those parts of the body that are not in pain. Such modes of attending serve to prevent a narrowing down of perspective and enable the establishing of a more open and accepting attitude towards the experience of being sick. Out of the various perceptions taught to Girimānanda, the present one seems most directly relevant to the actual experience of disease.

Another aspect of the perception of danger is that it provides a bridge from insight into the nature of the body, a theme taken up in the preceding perception, to awareness of feelings. According to the summary statement that introduces the instructions for the present perception, the body is subject to much pain and many diseases. Thus the experience of pain in various forms and degrees is an integral aspect of this meditation.

In fact the listing of afflictions in the discourse shows that this perception is not only concerned with what one would consider a sickness from a medical point of view, but also includes such aspects of bodily discomfort as the experience of cold and heat, hunger and thirst, or the need to defecate and urinate. Just like diseases, these types of discomfort are also productive of gradually increasing bodily pain if not attended to, and can even become the source of serious illness.

In practical terms, one could turn mindfulness to the need of the body to be constantly protected from being affected by outside temperature. The maintenance of the body requires a regular supply of food and drink, whose resultant wastage has to be disposed of with similar regularity. Even the very fact of sitting in meditation will eventually lead to the arising of various pains, forcing one to change posture.

Awareness of the basic discomfort implicit in having a body can either be part of formal practice by being combined with the body scan, or else be carried out during everyday activities. All that is required is a moment of mindful recognition when feeling an itch or any other type of bodily discomfort caused by one's posture or activity, when becoming hungry or thirsty, when feeling too hot or too cold, or when having to obey the calls of nature. Just for a moment one remains simply aware of the demands of the body and allows this to lead to a clear recognition of what this means from the viewpoint of the nature of one's own body. All of these aspects are avenues for developing insight into the "impediment" or "danger" inherent in having a human body. The proper implementation of the present perception will manifest in an increasingly non-attached and balanced attitude towards matters related to the body.

THE PERCEPTION OF ABANDONING (5)

At this juncture in the meditative progression, the groundwork in insight has been completed by cultivating four perceptions that are in direct contrast to the four perversions – of mistaking what is impermanent, *dukkha*, not-self, and unattractive – for being the opposite. The trajectory so far has been to cultivate two perceptions that embrace the entirety of one's experience, followed by two perceptions that focus on the body, with the second of these opening up the vista towards feelings. In line with the basic progression underlying the scheme of the four *satipaṭṭhānas*, at the present juncture the next topic is the condition of one's mind. The four types of thoughts or mental conditions that one should overcome are:

- sensual desire,
- ill will,
- harming,
- evil and unwholesome qualities.

In relation to each of these, the instructions in the Tibetan version are that one does "not dwell in arisen" sensual desire (or else ill will, harming, or evil and unwholesome qualities), "but removes it, eliminates it, does not become habituated to it, and does not cultivate it". The Pāli version similarly recommends that one should not "tolerate" such a thought: "abandon it, remove it, terminate it, and do away with it."

The topic of sensual desire naturally ties in with the previous perceptions. The perception of the absence of beauty in the body can offer a major contribution to undermining sensual desire of the sexual type and becoming well established in the opposite quality, an attitude of renunciation, *nekkhamma*, letting go of concern with sensual pleasures. This is the condition of the mind when sensual desire has gone into abeyance at least temporarily. Further support for the cultivation of renunciation comes from the perception of danger. The more one is able to let go of the quest for bodily pleasure through sensual indulgence, the less one will be affected by the impact of bodily pain when one becomes sick. Conversely, the more one realizes the body's natural tendency to become sick and lead to pain, the less one will be prone to getting lost in the quest for sensual pleasure and gratification.

A basic distinction between harmful and wholesome mental conditions underlies the instructions on contemplation of the mind in the *Satipaṭṭhāna-sutta* and its parallels. An important and easily overlooked aspect of such practice is that mindfulness has the task not only to recognize what is unwholesome, but also to recognize what is wholesome.[6]

The same perspective informs the approach I like to suggest for cultivating the present perception, which need not be confined to only those moments when one of these unwholesome thoughts manifests in the mind. Practice begins by examining whether the thought in question is present in one's mind. If it is,

6 See in more detail Anālayo 2013b: 159–62.

one makes an effort to remove and abandon it, in line with the instructions in the *Girimānanda-sutta* and its Tibetan parallel. If the thought is not present in the mind, however, one could keep dwelling in the condition that is directly opposed to it.

Applied to the case of sensual desire, if a first inspection of the mind has ascertained that no such thought is present in one's mind right now, practice can continue by dwelling with an attitude of renunciation of sensuality, inclining the mind towards renunciation. The peaceful and joyful condition of the mind experienced at this time will go a long way in strengthening one's readiness to let go of any incursion of sensual desire into this wholesome and agreeable mental condition.

After dwelling in the condition of renunciation, one next examines whether there is even a trace of ill will present in the mind. If ill will is present, one removes it. Once the mind is at least temporarily free from ill will, one continues dwelling in a condition that is free from ill will and anger. Such a condition naturally relates to *mettā*.[7] Dwelling in *mettā* could be done by way of the boundless radiation that I have discussed elsewhere.[8] Dwelling in this divine abiding, one gives particular emphasis to *mettā* as a condition of being entirely free from ill will and aversion.

The same procedure holds for thoughts of harming, in which case the opposite mental condition is compassion. By dwelling in compassion the mind is free from any intention to harm. At the same time such dwelling will make it much less probable that harmfulness arises again in the mind. Here, too, the dwelling in this divine abode is best done with an emphasis on the nature of compassion as being totally free from any intent to harm.

In relation to the absence of evil and unwholesome qualities in the mind, mentioned as the last aspect for the perception of abandoning, one could cultivate the divine abode of equanimity. The firm determination to continue dwelling in a mental condition free from any unwholesome influence can

7 As noted by Gunaratana 2014: 71, "when we abandon thoughts of hatred, loving-friendliness arises naturally to fill the void."
8 Anālayo 2015b: 159f.

become a form of dwelling in equanimity, ready to face the pull and push of anything unwholesome with the non-attachment of mental equipoise.

If one wishes to integrate all of the four *brahmavihāras* into the practice of the present perception, then sympathetic joy could be cultivated as a transition from compassion to equanimity, by way of rejoicing in relation to those whose mind is free from unwholesomeness and those who walk the path leading to this condition.

In short, my suggestion is to empower the perception of abandoning through the intentional cultivation of the mental conditions that are directly opposed to those types of thought one is required to abandon, thereby using this opportunity to integrate the divine abodes into the meditative progression.

Proper undertaking of this mode of practice manifests in an increasingly swift awareness of the occurrence of any of these unwholesome thoughts in the mind, and in the ever more frequent conscious experience of the pleasant and peaceful condition of a mind that is free from these.

THE PERCEPTION OF DISPASSION (6)

In the *Girimānanda-sutta*, the perception of dispassion is based on the following reflection:

> This is peaceful, this is sublime, namely the calming of all formations, the letting go of all supports, the extinguishing of craving, dispassion, Nirvāṇa.

A minor difference in the Tibetan formulation of this perception is that, instead of "letting go of all supports", it speaks of "the transformation of what has arisen". The main point behind this reflection is to incline the mind towards Nirvāṇa. Given the preceding trajectory of practice, where the perception of abandoning sets in with the removal of thoughts of sensual desire, freedom from passion naturally comes to the forefront with the present perception. In practical terms this can be implemented by inclining the mind towards Nirvāṇa as the freedom from all passion, by viewing freedom from passion and sensual craving as indeed peaceful and sublime.

THE PERCEPTION OF CESSATION (7)

The next perception is almost the same as the preceding one, with the difference that the term dispassion has been replaced by cessation:

> This is peaceful, this is sublime, namely the calming of all formations, the letting go of all supports, the extinguishing of craving, cessation, Nirvāṇa.

Cultivation of this perception can take up a complementary aspect of Nirvāṇa as the supreme cessation of all that is unwholesome, viewed as peaceful and sublime. When undertaken as part of the present meditative progression, this could be implemented by putting special emphasis on the cessation of thoughts of ill will and harming, mentioned earlier in relation to perception 5, concerned with abandoning. This would complement the relation of the preceding perception of dispassion to abandoning sensuality.

The final eradication of ill will and harming (just as of sensual desire) takes place at the time of attaining non-return. For progress to this lofty goal it can serve as a source of inspiration if the mind is regularly inclined towards dispassion and cessation as complementary aspects of mental freedom.

THE PERCEPTION OF NOT DELIGHTING IN THE WHOLE WORLD (8)

The *Girimānanda-sutta* formulates the perception of not delighting in the whole world in terms of letting go of and abandoning any "clinging, mental standpoints, adherences, or underlying tendencies". According to the Tibetan parallel, the same abandoning concerns "worldly knowledge, thoughts, positions, and underlying tendencies". These instructions can be understood as drawing out in more detail the implications of the reference to the "letting go of all supports" in the maxim quoted above for the previous two perceptions.

In practical terms, cultivating this perception can be implemented through a willingness to let go and relinquish whatever one is accustomed to clinging to, in particular one's opinions and preferences, judgements and views. In this way a refinement takes place compared to the two earlier perceptions, which in the way presented above are concerned with freedom from the more evident and gross manifestations of unwholesomeness, namely freedom from sensual desire through dispassion and freedom from ill will and harming through cessation. At the present juncture even the more subtle traces of unwholesomeness in the form of any type of clinging are being relinquished.

THE PERCEPTION OF IMPERMANENCE IN ALL FORMATIONS (9)

The Tibetan version recommends that one "has no attachment in relation to all formations, abandons them, and is disgusted by them". The *Girimānanda-sutta* employs stronger wording, as it uses three Pāli terms that are more or less equivalent to becoming disgusted. Here the Tibetan version seems to me preferable, in that it allows for a soft sense of letting go and non-attachment that gradually builds up, instead of presenting active disgust as the only mode in which to undertake this perception. In relation to the maxim for perceptions 6 and 7, the present perception can then be understood to draw out in more detail the full implications of the "calming of all formations" as an aspect of Nirvāṇa.

The name given to this perception can be considered as complementing the actual instructions. This name suggests that awareness of the "impermanence of all formations" offers a contribution to the attitude towards all formations described in the actual instructions.[9] The point behind this could be that impermanence is the foundation for insight, which then leads on to insight into *dukkha* and not-self. The maturing of insight into the three characteristics can indeed furnish the momentum for letting go of and becoming free from attachment in relation to all formations, in relation to all that is conditioned and subject to change.

In line with the gradual refinement underlying the previous three perceptions, the present exercise adds a further degree of subtlety by way of inclining the mind towards the

9 See also above p. 104 note 15.

unconditioned. All that is conditioned is necessarily impermanent. Seeing this clearly, one becomes free from being attached to it all, one lets go of it all, and one becomes sufficiently disgusted with it all to allow the inclination of the mind towards the unconditioned to gather momentum.

In sum, my suggestion is to cultivate perceptions 6 to 9 by inclining the mind towards Nirvāṇa as the supreme form of dispassion, the total cessation of all ill will and harming, the thorough giving up of all that is unwholesome, and the wholehearted abandoning of all that is conditioned and subject to change. A sign of successful practice of perceptions 6 to 9 is an increasing degree of clarity about one's priorities in life. The more one engages in these meditations, the more progress towards awakening will become the central reference point in one's activities, communications, and thoughts. Just as the ocean is pervaded by the taste of salt, so all one's actions and interactions with others will come to be pervaded by the taste of liberation.[10]

MINDFULNESS OF BREATHING (10)

From having inclined the mind towards the unconditioned, the meditative trajectory continues by turning back to what is conditioned. In fact practice turns to the one condition that is absolutely vital for the continuation of the body, which is the process of breathing. Mindfulness directed to the breath thereby becomes the last of the ten "perceptions" listed in the *Girimānanda-sutta*, and this tenth form of practice is in itself a whole programme of meditation that proceeds through sixteen distinct steps. The circumstance that this whole meditative programme is also reckoned a single "perception" seems to reflect its characteristic of converging on a single object. This is mindfulness of the changing nature of the breath, and therewith

10 A simile found in AN 8.19 at AN IV 203,6 (translated Bodhi 2012: 1144) compares the taste of liberation that pervades the teaching and discipline with the taste of salt that pervades the ocean. The simile of the salt pervading the ocean recurs in the parallel MĀ 35 at T I 476c11, where it illustrates pervasion with the tastes of dispassion, awakening, tranquillity, and the path. In yet another parallel, EĀ 42.4 at T II 753a28, the simile illustrates pervasion with the taste of the noble eightfold path.

awareness of the changing nature of all experiences that take place in conjunction with the process of breathing.

The function of mindfulness of breathing in the present context appears to be to bring the different aspects covered so far in the preceding nine perceptions together into a unified practice with the single object of the breath. Such bringing together of the range of insights cultivated up to this point in a way exemplifies the transition to be made from formal practice to daily activities, which similarly requires bringing together various insights in such a way that these converge on informing one's thoughts, words, and deeds in any circumstance.

A comparable function of the sixteen steps of mindfulness of breathing can be seen in the *Mahārāhulovāda-sutta*. Here instructions given in reply to a request to be taught mindfulness of breathing first take up contemplation of the not-self nature of the five elements earth, water, fire, wind, and space. The five elements are then employed to inspire mental attitudes of patience and equipoise. These attitudes then lead on to the divine abodes, which in turn are followed by contemplations of the lack of beauty and of impermanence.[11] It is only after this meditative tour that the practice of the sixteen steps of mindfulness of breathing falls into place in the *Mahārāhulovāda-sutta*. The meditative progression in the *Mahārāhulovāda-sutta* touches on several themes that are also relevant to the *Girimānanda-sutta*, a parallelism that supports the impression that in both instances mindfulness of breathing functions as a culmination point of practice.

This culmination point of practice operates within the framework of the four *satipaṭṭhāna*s by way of a constant pattern of fours, in that each set of four steps, each tetrad in the scheme of sixteen steps of mindfulness of breathing, corresponds to

---

11 MN 62 at MN I 421,27 (translated Ñāṇamoli 1995/2005: 528). The parallel EĀ 17.1 at T II 581c16 mentions cultivation of the absence of beauty and the four divine abodes, and then gives detailed instructions on mindfulness of breathing. Here this builds on earlier instructions in contemplation of the impermanent nature of the five aggregates of clinging. The absence of a reference to the elements as an inspiration for mental attitudes could be a case of a shifting of place of a textual passage within the collection, as such instructions occur in another discourse, EĀ 43.5 at T II 760a6, where they do not fit the context; see in more detail Anālayo 2014/2015: 75f.

one *satipaṭṭhāna*.[12] The entire scheme to be cultivated alongside awareness of inhalations and exhalations proceeds as follows:

Contemplation of the body:
- know breaths to be long
- know breaths to be short
- experience the whole body
- calm the bodily activity

Contemplation of feelings:
- experience joy
- experience happiness
- experience the mental activity
- calm the mental activity

Contemplation of the mind:
- experience the mind
- gladden the mind
- concentrate the mind
- liberate the mind

Contemplation of *dharmas*:
- contemplate impermanence
- contemplate dispassion
- contemplate cessation
- contemplate letting go

The sixteen steps are preceded by the injunction to sit down cross-legged in a secluded place and become mindful just of the inhalations and exhalations. In terms of actual practice I suggest observing the breath in whatever way one finds preferable. This could be at the point where the air strikes the nostrils or any other point where the air can be experienced in the body, such as the movement of the abdomen. It could also take place without focusing on any particular location. The main task is to be aware of breathing in and of breathing out, which can be executed in whatever way is most natural or suitable from the viewpoint of the individual meditator.

12 On the sixteen steps in other traditions see Anālayo 2013b: 228–33 and below p. 242.

According to the instructions given in the *Girimānanda-sutta*, the first four steps of mindfulness of breathing require being mindful of one's breath coming in as well as going out, and at the same time being aware of the following four aspects:

- know breaths to be long,
- know breaths to be short,
- experience the whole body,
- calm the bodily activity.

In practical terms this means that, after having become mindful of the breath moving in and out, the meditator becomes aware of the length of these breaths. These could be either long or short. Here it is noteworthy that in the *Girimānanda-sutta* the instructions for the first two steps are worded as alternatives, evident in the use of the disjunctive particle *vā*, which means "or". This suggests that the instructions need not be understood as requiring that one should first have long breaths and then short breaths, but rather that one is aware of either long or short breaths. Nevertheless, to cover both of these steps in the sequence in which they are described in the discourse, one might simply take a long and deep breath to start with, and after that mindfully observe how subsequent breaths become naturally shorter.

Whichever approach one prefers to adopt for the first two steps, the third step requires experiencing the whole body. Taking the instruction for the third step as referring to the whole physical body, a meaning that finds support in the formulation employed in several parallel versions,[13] awareness of the breath at this juncture would come combined with an awareness of the whole body in the sitting posture. Calming the bodily activity in the fourth step can then come about by allowing the breath to become calm and the body to relax until both reach a condition of natural stillness and stability.

The cultivation of mindfulness of breathing proceeds from contemplation of the body to contemplation of feelings by way of these four steps:

---

13 See in more detail Anālayo 2003: 131f and 2013b: 231, as well as the translations below p. 242.

- experience joy,
- experience happiness,
- experience the mental activity,
- calm the mental activity.

On the understanding that wholesome forms of joy and happiness can already be experienced when the mind has not yet reached absorption concentration,[14] one simply allows the calmness and stability of breath and body reached with the preceding step to give rise to joy. Such joy, which is the natural result of being established in calmness and being endowed with mindfulness in the present moment, can at first be barely noticeable. The arising of joy can be encouraged by becoming aware of even its most subtle manifestations and by consciously encouraging it through reviewing the pleasantness of the calmness reached so far.

The very condition of calmness also ensures that the arising of joy will lead to the more refined and tranquil experience of happiness. The progression from being aware of the body in the previous tetrad to experiencing joy and happiness in the first part of the present tetrad involves some degree of refinement, with mindfulness attending to aspects of the mind. These become the object of the next step, where the task is to experience whatever mental activity may manifest in the present moment, whatever perception or feeling there might be. The ensuing step is to calm any such mental activity. This continues a trajectory that already began with the shift from joy to happiness, where the willingness to let go of the more rapturous experience of joy results in greater calmness. The same principle holds here, in that the willingness to let go of mental activities of any type results in increasing depths of mental calmness.

Mindfulness of breathing proceeds to awareness of the mind with the next four steps:

- experience the mind,
- gladden the mind,
- concentrate the mind,
- liberate the mind.

14 Anālayo 2003: 133–6.

The calming of mental activities naturally leads to experiencing the mind as such, which involves a further refinement of one's meditative attention by becoming aware of that which knows, becoming aware of the mind itself. Practically speaking, the shift to the third tetrad requires turning awareness back to that which is aware of the breath, aware of the body, aware of happiness, etc. This further refinement naturally leads to a sense of gladness; simply becoming aware of this will encourage the pervasion of the mind with gladness. Such gladness of the mind in turn results in the mind becoming collected and concentrated. Precisely because of its profound calmness, the experience is so enjoyable that the alluring pull of any potential distraction fades in comparison. The present transition still involves a soft inclining of the mind towards concentration. This is followed by letting go even of this last vestige of inclining the mind, allowing it to be free from any interference at all, and at the same time remaining in a condition that is also liberated from any distraction.

The meditation undertaken up to this point builds up an ideal mental condition for the cultivation of insight, which according to the *Girimānanda-sutta* requires proceeding through four interrelated themes:

- contemplate impermanence,
- contemplate dispassion,
- contemplate cessation,
- contemplate letting go.

The first of these is a theme that has already been present throughout the preceding steps. At the present juncture impermanence moves to the forefront of awareness in the form of a clear recognition that all aspects of present-moment experience are merely a process, a flux; they are all subject to the nature of change. The breath keeps changing continuously, and in dependence on it the body keeps changing, just as the mind constantly changes.

Next one cultivates dispassion towards this changing process of experience. By allowing disenchantment to arise and transform one's affective attitude, attachment and passion gradually fade away. They yield to their opposites and are replaced by non-attachment and dispassion. From dispassion one turns to cessation, to becoming aware of the disappearance aspect of the process of experience. The present breath is barely noticed, and it is already gone. The present experience is barely noticed, and it is already gone.

This mode of attending sharpens insight into impermanence, bringing its most threatening aspect right to the forefront of meditative attention: everything is bound to disappear. The more this understanding ripens, the easier it is to let go. Letting go of attachment, passion, clinging, grasping, in whatever form they manifest. Letting go of any identification with present experience or any appropriation of it. With such letting go, practice points directly to what the previous perceptions 6 to 9 (dispassion, cessation, not delighting in the whole world, and impermanence in all formations) converge on, namely the realization of total mental health through the attainment of the deathless.

An alternative scheme for this last tetrad, found in some versions of the sixteen-step scheme (such as the Mūlasarvāstivāda *Vinaya* version translated in the appendix), proceeds instead through the following four steps:

- impermanence,
- eradication/abandoning,
- dispassion,
- cessation.

This could be implemented by proceeding from contemplating impermanence to eradicating and abandoning any clinging or holding on, followed by dispassion and cessation in the way described above.

With the last of the sixteen steps of mindfulness of breathing the whole meditative programme delineated in the *Girimānanda-sutta* has been completed. For the remainder of one's meditation session one could continue with an unstructured form of practice. With the continuity of awareness of the body in the sitting posture as a basic reference point, thereby being well established in an embodied form of mindfulness, one simply opens up to the changing process of present-moment experience in whatever way it unfolds. The mind remains with a wide-open attitude, anchored in the here and now of the flow of experience through its grounding in embodied mindfulness, which can include awareness of the process of breathing. If the mind has been distracted, a little more focus on the breath within the overall frame of whole-body awareness can be helpful to stabilize being in the present moment. Once practice has taken up momentum again, such focus can again be dispensed with, making room for a more relaxed and open type of embodied awareness.

Looking back on the entire meditative trajectory, the practice of the ten perceptions could be visualized as a spiral-like progression through a circular cone, proceeding from its base to its apex. The first two perceptions in the *Girimānanda-sutta*, the perceptions of impermanence (1) and of not-self (2), lay out the basic foundation in insight for what is to come and can be seen as establishing the axis of the cone. The central reference point for the entire practice is a comprehensive appreciation of the impermanent nature of all aspects of oneself, which has its complement in the empty nature of all aspects of experience.

The meditative progression from the third to the ninth perception can then be envisaged as taking off in a spiralling fashion along the circumference of the base of the cone and moving gradually towards the apex. This spiralling movement proceeds in two circles through the four cardinal directions, which correspond to the four *satipaṭṭhāna*s.

Here perception of lack of beauty (3) covers contemplation of the body (first *satipaṭṭhāna*) and perception of danger (4) offers a lead into contemplation of feelings (second *satipaṭṭhāna*). The perception of abandoning (5) reflects the basic distinction between wholesome and unwholesome states of mind underlying contemplation of the mind (third *satipaṭṭhāna*), and the perceptions of dispassion etc. (6 to 9) incline the mind towards awakening, a central aspect that emerges from a comparative study of contemplation of *dharma*s (fourth *satipaṭṭhāna*).

Having completed this first revolution through the four *satipaṭṭhāna*s, the tenth perception of mindfulness of breathing involves another such circle of the spiral at a section of the cone closer to its apex. This second revolution again proceeds through the same four cardinal directions of the four *satipaṭṭhāna*s, which correspond to each of the four tetrads of practice. With the last of the sixteen steps of mindfulness of breathing one reaches the apex of the cone, which is simply embodied present-moment awareness of the changing nature of empty phenomena with an attitude of letting go.

Awareness of change with an attitude of letting go, in particular letting go of any grasping and clinging, combines the foundational insight into impermanence and its complement of not-self. Just as the whole cone converges on its apex, so, too, the whole meditative programme can be viewed as converging on and moving towards ever deeper levels of letting go.

As mentioned earlier in this conclusion, a basic pattern of sets of four underlies the entire meditation programme delineated in the *Girimānanda-sutta*. The spiralling motion from the base to the apex of the cone, after having established the axis of the cone through the first two perceptions, can in turn be compared to a piece of music with a rhythm of four bars and a double crescendo that takes off from the main musical theme intonated with perceptions 1 and 2.

According to the way of practice I have suggested above, the perceptions of lack of beauty (3) and of danger (4) can be undertaken with the help of *four* body scans, which proceed from the outer parts of the body gradually towards its internal aspects and then to its propensity to give rise to pain and affliction. Next come *four* types of thought as the theme of the perception of abandoning (5), followed by *four* perceptions that incline the mind towards Nirvāṇa (6 to 9). These sets of four gradually progress towards what is more refined or profound, and the high point of this first crescendo is reached with the perception of impermanence in all formations (9).

The ensuing shift from the profound mode of inclining the mind towards Nirvāṇa with the ninth perception to the comparatively ordinary phenomenon of the long breath provides a starting point for a second crescendo. This second crescendo has the same rhythm of four bars, where mindfulness of breathing proceeds through *four* tetrads of *four* steps of practice.

Along with the double crescendo based on the basic rhythm of four bars, the circumference of the spiralling motion gradually draws closer to its culmination point at the apex, which comes with the last step in the last of the perceptions: letting go, the fruition of insight into the changing and empty nature of experience.

The second crescendo touches on the same basic tune of the four *satipaṭṭhāna*s that also underlie the first crescendo. Instead of employing an orchestra of different perceptions, it does so with a single musical instrument, the breath. After the four complementary modes of inclining the mind towards Nirvāṇa as the finale of the first crescendo, the transition to the solo performance by way of mindfulness of the breath brings things down to earth. Instead of leaving the practitioner to struggle with the contrast between the lofty heights of these four perceptions and one's own often less lofty condition, the ensuing shift maintains the same momentum but relates it to something very ordinary, the process of breathing. This helps to connect to present-moment experience just as it is, however painful or even close to death it may be.

The basic tune of the four *satipaṭṭhāna*s finds expression in complementary performances during the two crescendos. Perception 3 and the first tetrad of mindfulness of breathing are both concerned with aspects of the body closely related to its functionality, namely its different anatomical parts and the breath. Whereas with perception 3 the emphasis is on the body's lack of beauty and thereby on its not attractive and at times even disgusting aspects, the first tetrad counterbalances this by leading up to the peaceful experience of calming the bodily activity. Similarly, the concern with the inherent danger of the body to give rise to sickness and thereby to painful feeling in perception 4 finds its counterbalance in the pleasant feelings experienced with joy and happiness in the second tetrad of mindfulness of breathing. Perception 5 concerns the abandoning of unwholesome thoughts, an abandoning that is taken further with the third tetrad of mindfulness of breathing, where leaving behind any type of thought leads to experiencing the mind as such. Perceptions 6 to 9 as different modes of inclining the mind towards Nirvāṇa have their match in the last tetrad of mindfulness of breathing. After having first of all brought impermanence to the forefront of attention, this last tetrad takes up the very same themes of dispassion and cessation of perceptions 6 and 7, and its last step of letting go can be viewed as corresponding to the not delighting in the whole world of perception 8 and the giving up of all formations of perception 9.

A central theme relevant to all contemplations described in the *Satipaṭṭhāna-sutta* is impermanence, evident in the recurrent instruction to contemplate arising and passing away in relation to each of its exercises. In the case of the set of meditations in the *Girimānanda-sutta* and its Tibetan parallel, this musical theme of impermanence has been intonated right away, with the first perception concerned with the five aggregates. The same theme is echoed in perception 9, the perception of *impermanence* in all *formations*, which inclines the mind to the cessation of all formations. This leads to the solo performance by way of the sixteen steps of mindfulness of breathing, all of which continually play the musical theme of the *impermanent* nature of the bodily *formation* or activity of the breath,[15] evident in the alternation between inhalations and exhalations. Perceptions 9 and 10 together exemplify and actualize the potential of continuous awareness of impermanence in leading to the breakthrough to Nirvāṇa. This becomes particularly prominent with the last tetrad of mindfulness of breathing, where impermanence comes to be the sole object of attention with the first step. The remainder of this tetrad then builds on the meditative thrust that results from full appreciation of impermanence, namely inclining the mind towards Nirvāṇa through dispassion, cessation, and letting go (or alternatively through abandoning, dispassion, and cessation).

The apex of the meditative cone and finale movement in the entire concert performance, awareness of change with an attitude of letting go, not only serves as a converging point of the practices undertaken so far by those who have gone through the entire meditation programme, but also offers itself as an entry point for those who are in a situation that is not conducive to formal meditation practice. This is particularly relevant when one is seriously sick or on the verge of death. Although I hope the preceding pages have brought home the

15 SN 41.6 at SN IV 293,15 (translated Bodhi 2000: 1322) and its parallel SĀ 568 at T II 150a24 identify the breath as the "bodily formation" (par excellence).

importance of preparing oneself for such a situation as much as possible when one is still reasonably healthy, the present book would not completely fulfil its purpose if it did not also offer an entry into practice for those who find themselves in such a situation unprepared.

Suppose one has suddenly become seriously ill and is in pain and agony, physically unable to sit in formal meditation or just be quietly by oneself, perhaps even being close to passing away. What to do? The one thing to rely on in such a situation is mindfulness. From early Buddhist meditation to modern-day clinical pain relief, mindfulness is what empowers one to face disease and death. So the task is just to be aware of changing phenomena, as they really are, in the present moment. Just that much is more than enough. Whenever this is lost, which is only natural, one comes back to it, ideally with a smile, if one's pains allow for that.

In order to support the continuity of such present-moment awareness of the flow of experience, it is helpful to make this an embodied form of mindfulness, either by being with the breath or else by resting in a general manner aware of the body as a whole, whichever of these two alternatives suits one's sick condition better. The advantage of being mindful of the breath is that it naturally encourages awareness of the constantly changing nature of experience. The advantage of being mindful of the whole body is that it encourages a broad and encompassing type of awareness which is not so easily lost when a distraction occurs, and which counteracts the tendency to contract around physical pain.

Whether one chooses one of these two forms of embodied mindfulness or any combination of the two, one simply remains aware of the flux of what happens, just as it is, without choosing or rejecting, cultivating an attitude of letting go. Letting go of one's expectations. Letting go of one's ideas of how one would like things to be. Letting go of one's presumption that one is somehow entitled to a healthy body. Letting go of one's resistance to the fact that the body is manifesting its inherent nature of becoming sick and falling apart. Letting go of any attachment, in whatever way it might manifest.

In this way mindfully accompanying the present moment as a changing process, with an attitude of not giving in to the tendency to cling and react, can become a powerful way of facing disease and death. It not only offers a skilful way of handling the actual experience of being sick and perhaps even about to pass away, but it can even turn this experience into something profitable, in the sense that disease and death can become opportunities for deepening freedom from attachment.

The same emphasis on letting go and freedom from attachment is similarly relevant for those who take advantage of the opportunity to prepare themselves for facing disease and death through regular cultivation of the entire meditation programme described above. The spiralling progress through the meditative cone, from its base to its apex, leads to a form of embodied mindfulness of the flow of experience in the here and now, informed by the insights cultivated through the previous practices that have led up to the culmination point of letting go. With openly receptive and embodied awareness of the flow of experience in the present moment, one maintains this attitude of letting go; letting go of distractions and disturbances, of choosing and rejecting, of expectations and evaluations, of past and future. Training in letting go will eventually culminate in the supreme letting go, the realization of the total health of Nirvāṇa, the deathless.

APPENDIX ON MINDFULNESS OF BREATHING

This appendix offers translations of two *Vinaya* versions of the sixteen steps of mindfulness of breathing, the final exercise described in the *Girimānanda-sutta* and its Tibetan parallel. In my translation of the Tibetan version in Chapter 12, due to the original not being well enough preserved, I was unable to present a translation of its instruction and compare it with the Pāli parallel. Hence with the present appendix I hope to make up for this by providing some more comparative material on the practice of the sixteen steps.

In an earlier comparative study of *satipaṭṭhāna* meditation, I translated the instructions for the sixteen steps of mindfulness of breathing from the *Saṃyukta-āgama* as well as the Mahāsāṅghika *Vinaya*.[1] A noteworthy difference that emerges from comparing these to the Pāli presentation is that the injunction to "train" oneself is not found in all versions. Another point is that the Mahāsāṅghika *Vinaya* speaks of "pervading the body" in step 3, which supports an understanding of this step as involving an awareness of the whole body. Moreover, steps 14, 15, and 16 in these two versions require contemplation of eradication, dispassion, and cessation, instead of being concerned with contemplating dispassion, cessation, and letting go.

The same points also emerge from the two *Vinaya* versions translated below. For the last three steps the Mūlasarvāstivāda

1 Anālayo 2013b: 228–30.

Vinaya has abandoning, dispassion, and cessation. The Sarvāstivāda *Vinaya* instead follows the sequence also found in Pāli sources, namely eradication, dispassion, and cessation. In relation to the third step of mindfulness of breathing, the Mūlasarvāstivāda and Sarvāstivāda *Vinaya* versions both speak of pervading the body. Neither of the two refers to training. No reference to training is found even in the *Saṃyutta-nikāya* parallel to the Mūlasarvāstivāda *Vinaya* account. This appears to be due to the circumstance that the episode in question concerns the Buddha's own practice. As explained in the Pāli commentary, the Buddha had no need to train when practising mindfulness of breathing.[2]

The text translated first stems from this episode, reported in the Mūlasarvāstivāda *Vinaya* and a *Saṃyutta-nikāya* parallel.[3] The two versions agree that on this occasion the Buddha had been on a longer retreat, during which he undertook the practice of mindfulness of breathing.

The second translation is from the Sarvāstivāda *Vinaya*, where the Buddha gives instructions on mindfulness of breathing after unbalanced practice of contemplation of the body's lack of beauty has led some monastics to become so disgusted with their own bodies that they committed suicide. The same is also recorded in a range of *Vinaya*s as well as in a discourse in the *Saṃyutta-nikāya* and its *Saṃyukta-āgama* parallel.[4] On finding out what had happened, the Buddha is on record for recommending to his monastics the cultivation of mindfulness of breathing.

These two markedly different occasions are helpful for an appreciation of the nature of mindfulness of breathing as a meditation practice. In the case of the disgusted monastics, mindfulness of breathing has the purpose of replacing an unbalanced form of practice, the undertaking of which has led to rather serious problems. The *Saṃyutta-nikāya* discourse and its *Saṃyukta-āgama* parallel agree that the Buddha explicitly

---

2 Spk III 273,31.

3 SN 54.11 at SN V 326,1 (translated Bodhi 2000: 1778), see also SĀ 807 at T II 207a12.

4 SN 54.9 at SN V 321,21 (translated Bodhi 2000: 1774) and its parallel SĀ 809 at T II 208a3; for a comparative study of this episode see Anālayo 2014f.

introduced the sixteen steps of mindfulness of breathing as a sublime way of practice that quickly leads to the overcoming of unwholesome states. The *Saṃyukta-āgama* version illustrates this potential of mindfulness of breathing with the example of heavy rain that will make any dust quickly disappear.[5]

The nuance of a balanced and sublime practice with remarkable liberating potential is similarly relevant to the Buddha's own practice, although in this case some further exploration is needed to substantiate this.

Relevant to the Buddha's apparent preference for the practice of mindfulness of breathing in sixteen steps would be his own practices related to the breath during the time before his awakening. The *Mahāsaccaka-sutta* and its parallels report that, besides an attempt to control the mind through force and the practice of fasting, the Buddha-to-be engaged in several ways in breath control.[6] When the attempt to control the mind by sheer force did not work, he tried in various ways to achieve the same by forcefully stopping the breath, practising the "breathingless meditation". When repeated practice of this type did not work, he tried to achieve his aim by controlling his food intake.

What all these attempts have in common is forceful control. None of these led the Buddha-to-be to awakening. Instead, the way to awakening he eventually found and taught to others was the cultivation of insight through the receptivity of mindful observation.

The practice of mindful observation of the process of breathing in sixteen steps can be seen to build on the Buddha's pre-awakening interest in the breath, but put into practice in an entirely different manner. Instead of trying to control the breath, the task is rather to bring into play receptive and non-interfering observation through mindfulness. This takes place in such a way that all four *satipaṭṭhāna*s are covered against the background of the continuously changing alternation between inhalations and exhalations. In this way the sixteen steps of

---

5 SĀ 809 at T II 207c28 (translated Anālayo 2014f: 14).

6 MN 36 at MN I 243,4 (translated Ñāṇamoli 1995/2005: 337), Sanskrit fragment 333r3, Liu 2010: 171, and EĀ 31.8 at T II 671a12; see also the *Lalitavistara*, Lefmann 1902: 251,14, the *Mahāvastu*, Senart 1890: 124,9 (translated Jones 1952/1976: 120), and the *Saṅghabhedavastu*, Gnoli 1977: 100,16.

mindfulness of breathing could be considered a practical expression of the change of attitude that led the Buddha to awakening.

From this viewpoint, the Buddha's preference for mindfulness of breathing to the extent that he would spend an entire retreat period engaged in this practice conveys the same message as his recommendation of this form of meditation to monastics who had been practising in an unbalanced manner. In both situations mindfulness of breathing stands out as a balanced meditation practice which inculcates insight into impermanence by way of cultivating the four *satipaṭṭhānas*. This can equally serve as the path to liberation or else as the dwelling appropriate for one who has been liberated.

TRANSLATION (1) FROM THE MŪLASARVĀSTIVĀDA *VINAYA*[7]

Then, when the two months were over,[8] the Blessed One rose from his concentration and sat down on a seat prepared in front of the community of monastics. He said to the monastics: "If heterodox practitioners come and ask you: 'During these two months, what practice did the recluse Gotama undertake to abide in concentration?', you should reply: 'He undertook concentration through mindfulness of breathing.' What is the reason? During these two months I undertook contemplation through mindfulness of breathing, calmly sitting and abiding in it.

"When I practised this contemplation, while breathing in I was without confusion, understanding it as it really is; while breathing out I was also without confusion, understanding it as it really is.[9]

"*While breathing in* long *I was without confusion, understanding it as it really is; while breathing out long I was also without confusion,*

7 The translated text is found in T 1448 at T XXIV 32c7 to 32c21. The instructions on the sixteen steps in the Tibetan translation of the Mūlasarvāstivāda *Vinaya*, D 1 *kha* 62b6 or Q 1030 *ge* 58a6, are abbreviated and only offer material for comparison up to step 4 and for step 16.

8 According to SN 54.11 at SN V 326,1, the Buddha had been on retreat for three months.

9 SN 54.11 does not mention being without confusion or understanding as it really is.

understanding it as it really is. While breathing in short *I was without confusion, understanding it as it really is; while breathing out short I was also without confusion, understanding it as it really is their* arising and passing away.[10] Pervading the body when breathing ⟨in⟩,[11] I understood it completely; pervading the body when breathing ⟨out⟩, I also understood it completely. Calming the [bodily] activity when breathing ⟨in⟩,[12] *I understood it as it really is;* calming the [bodily] activity when breathing ⟨out⟩, I understood it as it really is.

"Experiencing [joy] *when breathing in,* I understood it *as it really is; experiencing joy when breathing out, I understood it as it really is.* [Experiencing] happiness *when breathing in,* I understood it *as it really is; experiencing happiness when breathing out, I understood it as it really is.* [Experiencing] the ⟨mental⟩ activity *when breathing in,* I understood it *as it really is; experiencing the mental activity when breathing out, I understood it as it really is.*[13] Calming the mental activity when breathing in, I understood it as it really is; calming the mental activity when breathing out, I understood it as it really is.

---

10 This remark on arising and passing away, which has no counterpart in SN 54.11, could be the result of a textual error.

11 My translation here and in the next step is based on an emendation. T 1448 at T XXIV 32c13 speaks first of breathing out and then of breathing in for steps 3 and 4. The Tibetan translation of the Mūlasarvāstivāda *Vinaya*, D 1 *kha* 62b7 or Q 1030 *ge* 58a7, instead starts with breathing in for these two steps. The same is also the case for a Mūlasarvāstivāda discourse version; see SĀ 810 at T II 208a25 (translated Anālayo 2007a: 139). Since even T 1448 itself mentions first breathing in for the preliminary step as well as in the remainder of the scheme, it can safely be concluded that its presentation of steps 3 and 4 has suffered from a textual corruption.

12 The supplementation of "activity" (for this rendering of equivalents to *saṅkhāra* in the present context see above p. 105 note 18) is supported by the Tibetan parallel, D 1 *kha* 63a1 or Q 1030 *ge* 58a8.

13 My rendering is based on an emendation. T 1448 at T XXIV 32c15 has a reference to knowing just the mind as step 6, and after the reference to happiness in step 7 then has an isolated occurrence of the Chinese character for formation or activity, before coming to step 8. This clearly is the result of textual confusion; in fact the corresponding presentation in the *Saṃyukta-āgama* agrees with other sources that the progression in this tetrad involves experiencing joy, happiness, the mental activity, and calming the mental activity; see SĀ 810 at T II 208b1. So my emendation involves shifting the reference to mind and to knowing so that they come after step 7 and thereby complement the reference found there to activity.

"Cognizing the mind *when breathing in, I understood it as it really is; cognizing the mind when breathing out, I understood it as it really is.* Gladdening the mind *when breathing in, I understood it as it really is; gladdening the mind when breathing out, I understood it as it really is.* Concentrating the mind *when breathing in, I understood it as it really is; concentrating the mind when breathing out, I understood it as it really is.* Liberating the mind when breathing in, I understood it as it really is; liberating the mind when breathing out, I understood it as it really is.

"Discerning impermanence *when breathing in, I understood it as it really is; discerning impermanence when breathing out, I understood it as it really is.* Discerning abandoning *when breathing in, I understood it as it really is; discerning abandoning when breathing out, I understood it as it really is.* Discerning dispassion *when breathing in, I understood it as it really is; discerning dispassion when breathing out, I understood it as it really is.* Discerning cessation when breathing in, I understood it as it really is; up to discerning cessation when breathing out,[14] I understood it as it really is."

TRANSLATION (2) FROM THE SARVĀSTIVĀDA *VINAYA*[15]

The Buddha said to Ānanda: "When the time in the morning has come for a monastic, according to wherever one has come to stay in dependence on a town or village, one puts on the robes, takes the bowl, and enters the village to beg for food with collected body, with sense faculties restrained, being single-mindedly mindful. Having partaken of the meal, one spreads out the sitting mat in an empty place, at the foot of a tree or in an empty hut, sits down properly with straight body and collects mindfulness in front.

"One abandons covetousness in the world, being far removed from greedy attachment to the possessions of others. Proceeding in this way one then ably removes ill will, sloth-and-torpor, restlessness-and-worry, and doubt. These are the

14 The occurrence of the expression "up to", which usually indicates an abbreviation, seems out of place at this point and would much rather fit the Tibetan version, which indeed abbreviates up to step 16 of contemplating cessation when breathing out.

15 The translated section is found in T 1435 at T XXIII 8a17 to 8b2.

types of hindrance that are able to vex the mind. They result in weakening the power of wisdom and do not lead to Nirvāṇa, therefore they should be abandoned.

"When breathing in, one should know to be breathing in single-mindedly; when breathing out, one should know to be breathing out single-mindedly.

"*When breathing in* long, *one should know to be breathing in long and single-mindedly; when breathing out long, one should know to be breathing out long and single-mindedly. When breathing in* short, *one should know to be breathing in short and single-mindedly; when breathing out short, one should know to be breathing out short and single-mindedly.* When breathing in pervading the body, one should know from the whole of the body to be breathing in single-mindedly; when breathing out pervading the body, one should know from the whole of the body to be breathing out single-mindedly. When abandoning the bodily activity, one should be mindful of breathing in single-mindedly; *when abandoning the bodily activity, one should be mindful of* breathing out *single-mindedly.*

"When experiencing joy, *one should be mindful of breathing in single-mindedly; when experiencing joy, one should be mindful of breathing out single-mindedly.* When experiencing happiness, *one should be mindful of breathing in single-mindedly; when experiencing happiness, one should be mindful of breathing out single-mindedly.* When experiencing the mental activity, *one should be mindful of breathing in single-mindedly; when experiencing the mental activity, one should be mindful of breathing out single-mindedly.* When abandoning the mental activity, one should be mindful of breathing in single-mindedly; *when abandoning the mental activity, one should be mindful* of breathing out *single-mindedly.*

"When apprehending the mind, *one should be mindful of breathing in single-mindedly; when apprehending the mind, one should be mindful of breathing out single-mindedly.* When gladdening the mind, *one should be mindful of breathing in single-mindedly; when gladdening the mind, one should be mindful of breathing out single-mindedly.* When collecting the mind, *one should be mindful of breathing in single-mindedly; when collecting the mind, one should be mindful of breathing out single-mindedly.* When liberating the mind, one should be mindful of breathing in single-mindedly; *when liberating the mind, one should be mindful* of breathing out *single-mindedly.*

"[When] contemplating impermanence [by] contemplating change, *one should be mindful of breathing in single-mindedly; when contemplating impermanence [by] contemplating change, one should be mindful of breathing out single-mindedly.*[16] [When] contemplating dispassion, *one should be mindful of breathing in single-mindedly; when contemplating dispassion, one should be mindful of breathing out single-mindedly.* [When] contemplating cessation, *one should be mindful of breathing in single-mindedly; when contemplating cessation, one should be mindful of breathing out single-mindedly.* [When] contemplating letting go, one should be mindful of breathing in single-mindedly; *when contemplating letting go, one should be mindful* of breathing out *single-mindedly.*"

16 I take the double reference in the original to "impermanence" and "change" to be the result of a textual error. This appears to have affected other works; see T 614 at T XV 275c26 and T 1509 at T XXV 138a14 (translated Lamotte 1949/1981: 642). Dhammajoti 2008: 263 notes that T 614 and T 1509 were translated by the same Kumārajīva who was also one of the translators of the Sarvāstivāda *Vinaya*, T 1435, making it probable that what would originally have been a textual corruption affecting T 1435 was subsequently applied during translation to the presentation in T 614 and T 1509. In order to make sense of this error in the present context I have supplemented "[by]".

POSTSCRIPT BY AMING TU[1]

When I was first diagnosed with cancer and had to be hospitalized, I was shocked to discover that, out of the thousands of books in my collection, I could not find a single book that I could bring with me; in spite of having read countless books during my life, there was not a single one that could accompany me in my life's final journey.

A GIFT IN DISGUISE

Towards the end of 2005 I accompanied my mother to the hospital for a health check. Because it was taking quite a while, I took the opportunity to get a check-up myself. As soon as an ultrasound scan was performed, something wrong was detected in my liver. The doctor immediately scheduled an MRI scan and made arrangements for my hospitalization. I remember that the day I was diagnosed with cancer I went to the Yángmíng mountains for a walk, just as I always had, to enjoy the flowers and eat some local vegetables; emotionally I didn't experience much of an upset and was able to enjoy a serene afternoon. Yet after that I quickly wrote down my will and wrapped up as many engagements as possible before taking ten days of leave for my upcoming hospitalization.

---

1 In this postscript Aming Tu explains what led to the writing of this book; see also above p. 6.

Being hospitalized is a bit like going on a retreat; one is left to face oneself and come to terms with life and death. I was to go on a ten-day voyage of the body and mind. Bringing with me a small bag, I entered the hospital ward and began an encounter with my life and this sickness. From one point of view this was a precious opportunity; I could no longer use my busy schedule as an excuse. This ten-day retreat was an invaluable chance for me to calm down and reconnect with my own body and mind.

MIND AND BODY DURING MY TEN-DAY "HOSPITALIZATION RETREAT"

Because this was my first time being hospitalized, everything was new to me, and these experiences are indeed quite different from one's daily routine. The eyes could only see people, events, and things related to illness; the ears for the most part could only hear moans and sorrowful sighs; the nose was filled with the scent of medicine and disease; the tongue could only taste flavourless and bitter substances; and the body experienced the cold surfaces of medical equipment or the piercing sensation of a needle. The mental and physical experience of the five aggregates of bodily form, feeling, perception, mental formations, and consciousness was equally alien and unpleasant.

I experienced much anguish during this period, but the most unbearable aspect of the ordeal was the physical pain. This kind of pain doesn't let you sit, lie down, or sleep and, at times, even makes breathing difficult; the feeling of trying to catch one's breath during one of those bouts of intense pain can hardly be put into words and describing the sensation to the doctor proved challenging. This kind of unspeakable pain was akin to that expressed by the venerable Khemaka in the *Saṃyukta-āgama*: "It is just as if a cow butcher with a sharp knife were to cut open a living [cow's] belly to take its internal organs. How could that cow endure the pains in its belly? My belly is now more painful than that cow's."[2] When I first read this passage I

2 See above p. 91.

was deeply moved; I was shocked to find in the discourses such an accurate and vivid description of my predicament.

THE KOAN OF PAIN

This kind of unbearable pain led me to ask myself: what kind of teaching could help me overcome this intense suffering? Apart from the physical pain, finding a way of facing the feeling of uncertainty brought about by my illness was also a question which troubled me deeply. In the newspapers and magazines cancer was presented as leading inevitably to death; for this reason the problem of death would often surface in my mind, bringing with it much unease and worry. It is perhaps fair to say that this feeling of pain and helplessness cannot be fully grasped by the sympathetic observer by means of mere empathy.

In this situation, as I started to look for ways of facing pain and death, I also began a deeper reflection: what teaching could I find refuge and guidance in for the remainder of this life? How did the Buddha guide the ill and the dying? How did he teach them to face death? These questions would keep swirling in my mind just like a "head phrase" (*huàtóu*), the word or short sentence one contemplates in Chan practice, also referred to as koan (*gōng'àn*).

FINDING INSPIRATION IN THE SCRIPTURES

After leaving the hospital I started surveying the discourses in search of methods of practice suitable for the ill and dying. Eventually I came across a group of discourses in the *Saṃyukta-āgama* which offer a detailed account of the teachings given by the Buddha to his disciples on practices for facing illness, pain, and death. These texts provide a record of how the Buddha taught disciples who had fallen ill, including both senior and novice monks, as well as elderly and young laymen.

As I started perusing the discourses, I discovered to my great surprise that, even though the discourses from this collection had been delivered haphazardly in response to particular situations, one could find in these neatly arranged, concise, and simple discourses a systematic and profound exposition of the practice and its conceptual framework; the more I read and analysed the contents of these discourses, the more appreciative and filled with joy I became.

As I worked my way through the Pāli parallels, I also found that a comparative side-by-side study of the texts enhanced my understanding of the teachings and helped me identify the essence of the Buddha's message. My work eventually led me to delineate the teaching's overall framework as well as identify the sequential stages of practice, revealing the collection as a precious resource for practice.

Later on, having been in and out of hospital several times already, these discourses not only proved to be a precious companion for facing my illness, they also became something that I would share with people around me, whether it be in the classroom with my students, or in casual conversations with friends. My sharing of these texts slowly aroused the curiosity of various people around me. Yet, perhaps because for most of us death feels like a very distant prospect, the people I encountered did not take the time to look more closely at the discourses. I felt as if I had failed to help people understand the significance of these teachings. For this reason I decided to sort the texts into a book with the hope that, with my preliminary attempts at analysing and classifying the contents in hand, it would be easier for me to share the teachings with others.

THE STORY OF ANĀTHAPIṆḌIKA

In all my readings of this collection, the most moving story was certainly that of Anāthapiṇḍika. Ānanda and Sāriputta visited him when he had become very ill. When the two monks asked Anāthapiṇḍika how he felt, the householder said, "My affliction is now extreme and there is little to rely on. I experience an increase, I do not experience a decrease."[3] Then Sāriputta offered him guidance to help him face pain and death. At that moment Anāthapiṇḍika burst into tears; this strong emotional reaction was triggered by Sāriputta's exposition of the wonderful Dharma. Indeed, Anāthapiṇḍika had practised

3 See above p. 138.

the Dharma for more than twenty years and had, as a result, been able to face the growing pain with great courage. I was deeply moved when I came across this passage. It also made me think, "I have studied the Dharma for so many years. What really have I learned?"

Over the course of my twenty to thirty years of study of the teachings, my main area of research had revolved around textual study and the digitization of Buddhist scriptures. Yet this illness had drawn my attention back to a more fundamental question: what is the core of the Buddha's teaching? Was it not his encounter with old age, sickness, and death that led the prince Siddhartha to leave his palace and begin his quest to find freedom from this suffering?

It was only then that I truly understood the following two passages: "There are these three things which the whole world does not like to think about. What are the three? That is, they are old age, disease, and death" and "Because there are these three things in the world that one does not like to think about, that is, old age, disease, and death, therefore Buddhas, Tathāgatas, appear in the world and the world comes to know the teaching realized by Buddhas, Tathāgatas, being widely taught [to people]."[4] I understood that this cultivation and this realization are truly at the core of the Buddha's message. In a way, this sickness allowed me to rediscover the Buddha's teaching.

THE DISCOURSES AS MEDICAL RECORDS

As I first read the discourses on illness, it struck me that each small discourse resembled a kind of condensed medical record of the "treatment" undergone by the person receiving the teachings. During my hospitalization I had learned a bit about how doctors fill out patient-information forms to help me understand my own medical history sheet. I learned that often doctors will use a framework called SOAP (Subjective,

4 See above p. 116.

Objective, Assessment, and Plan) when creating the medical records of patients.[5]

Later I made use of this SOAP model and created a "patient-information form" for each one of the discourses on illness with information on the patient himself, the time and place of the teacher's visit, the subjective description of the illness by the patient, the observable symptoms, the prescription, the prognosis, and so on. Using this method to analyse the discourses allowed me to identify a comprehensive set of practices.

In my experience, this kind of SOAP framework, which closely resembles the structure of the four noble truths described in the discourse on the Buddha as a physician,[6] is especially well suited to modern people. By presenting the contents of the discourses in this way, people, and doctors and carers in particular, are able to look at these texts in a different way, giving them a fresh outlook on illness and death. Having sorted, compared, and analysed the contents of this corpus, I arrived at the following list of people who could benefit from these teachings:

- patients could rely on them for their personal practice as well as for recitation;
- doctors, carers, and chaplains could use them as a supplementary reference book in their interactions with patients;
- people in good health might use them as a guide or an introductory exposition to be used in one's daily practice to prepare for disease and death.

In short, I believe the selection of discourses in this book is especially well suited to those with busy lives who do not have the time to study all the discourses extensively. As such, this collection constitutes very good introductory reading which

5 "Subjective" refers to the patient's subjective description of the ailment, "objective" documents the results from the medical check, "assessment" corresponds to the physician's diagnosis, and "plan" delineates the prescribed treatment.

6 See above p. 9.

also provides precious guidance for meditative practice as presented in this book.

LAST THOUGHTS

"Today is the last day of my life." Since the onset of my illness, I have used this phrase as a guiding principle for my life: I have viewed every class, every meeting, every get-together, and every conversation as a farewell ceremony.[7] With this attitude, the mind is filled with gratitude and a deep appreciation of each moment. Each morning is like the beginning of a new life: "Today is the first day of my life."

Having read the discourses on illness after a new close encounter with death, I felt that it was truly a shame that this treasure had been buried deep in the vast Buddhist canon for so long; few had ever taken notice of it and even fewer had used it as a guide to their practice. I am grateful for venerable Anālayo's dedication in carrying out the selection's translation and writing accompanying explanations. I feel deeply blessed to be able to finally hold this book in my hands, a book that can accompany me in this life's final journey!

7 See above p. 203.

REFERENCES

Amore, R.C. 1974: "The Heterodox Philosophical Systems", in *Death and Eastern Thought: Understanding Death in Eastern Religions and Philosophies*, F. Holck (ed.), 114–63, Nashville: Abingdon Press.

Anālayo 2003: *Satipaṭṭhāna, the Direct Path to Realization*, Birmingham: Windhorse Publications.

— 2007a: "Mindfulness of Breathing in the Saṃyukta-āgama", *Buddhist Studies Review*, 24/2: 137–50.

— 2007b: "Sukha", in *Encyclopaedia of Buddhism*, W.G. Weeraratne (ed.), 8/1: 164–8, Sri Lanka: Department of Buddhist Affairs.

— 2008a: "Uttarimanussadhamma", in *Encyclopaedia of Buddhism*, W.G. Weeraratne (ed.), 8/2: 462–5, Sri Lanka: Department of Buddhist Affairs.

— 2008b: "Tathāgata", in *Encyclopaedia of Buddhism*, W.G. Weeraratne (ed.), 8/2: 277–83, Sri Lanka: Department of Buddhist Affairs.

— 2009a: "The Development of the Pāli Udāna Collection", *Bukkyō Kenkyū*, 37: 39–72.

— 2009b: "The Lion's Roar in Early Buddhism – A Study Based on the Ekottarika-āgama Parallel to the Cūḷasīhanāda-sutta", *Chung-Hwa Buddhist Journal*, 22: 3–23.

— 2009c: "Waxing Syllables", in *Encyclopaedia of Buddhism*, W.G. Weeraratne (ed.), 8/3: 740–1, Sri Lanka: Department of Buddhist Affairs.

— 2010a: "Paccekabuddhas in the Isigili-sutta and Its Ekottarika-āgama Parallel", *Canadian Journal of Buddhist Studies*, 6: 5–36.

— 2010b: "Teachings to Lay Disciples – The Saṃyukta-āgama Parallel to the Anāthapiṇḍikovāda-sutta", *Buddhist Studies Review*, 27/1: 3–14.

— 2011a: *A Comparative Study of the Majjhima-nikāya*, Taipei: Dharma Drum Publishing Corporation.

— 2011b: "Right View and the Scheme of the Four Truths in Early Buddhism, The Saṃyukta-āgama Parallel to the Sammādiṭṭhi-sutta and the Simile of the Four Skills of a Physician", *Canadian Journal of Buddhist Studies*, 7: 11–44.

— 2011c: "The Tale of King Ma(k)hādeva in the Ekottarika-āgama and the Cakravartin Motif", *Journal of the Centre for Buddhist Studies, Sri Lanka*, 9: 43–77.

— 2011d: "Vakkali's Suicide in the Chinese Āgamas", *Buddhist Studies Review*, 28/2: 155–70.

— 2012a: "The Chinese Parallels to the Dhammacakkappavattana-sutta (1)", *Journal of the Oxford Centre for Buddhist Studies*, 3: 12–46.

— 2012b: "The Case of Sudinna: On the Function of Vinaya Narrative, Based on a Comparative Study of the Background Narration to the First Pārājika Rule", *Journal of Buddhist Ethics*, 19: 396–438.

— 2012c: "The Dynamics of Theravāda Insight Meditation", in 佛教禪坐傳統國際學術研討會論文集 [*Buddhist Meditation Traditions: An International Symposium*], Kuo-pin Chuang (ed.), 23–56, Taiwan: Dharma Drum Publishing Corporation.

— 2012d: "On the Five Aggregates (1) – A Translation of Saṃyukta-āgama Discourses 1 to 32", *Dharma Drum Journal of Buddhist Studies*, 11: 1–61.

— 2012e: "Purification in Early Buddhist Discourse and Buddhist Ethics", *Bukkyō Kenkyū*, 40: 67–97.

— 2012f: "The Tale of King Nimi in the Ekottarika-āgama", *Journal of the Centre for Buddhist Studies, Sri Lanka*, 10: 69–94.

— 2013a: "The Chinese Parallels to the Dhammacakkappavattana-sutta (2)", *Journal of the Oxford Centre for Buddhist Studies*, 5: 9–41.

— 2013b: *Perspectives on Satipaṭṭhāna*, Cambridge: Windhorse Publications.

— 2014a: "The Buddha's Last Meditation in the Dīrgha-āgama", *Indian International Journal of Buddhist Studies*, 15: 1–43.

— 2014b: "Defying Māra – Bhikkhunīs in the Saṃyukta-āgama", in *Women in Early Indian Buddhism: Comparative Textual Studies*, A. Collett (ed.), 116–39, New York: Oxford University Press.

— 2014c: "Exploring the Four Satipaṭṭhānas in Study and Practice", *Canadian Journal of Buddhist Studies*, 10: 73–95.

— 2014d: "The First Absorption (Dhyāna) in Early Indian Buddhism – A Study of Source Material from the Madhyama-āgama", in *Hindu, Buddhist and Daoist Meditation Cultural Histories*, H. Eifring (ed.), 69–90, Oslo: Hermes Publishing.

— 2014e: "Maitreya and the Wheel-turning King", *Asian Literature and Translation: A Journal of Religion and Culture*, 2/7: 1–29.

— 2014f: "The Mass Suicide of Monks in Discourse and Vinaya Literature", *Journal of the Oxford Centre for Buddhist Studies*, 7: 11–55.

— 2014g: "On the Five Aggregates (4) – A Translation of Saṃyukta-āgama Discourses 33 to 58", *Dharma Drum Journal of Buddhist Studies*, 14: 1–71.

— 2014h: "On the Five Aggregates (5) – A Translation of Saṃyukta-āgama Discourses 103 to 110", *Dharma Drum Journal of Buddhist Studies*, 15: 1–64.

— 2014/2015: "Discourse Merger in the Ekottarika-āgama (2), The Parallels to the Kakacūpama-sutta and the Alagaddūpama-sutta", *Journal of the Centre for Buddhist Studies, Sri Lanka*, 12: 63–90.

— 2015a: "The Buddha's Fire Miracles", *Journal of the Oxford Centre for Buddhist Studies*, 9: 9–42.

— 2015b: *Compassion and Emptiness in Early Buddhist Meditation*, Cambridge: Windhorse Publications.

— 2015c: "Healing in Early Buddhism", *Buddhist Studies Review*, 32/1: 19–33.

— 2015d: "Pratyekabuddhas in the Ekottarika-āgama", *Journal of the Oxford Centre for Buddhist Studies*, 8: 10–27.

— 2016: "The Second Absorption in Early Buddhist Discourse", in *Buddhist Meditative Traditions: A Comparison and Dialogue*, Chuang Kuo-pin (ed.), 25–58, Taiwan: Dharma Drum Publishing Corporation.

Bareau, André 1991: "Les agissements de Devadatta selon les chapitres relatifs au schisme dans les divers Vinayapiṭaka", *Bulletin de l'École Française d'Extrême-Orient*, 78: 87–132.

Bechert, Heinz and K. Wille 1989: *Sanskrithandschriften aus den Turfanfunden, Teil 6*, Stuttgart: Franz Steiner.

Becker, Ernest 1973: *The Denial of Death*, New York: Simon & Schuster.

Bernhard, Franz 1965 (vol. 1): *Udānavarga*, Göttingen: Vandenhoeck & Ruprecht.

Bingenheimer, Marcus (forthcoming): "Three Saṃyuktāgama-type Sutras on Healing and Healers from the Chinese Canon", in *Buddhism & Healing in East Asia*, C.P. Salguero (ed.).

Bingenheimer, Marcus, Bh. Anālayo, and R. Bucknell 2013 (vol. 1): *The Madhyama Āgama (Middle Length Discourses)*, Berkeley: Numata Center for Buddhist Translation and Research.

Bodhi, Bhikkhu 2000: *The Connected Discourses of the Buddha: A New Translation of the Saṃyutta Nikāya*, Boston: Wisdom Publications.

— 2012: *The Numerical Discourses of the Buddha: A Translation of the Aṅguttara Nikāya*, Boston: Wisdom Publications.

Boisvert, Mathieu 1996: "Death as a Meditation Subject in the Theravāda Tradition", *Buddhist Studies Review*, 13/1: 37–54.

Bowker, John 1991: *The Meanings of Death*, Cambridge: Cambridge University Press.

Brough, John 1962/2001: *The Gāndhārī Dharmapada, Edited with an Introduction and Commentary*, Delhi: Motilal Banarsidass.

Burke, Brian L., A. Martens, and E.H. Faucher 2010: "Two Decades of Terror Management Theory: A Meta-Analysis of Mortality Salience Research", *Personality and Social Psychology Review*, 14/2: 155–95.

Catherine, Shaila 2008: *Focused and Fearless: A Meditator's Guide to States of Deep Joy, Calm, and Clarity*, Boston: Wisdom Publications.

Chokyi Nyima Rinpoche 2002: *Present Fresh Wakefulness: A Meditation Manual on Nonconceptual Wisdom*, Boudhanath: Rangjung Yeshe.

Collett, Alice and Anālayo 2014: "Bhikkhave and Bhikkhu as Gender-inclusive Terminology in Early Buddhist Texts", *Journal of Buddhist Ethics*, 21: 760–97.

Cone, Margaret 1989: "Patna Dharmapada", *Journal of the Pali Text Society*, 13: 101–217.

Cowell, E.B. and R.A. Neil 1886: *The Divyāvadāna: A Collection of Early Buddhist Legends, Now First Edited from the Nepalese Sanskrit Mss. in Cambridge and Paris*, Cambridge: Cambridge University Press.

Deeg, Max 1999: "The Saṅgha of Devadatta: Fiction and History of a Heresy in the Buddhist Tradition", *Journal of the International College for Advanced Buddhist Studies*, 2: 183–218.

Demiéville, Paul 1974: "Byō", in *Hôbôgirin, dictionnaire encyclopédique du bouddhisme d'après les sources chinoises et japonaises*, Paris: Adrien Maisonneuve, 3: 224–65.

de Silva, Lily, 1993: "Ministering to the Sick and Counselling the Terminally Ill", in *Studies on Buddhism in Honour of Professor A.K. Warder*, N.K. Wagle et al. (ed.), 29–39, Toronto: University of Toronto, Centre for South Asian Studies.

Dhammajoti, Bhikkhu K.L. 2008: "The Sixteen-mode Mindfulness of Breathing", *Journal of the Centre for Buddhist Studies, Sri Lanka*, 6: 251–88.

Feer, Léon 1883: *Fragments extraits du Kandjour, traduits du tibétain*, Paris: Ernest Leroux.

Filliozat, Jean 1934: "La médecine indienne et l'expansion bouddhique en Extrême-Orient", *Journal Asiatique*, 224: 301–7.

Frauwallner, Erich 1956: *The Earliest Vinaya and the Beginnings of Buddhist Literature*, Rome: Istituto Italiano per il Medio ed Estremo Oriente.

Geng, Shimin and H.-J. Klimkeit 1988: *Das Zusammentreffen mit Maitreya: Die ersten fünf Kapitel der Hami-Version der Maitrisimit*, Wiesbaden: Otto Harrassowitz.

Gethin, Rupert 1992: *The Buddhist Path to Awakening: A Study of the Bodhi-Pakkhiyā Dhammā*, Leiden: E.J. Brill.

— 1997: "Cosmology and Meditation: From the Aggañña-sutta to the Mahāyāna", *History of Religions*, 36: 183–217.

Glass, Andrew 2007: *Four Gāndhārī Saṃyuktāgama Sūtras: Senior Kharoṣṭhī Fragment 5*, Seattle: University of Washington Press.

Gnoli, Raniero 1977 (part 1): *The Gilgit Manuscript of the Saṅghabhedavastu, Being the 17th and Last Section of the Vinaya of the Mūlasarvāstivādin*, Rome: Istituto Italiano per il Medio ed Estremo Oriente.

Greenberg, Jeff, T. Pyszczynski, and S. Solomon 1986: "The Causes and Consequences of a Need for Self-esteem: A Terror Management

Theory", in *Public Self and Private Self*, R.F. Baumeister (ed.), 189–212, New York: Springer-Verlag.

Griffiths, Paul J. 1986/1991: *On Being Mindless: Buddhist Meditation and the Mind–Body Problem*, La Salle: Open Court.

Gunaratana, Bhante 2014: *Meditation on Perception: Ten Healing Practices to Cultivate Mindfulness*, Boston: Wisdom Publications.

Gunaratne, V.F. 1982: *Buddhist Reflections on Death*, Kandy: Buddhist Publication Society.

Har Dayal 1932/1970: *The Bodhisattva Doctrine in Buddhist Sanskrit Literature*, Delhi: Motilal Banarsidass.

Harmon-Jones, Eddie, L. Simon, J. Greenberg, T. Pyszczynski, S. Solomon, and H. McGregor 1997: "Terror Management Theory and Self-esteem: Evidence that Increased Self-esteem Reduces Mortality Salience Effects", *Journal of Personality and Social Psychology*, 72/1: 24–36.

Horner, I.B. 1951/1982 (vol. 4) and 1952/1975 (vol. 5): *The Book of the Discipline (Vinaya-piṭaka)*, London: Pali Text Society.

Ichimura Shohei 2015 (vol. 1): *The Canonical Book of the Buddha's Lengthy Discourses*, Berkeley: Bukkyo Dendo Kyokai America.

Ireland, John D. 1990: *The Udāna: Inspired Utterances of the Buddha*, Kandy: Buddhist Publication Society.

Jin Siyan 2013: 遊行經 *Soutra de l'ultime voyage ou le dernier discours du Bouddha, Mahā-Parinibbāna-sutta, traduit et annoté*, Paris: Éditions You-Feng Libraire & Éditeur.

Ji Xianlin, W. Winter, and G.-J. Pinault 1998: *Fragments of the Tocharian A Maitreyasamiti-Nāṭaka of the Xinjiang Museum, China, Transliterated, Translated and Annotated*, Berlin: Mouton de Gruyter.

Jones, J.J. 1949/1973 (vol. 1), 1952/1976 (vol. 2), and 1956/1978 (vol. 3): *The Mahāvastu, Translated from the Buddhist Sanskrit*, London: Pali Text Society.

Kabat-Zinn, Jon 1982: "An Out-patient Program in Behavioral Medicine for Chronic Pain Patients Based on the Practice of Mindfulness Meditation: Theoretical Considerations and Preliminary Results", *General Hospital Psychiatry*, 4: 33–47.

— 1990/2013: *Full Catastrophe Living, Using the Wisdom of Your Body and Mind to Face Stress, Pain, and Illness*, New York: Bantam Books.

— 2005: *Coming to Our Senses*, New York: Hachette Books.

— 2010: "Foreword", in *Teaching Mindfulness*, D. McCown, D. Reibel, and M.S. Micozzi (ed.), ix–xxii, New York: Springer.

— 2013: "Some Reflections on the Origins of MBSR, Skillful Means, and the Trouble with Maps", in *Mindfulness: Diverse Perspectives on Its Meaning, Origins, and Applications*, J.M.G. Williams and J. Kabat-Zinn (ed.), 281–306, Abingdon: Routledge.

Kabat-Zinn, J., L. Lipworth, and R. Burney 1985: "The Clinical Use of Mindfulness Meditation for the Self-regulation of Chronic Pain", *Journal of Behavioural Medicine*, 8: 163–90.

Kabat-Zinn, J., L. Lipworth, R. Burney, and W. Sellers 1986: "Four Year Follow-up of a Meditation-based Program for the Self-regulation of Chronic Pain: Treatment Outcomes and Compliance", *Clinical Journal of Pain*, 2: 159–73.

Kapleau, Philip 1967: *The Three Pillars of Zen: Teaching, Practice, Enlightenment*, Boston: Beacon Press.

Karunaratne, Suvimalee 2002: "Maraṇānussati", in *Encyclopaedia of Buddhism*, W.G. Weeraratne (ed.), 6/4: 636–9, Sri Lanka: Department of Buddhist Affairs.

Klima, Alan 2002: *The Funeral Casino, Meditation, Massacre, and Exchange with the Dead in Thailand*, Princeton: Princeton University Press.

Kübler-Ross, Elisabeth 1969/1982: *On Death and Dying*, London: Tavistock Publications.

Kudara Kōgi and P. Zieme 1995: "Uigurische Āgama-Fragmente (3)", *Bukkyō Bunka Kenkyūū sho Kiyō*, 34: 23–84.

Lamotte, Étienne 1949/1981 (vol. 2) and 1970 (vol. 3): *Le traité de la grande vertu de sagesse de Nāgārjuna (Mahāprajñāpāramitāśāstra)*, Louvain-la-Neuve: Institut Orientaliste.

Lefmann, S. 1902: *Lalita Vistara, Leben und Lehre des Çâkya-Buddha, Textausgabe mit Varianten-, Metren- und Wörterverzeichnis*, Halle: Verlag der Buchhandlung des Waisenhauses.

Leslie, Julia and D. Wujastyk 1991: "The Doctor's Assistant, Nursing in Ancient Indian Medical Texts", in *Anthropology and Nursing*, P. Holden and J. Littlewood (ed.), 25–30, London: Routledge.

Liu Zhen 2010: *Dhyānāni tapaś ca*, 禅定与苦修, Shanghai: 古籍出版社.

Malalasekera, G.P. 1937/1995 (vol. 1) and 1938/1998 (vol. 2): *Dictionary of Pāli Proper Names*, Delhi: Munshiram Manoharlal.

Martini, Giuliana 2011: "Meditative Dynamics of the Early Buddhist Appamāṇas", *Canadian Journal of Buddhist Studies*, 7: 137–80.

Minh Chau, Thich 1964/1991: *The Chinese Madhyama Āgama and the Pāli Majjhima Nikāya*, Delhi: Motilal Banarsidass.

Mukherjee, Biswadeb 1966: *Die Überlieferung von Devadatta dem Widersacher des Buddha in den Kanonischen Schriften*, Munich: Kitzinger.

Mu Soeng 2004: *Trust in Mind: The Rebellion of Chinese Zen*, Boston: Wisdom Publications.

Ñāṇamoli, Bhikkhu 1995/2005: *The Middle Length Discourses of the Buddha: A Translation of the Majjhima Nikāya*, Bhikkhu Bodhi (ed.), Boston: Wisdom Publications.

Nattier, Jan 2003: "The Ten Epithets of the Buddha in the Translations of Zhi Qian 支謙", *Annual Report of the International Research Institute for Advanced Buddhology at Soka University*, 6: 207–50.

Niemic, Christopher P., K.W. Brown, T.B. Kashdan, P.J. Cozzolino, W.E. Breen, C. Levesque-Bristol, and R.M. Ryan 2010: "Being Present in the Face of Existential Threat: The Role of Trait Mindfulness in Reducing

Defensive Responses to Mortality Salience", *Journal of Personal and Social Psychology*, 99/2: 344–65.

Norman, K.R. 1969: *The Elder's Verses I, Theragāthā, Translated with an Introduction and Notes*, London: Pali Text Society.

— 1997/2004: *The Word of the Doctrine (Dhammapada)*, Oxford: Pali Text Society.

Nyanaponika Thera 1962: *The Heart of Buddhist Meditation*, Kandy: Buddhist Publication Society.

— 1967/1981: *The Four Nutriments of Life*, Kandy: Buddhist Publication Society.

— 1968/1986: *The Power of Mindfulness*, Kandy: Buddhist Publication Society.

Nyanaponika Thera and H. Hecker 1997: *Great Disciples of the Buddha: Their Lives, Their Works, Their Legacy*, Bhikkhu Bodhi (ed.), Kandy: Buddhist Publication Society.

Pāsādika, Bhikkhu 1972: "Some Notes on the Vimalakīrtinirdeśa Sūtra", *Jagajjyoti: A Buddha Jayanti Annual*, 22–6.

Pruitt, William 1998/1999: *The Commentary on the Verses of the Therīs (Therīgāthā-aṭṭhakathā, Paramatthadīpanī VI) by Ācariya Dhammapāla*, Oxford: Pali Text Society.

Pyszczynski, Tom, J. Greenberg, S. Solomon, J. Arndt, and J. Schimel 2004: "Why Do People Need Self-esteem? A Theoretical and Empirical Review", *Psychological Bulletin*, 130/3: 435–68.

Ray, Reginald A. 1994: *Buddhist Saints in India: A Study in Buddhist Values & Orientations*, New York: Oxford University Press.

Reynolds, Frank E. 1992: "Death as Threat, Death as Achievement: Buddhist Perspectives with Particular Reference to the Theravada Tradition", in *Death and Afterlife: Perspectives of World Religions*, Hiroshi Obayashi (ed.), 157–67, New York: Greenwood Press.

Rotman, Andy 2008: *Divine Stories, Divyāvadāna, Part 1*, Boston: Wisdom Publications.

Samtani, N.H. 1971: *The Arthaviniścaya-sūtra & Its Commentary (Nibandhana) (Written by Bhikṣu Vīryaśrīdatta of Śrī-Nālandāvihāra), Critically Edited and Annotated for the First Time with Introduction and Several Indices*, Patna: K.P. Jayaswal Research Institute.

Saunders, Cicely and M. Baines 1983/1989: *Living with Dying: The Management of Terminal Disease*, New York: Oxford University Press.

Schmidt-Leukel, Perry 1984: *Die Bedeutung des Todes für das menschliche Selbstverständnis im Pali-Buddhismus*, Munich: Missio Verlags- und Vertriebsgesellschaft.

Senart, Émile 1882 (vol. 1), 1890 (vol. 2), and 1897 (vol. 3): *Le Mahāvastu, texte sanscrit publié pour la première fois et accompagné d'introductions et d'un commentaire*, Paris: Imprimerie Nationale.

Sheng Yen 2012: *The Method of No-method: The Chan Practice of Silent Illumination*, Boston: Shambhala.

Silk, Jonathan A. 2006: *Body Language, Indic Śarīra and Chinese Shèlì in the Mahāparinirvāṇa-sūtra and Saddharmapuṇḍarīka*, Tokyo: International Institute for Buddhist Studies.

Skilling, Peter 1993: "Theravādin Literature in Tibetan Translation", *Journal of the Pali Text Society*, 19: 69–201.

Spellman, John W. 1962: "The Symbolic Significance of the Number Twelve in Ancient India", *Journal of Asian Studies*, 22: 79–88.

Śrāvakabhūmi Study Group 1998: *Śrāvakabhūmi, Revised Sanskrit Text and Japanese Translation, the First Chapter*, Tokyo: Sankibo.

Suvimalee, Bhikkhunī W. 2012: "Anusārani Pātihāri: The Miracle of Instruction in the Bojjhaṅga-sutta and the Girimānanda-sutta", *Sri Lanka International Journal of Buddhist Studies*, 2: 171–86.

Tanahashi K. 2014: *The Heart Sutra: A Comprehensive Guide to the Classic of Mahayana Buddhism*, Boston: Shambhala.

Thurman, R.A.F. 1976: *The Holy Teaching of Vimalakirti*, University Park, PA: Pennsylvania State University Press.

Tripāṭhī, Chandrabhāl 1962: *Fünfundzwanzig Sūtras des Nidānasaṃyukta*, Berlin: Akademie Verlag.

von Gabain, Annemarie 1954: *Türkische Turfan-Texte VIII*, Berlin: Akademie Verlag.

Waldschmidt, Ernst 1944 (vol. 1) and 1948 (vol. 2): *Die Überlieferung vom Lebensende des Buddha, Eine vergleichende Analyse des Mahāparinirvāṇasūtra und seiner Textentsprechungen*, Göttingen: Vandenhoeck & Ruprecht.

— 1951 (vol. 2): *Das Mahāparinirvāṇasūtra, Text in Sanskrit und Tibetisch, verglichen mit dem Pāli nebst einer Übersetzung der chinesischen Entsprechung im Vinaya der Mūlasarvāstivādins, auf Grund von Turfan-Handschriften herausgegeben und bearbeitet*, Berlin: Akademie Verlag.

— 1967: "Zu einigen Bilinguen aus den Turfan-Funden", in *Von Ceylon bis Turfan, Schriften zur Geschichte, Literatur, Religion und Kunst des indischen Kulturraums, Festgabe zum 70. Geburtstag am 15. Juli 1967 von Ernst Waldschmidt*, 238–57, Göttingen: Vandenhoeck & Ruprecht.

Walshe, M. O'C. 1978: *Buddhism and Death*, Kandy: Buddhist Publication Society.

Walshe, Maurice 1987: *Thus Have I Heard: The Long Discourses of the Buddha*, London: Wisdom Publications.

Wayman, Alex 1982: "The Religious Meaning of Concrete Death in Buddhism", in *Sens de la mort, dans le christianisme et les autres religions*, M. Dhavamony et al. (ed.), 273–95, Rome: Gregorian University.

Weller, Friedrich 1939 and 1940: "Buddhas letzte Wanderung, Aus dem Chinesischen", *Monumenta Serica*, 4: 40–84 and 406–40; 5: 141–207.

Wezler, A. 1984: "On the Quadruple Division of the Yogaśāstra: The Caturvyūhatva of the Cikitsāśāstra and the 'Four Noble Truths' of the Buddha", *Indologica Taurinensia*, 12: 289–337.

Wilson, Jeff 2014: *Mindful America: The Mutual Transformation of Buddhist Meditation and American Culture*, Oxford: Oxford University Press.

Wogihara, Unrai 1936: *Sphuṭārthā Abhidharmakośavyākhyā by Yaśomitra, Part II*, Tokyo: The Publishing Association of Abhidharmakośavyākhyā.

Yamada, Isshi 1972: "Anityatāsūtra", *Indogaku Bukkyōgaku Kenkyū*, 20/2: 30–5.

Yìnshùn 印順法師 1983a (vol. 1), 1983b (vol. 2), and 1983c (vol. 3): 雜阿含經論會編, Tapei: 正聞出版社.

Zeidan, F., N.M. Emerson, S.R. Farris, et al. 2015: "Mindfulness-based Pain Relief Employs Different Neural Mechanisms than Placebo and Sham Mindfulness Meditation-induced Analgesia", *Journal of Neuroscience*, 35/46: 15307–25.

Zeidan, F., A.L. Adler-Neal, R.E. Wells, et al. 2016: "Mindfulness-meditation-based Pain Relief Is Not Mediated by Endogenous Opiods", *Journal of Neuroscience*, 36/11: 3391–7.

LIST OF ABBREVIATIONS

AN	*Aṅguttara-nikāya*
CBETA	Chinese Buddhist Electronic Text Association
D	Derge edition
DĀ	*Dīrgha-āgama* (T 1)
Dhp	*Dhammapada*
DN	*Dīgha-nikāya*
EĀ	*Ekottarika-āgama* (T 125)
EĀ²	*Ekottarika-āgama* (T 150A)
MĀ	*Madhyama-āgama* (T 26)
MN	*Majjhima-nikāya*
Mp	*Manorathapūraṇī*
Nett	*Nettipakaraṇa*
Ps	*Papañcasūdanī*
PTS	Pali Text Society
Q	Peking edition
SĀ	*Saṃyukta-āgama* (T 99)
SĀ²	*Saṃyukta-āgama* (T 100)
SHT	Sanskrithandschriften aus den Turfanfunden
SN	*Saṃyutta-nikāya*
Sn	*Sutta-nipāta*
Spk	*Sāratthappakāsinī*
T	Taishō edition (CBETA)
Th	*Theragāthā*
Th-a	*Theragāthā-aṭṭhakathā*
Thī-a	*Therīgāthā-aṭṭhakathā* (1998 edition)
Ud	*Udāna*
Vin	*Vinaya*
〈〉	emendation
[]	supplementation

INDEX OF SUBJECTS

INDEX LOCORUM

WINDHORSE PUBLICATIONS

Windhorse Publications is a Buddhist charitable company based in the UK. We place great emphasis on producing books of high quality that are accessible and relevant to those interested in Buddhism at whatever level. We are the main publisher of the works of Sangharakshita, the founder of the Triratna Buddhist Order and Community. Our books draw on the whole range of the Buddhist tradition, including translations of traditional texts, commentaries, books that make links with contemporary culture and ways of life, biographies of Buddhists, and works on meditation.

As a not-for-profit enterprise, we ensure that all surplus income is invested in new books and improved production methods, to better communicate Buddhism in the 21st century. We welcome donations to help us continue our work – to find out more, go to windhorsepublications.com.

The Windhorse is a mythical animal that flies over the earth carrying on its back three precious jewels, bringing these invaluable gifts to all humanity: the Buddha (the 'awakened one'), his teaching, and the community of all his followers.

Windhorse Publications
169 Mill Road
Cambridge CB1 3AN
UK
info@windhorsepublications.com

Perseus Distribution
210 American Drive
Jackson TN 38301
USA

Windhorse Books
PO Box 574
Newtown NSW 2042
Australia

THE TRIRATNA BUDDHIST COMMUNITY

Windhorse Publications is a part of the Triratna Buddhist Community, which has more than sixty centres on five continents. Through these centres, members of the Triratna Buddhist Order offer classes in meditation and Buddhism, from an introductory to a deeper level of commitment. Members of the Triratna community run retreat centres around the world, and the Karuna Trust, a UK fundraising charity that supports social welfare projects in the slums and villages of South Asia.

Many Triratna centres have residential spiritual communities and ethical Right Livelihood businesses associated with them. Arts activities and body awareness disciplines are encouraged also, as is the development of strong bonds of friendship between people who share the same ideals. In this way Triratna is developing a unique approach to Buddhism, not simply as a set of techniques, but as a creatively directed way of life for people living in the modern world.

If you would like more information about Triratna please visit thebuddhistcentre.com or write to:

London Buddhist Centre
51 Roman Road
London E2 0HU
UK

Aryaloka
14 Heartwood Circle
Newmarket NH 03857
USA

Sydney Buddhist Centre
24 Enmore Road
Sydney NSW 2042
Australia

Also by Anālayo

Satipaṭṭhāna: The Direct Path to Realization

Anālayo

This best-selling book offers a unique and detailed textual study of the Satipaṭṭhāna Sutta, a foundational Buddhist discourse on meditation practice.

This book should prove to be of value both to scholars of Early Buddhism and to serious meditators alike. – Bhikku Bodhi

. . . a gem . . . I learned a lot from this wonderful book and highly recommend it. – Joseph Goldstein

An indispensible guide . . . surely destined to become the classic commentary on the Satipaṭṭhāna. – Christopher Titmuss

Very impressive and useful, with its blend of strong scholarship and attunement to practice issues. – Prof. Peter Harvey, author of *An Introduction to Buddhist Ethics*

ISBN 9781 899579 54 9
£17.99 / $27.95 / €19.95
336 pages

Perspectives on Satipaṭṭhāna

Anālayo

As mindfulness is increasingly embraced in the contemporary world as a practice that brings peace and self-awareness, Bhikkhu Anālayo casts fresh light on the earliest sources of mindfulness in the Buddhist tradition.

The Satipaṭṭhāna Sutta is well known as the main source for Buddhist teachings on mindfulness and its place in the Buddhist path. Ten years after Anālayo's acclaimed study of the Sutta, his current work, *Perspectives on Satipaṭṭhāna*, brings a new dimension to our understanding by comparing the Pali text with versions that have survived in Chinese. Anālayo also draws on the presentation of mindfulness in a number of other discourses as they survive in Chinese and Tibetan translations as well as in Pali.

The result is a wide-ranging exploration of what mindfulness meant in early Buddhism. Informed by Anālayo's outstanding scholarship, depth of understanding and experience as a practitioner, this book sheds fresh light on material that is central to our understanding of Buddhist practice, bringing us as close as we can come to the mindfulness teachings of the Buddha himself.

Anālayo builds on his earlier ground-breaking work, Satipaṭṭhāna: The Direct Path to Realization. *The brilliance of his scholarly research, combined with the depth of his meditative understanding, provides an invaluable guide to these liberating practices.* – Joseph Goldstein

He offers us a work of great scholarship and wisdom that will be of immense benefit to anyone who wants to seriously study or to establish a practice of mindfulness. – Sharon Salzberg

A treasury of impeccable scholarship and practice, offering a wise, open-minded and deep understanding of the Buddha's original teaching. – Jack Kornfield

1SBN: 9781 909314 03 0
£15.99 / $24.95 / €19.95
336 pages

Compassion and Emptiness in Early Buddhist Meditation

Anālayo

Exploring the meditative practices of compassion and emptiness, Anālayo casts fresh light on their earliest sources in the Buddhist tradition.

This book is the result of rigorous textual scholarship that can be valued not only by the academic community, but also by Buddhist practitioners. This book serves as an important bridge between those who wish to learn about Buddhist thought and practice and those who wish to learn from it. As a monk engaging himself in Buddhist meditation as well as a professor applying a historical-critical methodology, Bhikkhu Anālayo is well positioned to bridge these two communities. – 17th Karmapa Ogyen Trinley Dorje

In this study, Venerable Anālayo brings a meticulous textual analysis of Pali texts, the Chinese Āgamas and related material from Sanskrit and Tibetan to the foundational topics of compassion and emptiness. While his analysis is grounded in a scholarly approach, he has written this study as a helpful guide for meditation practice. – Jetsunma Tenzin Palmo

This is an intriguing and delightful book that presents these topics from the viewpoint of the early suttas as well as from other perspectives, and grounds them in both theory and meditative practice. – Bhikshuni Thubten Chodron

Anālayo holds a lamp to illuminate how the earliest teachings wed the great heart of compassion and the liberating heart of emptiness and invites us to join in this profound training. – Jack Kornfield

This scholarly book is more than timely with its demonstrations that teachings on emptiness and compassion that are helpful to practitioners of any form of Buddhism are abundant in early Buddhist texts. – Rita M. Gross

Arising from the author's long-term, dedicated practice and study, this book provides a window into the depth and beauty of the Buddha's liberating teachings. Serious meditation students will benefit tremendously from the clarity of understanding that Venerable Anālayo's efforts have achieved. – Sharon Salzberg

ISBN 978 1 909314 55 9
£11.99 / $17.95 / €16.95
232 pages

Mind in Harmony: The Psychology of Buddhist Ethics

Subhuti

It's not our bank balance, looks, social status or popularity that determines how happy, free and fulfilled we are in life. Finally, what really counts is our state of mind. Subhuti helps us to identify what's going on in our mind, including our moods and emotions, and see clearly what's helpful and what will end in tears. – Vessantara, author of *The Breath* and *A Guide to the Buddhas*

This is a refreshing approach to the classical Abhidharma material, relentlessly experiential and eminently practical. It offers a way of engaging directly with the sophisticated elements of Buddhist psychology that is immediately accessible and offers a real prospect of transformation. I heartily recommend it to anyone who wants to use Buddhist wisdom to explore and clarify their minds. – Andrew Olendzki, author of *Unlimiting Mind*, senior scholar at Barre Center for Buddhist Studies

'What exactly should I be working on in my spiritual life?'

This is the question that Subhuti sets before us, along with what we most need to answer it for ourselves.

Long before the discoveries of contemporary neuroscience and psychology, the Buddha gained insight into the nature of mind. In early Buddhism this profound insight informed the Abhidharma – a 'training manual' to help us understand and transform our own minds. Subhuti brings this manual to life, and shows us the ways in which it illuminates our mind's patterns.

Outlining the processes whereby the mind attends to the world, and explaining how mindfulness fits into the pattern of spiritual development from the perspective of the Abhidharma, Subhuti guides us expertly to an appreciation of how mental states arise, and how to distinguish between skilful mental states and their opposites. In this way, we are given the means to live a happier and more fruitful life, and ultimately a pathway to liberation from all suffering. We are also offered a glimpse of how the enlightened mind of a Buddha works – the mind in its ultimate harmony.

Subhuti has led retreats in Europe, the United States and India on the Buddhist texts of the Yogacara Abhidharma, the source of this system of mind training. This book is the fruit of that teaching experience.

ISBN 978 1 909314 08 5
£12.99 / $19.95 / €12.95
272 pages

The Buddha on Wall Street: What's Wrong with Capitalism and What We Can Do about It

Vaḍḍhaka Linn

After his Enlightenment the Buddha set out to help liberate the individual, and create a society free from suffering. The economic resources now exist to offer a realistic possibility of providing everyone with decent food, shelter, work and leisure, to allow each of us to fulfil our potential as human beings, whilst protecting the environment. What is it in the nature of modern capitalism which prevents that happening? Can Buddhism help us build something better than our current economic system, to reduce suffering and help the individual to freedom? In this thought-provoking work, Vaḍḍhaka Linn explores answers to these questions by examining our economic world from the moral standpoint established by the Buddha.

An original, insightful, and provocative evaluation of our economic situation today. If you wonder about the social implications of Buddhist teachings, this is an essential book. – David Loy, author *Money, Sex, War, Karma*

Lays bare the pernicious consequences of corporate capitalism and draws forth from Buddhism suggestions for creating benign alternatives conducive to true human flourishing. – Bhikkhu Bodhi, editor *In the Buddha's Words*

Questions any definition of wellbeing that does not rest on a firm ethical foundation, developing a refreshing Buddhist critique of the ends of economic activity. – Dominic Houlder, Adjunct Professor in Strategy and Entrepreneurship, London Business School

ISBN 978 1 909314 44 3
£9.99 / $16.99 / €12.95
272 pages

Buddhist Meditation: Tranquillity, Imagination & Insight

Kamalashila

First published in 1991, this book is a comprehensive and practical guide to Buddhist meditation, providing a complete introduction for beginners, as well as detailed advice for experienced meditators seeking to deepen their practice. Kamalashila explores the primary aims of Buddhist meditation: enhanced awareness, true happiness, and – ultimately – liberating insight into the nature of reality. This third edition includes new sections on the importance of the imagination, on Just Sitting, and on reflection on the Buddha. Kamalashila has been teaching meditation since becoming a member of the Triratna Buddhist Order in 1974. He has developed approaches to meditation practice that are accessible to people in the contemporary world, whilst being firmly grounded in the Buddhist tradition.

A wonderfully practical and accessible introduction to the important forms of Buddhist meditation. From his years of meditation practice, Kamalashila has written a book useful for both beginners and longtime practitioners. – Gil Fronsdal, author of *A Monastery Within*, founder of the Insight Meditation Center, California, USA

This enhanced new edition guides readers more clearly into the meditations and draws out their significance more fully, now explicitly oriented around the 'system of meditation'. This system provides a fine framework both for understanding where various practices fit in and for reflecting on the nature of our own spiritual experiences. Kamalashila has also woven in an appreciation of a view of the nature of mind that in the Western tradition is known as the imagination, helping make an accessible link to our own philosophical and cultural traditions. – Lama Surya Das, author of *Awakening the Buddha Within*, founder of Dzogchen Center and Dzogchen Meditation Retreats, USA

His approach is a clear, thorough, honest, and, above all, open-ended exploration of the practical problems for those new to and even quite experienced in meditation. – Lama Shenpen Hookham, author of *There's More to Dying than Death*, founder of the Awakened Heart Sangha, UK

ISBN 9781 907314 09 4
£14.99 / $27.95 / €19.95
272 pages